Analogy and Morphological Change

David Fertig

EDINBURGH
University Press

© David Fertig, 2013

Edinburgh University Press Ltd
22 George Square, Edinburgh EH8 9LF

www.euppublishing.com

Typeset in Times New Roman by
Servis Filmsetting Ltd, Stockport, UK

A CIP record for this book is available from the British Library

ISBN 978 0 7486 4622 7 (hardback)
ISBN 978 0 7486 4621 0 (paperback)
ISBN 978 0 7486 4623 4 (webready PDF)
ISBN 978 0 7486 8422 9 (epub)

The right of David Fertig
to be identified as author of this work
has been asserted in accordance with
the Copyright, Designs and Patents Act 1988.

Contents

Series Editors' Preface		vii
Preface and Acknowledgements		viii

1 Fundamental Concepts and Issues — 1
- 1.1 Introduction — 1
- 1.2 Essential Historical Background: Hermann Paul and the Neogrammarian Period — 2
- 1.3 Preliminary (Narrow) Definitions — 4
- 1.4 Conceptual and Terminological Fundamentals — 4
  - 1.4.1 The term 'analogy' — 4
  - 1.4.2 Analogy vs. analogical innovation/change — 5
  - 1.4.3 Speaker-oriented approaches — 6
  - 1.4.4 Change vs. diachronic correspondence — 7
  - 1.4.5 Innovation vs. change — 7
  - 1.4.6 Defining historical linguistics — 9
- 1.5 Clarifying the Definition of Analogical Innovation/Change — 9
  - 1.5.1 Narrow vs. broad definitions of analogical innovation — 9
  - 1.5.2 Toward a more adequate definition of analogical innovation/change — 11
  - 1.5.3 Some other definitions — 12
- 1.6 Analogical Change as Opposed to What? — 13
  - 1.6.1 Analogy vs. reanalysis — 13
  - 1.6.2 Analogy$_2$ and sound change — 13
  - 1.6.3 Analogy$_2$ and language contact — 14
  - 1.6.4 Changes attributable to extra-grammatical factors — 15
  - 1.6.5 What about grammaticalization? — 15
- 1.7 Proportions and Proportional Equations — 15
- 1.8 Why Study Analogy and Morphological Change? — 16

2 Basic Mechanisms of Morphological Change — 19
- 2.1 Introduction — 19
- 2.2 Defining (Re)analysis — 20

	2.3	Associative Interference	21
	2.4	(Re)analysis, Analogy$_2$ and Grammatical Change	21
		2.4.1 History, synchrony, diachrony, panchrony	22
		2.4.2 'Language change is grammar change'?	23
		2.4.3 The role of transmission/acquisition in grammatical innovation	24
		2.4.4 The relationship of analogical innovation to grammatical change in static and dynamic models of mental grammar	25
	2.5	Types of Morphological Reanalysis	27
		2.5.1 D-reanalysis	28
		2.5.2 C-reanalysis	29
		2.5.3 B-reanalysis	32
		2.5.4 A-reanalysis	35
		2.5.5 Summary of A-, B-, C- and D-reanalysis	36
		2.5.6 Exaptation	37
	2.6	Chapter Summary	40

3 Types of Analogical Change, Part 1: Introduction and Proportional Change   42

	3.1	Introduction	42
	3.2	Outcome-Based vs. Motivation-Based Classifications	42
	3.3	Terminology and Terminological Confusion	43
	3.4	Proportional vs. Non-Proportional Analogy	43
	3.5	Morphological vs. Morphophonological Change	47
	3.6	A Critical Overview of Traditional Subtypes of Proportional Change	47
		3.6.1 Four-part analogy	47
		3.6.2 Extension	48
		3.6.3 Backformation	51
		3.6.4 Regularization and irregularization	55
		3.6.5 Item-by-item vs. across-the-board change	56

4 Types of Analogical Change, Part 2: Non-Proportional Change   57

	4.1	Introduction	57
	4.2	Folk Etymology	57
	4.3	Confusion of Similar-Sounding Words	61
	4.4	Contamination and Blends	62
		4.4.1 Contamination	62
		4.4.2 Double marking of grammatical categories	65
		4.4.3 Blends and related phenomena	66

5 Types of Analogical Change, Part 3: Problems and Puzzles   71

	5.1	A Problem Child for Classification Schemes: Paradigm Leveling	71

	5.2	Analogical Non-Change	76
	5.3	Phantom Analogy	77
		5.3.1 'Regularization is much more common than irregularization': a case study in circular reasoning	80
	5.4	Summary of Types of Analogical Change (Chapters 3–5)	83

6 Analogical Change beyond Morphology — 85
6.1 Introduction — 85
6.2 Syntactic Change — 85
6.3 Lexical (Semantic) Change — 88
6.4 Morphophonological Change — 90
6.5 Phonological Change — 92
6.6 Regular Sound Change as Analogy — 94
6.7 The Interaction of Analogy$_2$ and Sound Change — 95
  6.7.1 Sturtevant's so-called paradox — 97
  6.7.2 'Therapy, not Prophylaxis' — 98
6.8 Chapter Summary — 101

7 Constraints on Analogical Innovation and Change — 102
7.1 Introduction — 102
7.2 Predictability and Directionality — 104
7.3 Constraints on the Interparadigmatic Direction of Change — 104
  7.3.1 Analogical change as 'optimization' — 104
  7.3.2 Formal simplification/optimization of the grammar — 105
  7.3.3 Preference theories — 106
  7.3.4 System-independent constraints — 106
  7.3.5 System-dependent constraints — 110
  7.3.6 Analogical extension of patterns with initially low type frequency — 113
  7.3.7 System-dependent naturalness vs. formal simplicity/optimality — 114
  7.3.8 Universal preferences and 'evolutionary' grammatical theory — 114
7.4 Constraints on the Intraparadigmatic Direction of Change — 116
7.5 Token Frequency — 118
7.6 Teleology — 118
7.7 Chapter Summary — 120

8 Morphological Change and Morphological Theory — 122
8.1 Introduction — 122
8.2 Grammatical Theory and Acquisition — 123
8.3 The Nature and Significance of Linguistic Universals — 124
8.4 Static vs. Dynamic Conceptions of Grammar — 125
8.5 Exemplar-Based vs. Rule-Based Models — 129
8.6 Analogy vs. Rules — 130
  8.6.1 Dual-mechanism models — 131
8.7 Rules vs. Constraints — 132

8.8	Syntagmatic/Compositional vs. Paradigmatic/ Configurational Approaches to Morphology		134
	8.8.1	Asymmetric vs. symmetric paradigmatic models	137
	8.8.2	Paul's proportional model	138
8.9	Chapter Summary		139

References 141
Index 157

Series Editors' Preface

With this volume, we are delighted to introduce to the world of linguistics *Historical Linguistics*, a series of advanced textbooks on language change and comparative linguistics, where individual volumes cover key subfields within Historical Linguistics in depth. As a whole, the series will provide a comprehensive introduction to this broad and increasingly complex field.

The present volume, we believe, exemplifies the kind of content, tone and format we aim for in the series, and the volumes that are coming down the pike do as well. The series is aimed at advanced undergraduates in Linguistics and students in language departments, as well as beginning postgraduates who are looking for an entry point. Volumes in the series are serious and scholarly university textbooks, theoretically informed and substantive in content. Every volume will contain pedagogical features such as recommendations for further reading, but the tone of the volumes is discursive, explanatory and critically engaged, rather than 'activity-based'.

Authors interested in writing for the series should contact us.

Joseph Salmons (jsalmons@wisc.edu)
David Willis (dwew2@cam.ac.uk)

Preface and Acknowledgements

Analogy and morphological change are among the major topics covered in any introductory historical linguistics textbook, but advanced students and interested scholars looking for a coherent book-length survey of the subject will find a very limited selection. This book is intended for readers who have at least some basic background in historical linguistics and are trying to make sense of morphological change, especially of the various things historical linguists mean when they describe a development as 'analogical'. Important theoretical work on analogy and morphological change spans the history of modern linguistics, and one of the major goals of this book is to do justice to both the crucial foundational work of the Neogrammarians and their contemporaries in the late nineteenth century, and the major advances and new insights that have come from scholars working in a wide variety of theoretical frameworks in recent years and decades.

I could fill many pages with a list of people who have contributed to the completion of this project. The support from family, friends, and colleagues has been constant and wonderful throughout the process. Steady encouragement and inspiration has come from all of my colleagues in the Department of Linguistics and many others at the University at Buffalo. Our current chair Jean-Pierre Koenig and former chairs Karin Michelson and Robert Van Valin deserve special mention in this regard, as does Wolfgang Wölck, whose time as chair was before my time but whose leadership continues to be a big part of what makes our department such a great place to work.

I cannot possibly name all of the colleagues in historical and Germanic linguistics whose ideas and constructive feedback have been so important in shaping my own thinking. One person I do want to single out is Neil Jacobs, whose friendship matters so much to so many of us. The greatest professional thanks must be reserved for Joe Salmons. It was a stroke of extraordinary good fortune for me that I got to know Joe while I was still in graduate school. If even a few of us had the means to repay Joe for everything he has done for us, he would be a very rich man.

Finally, I am so grateful to my terrific family, to my brother, Lamar, my sisters, Pat and Melinda, and to my mother for love and support, and most of all to my wife, Sigrid, and my kids Elisabeth, Alexander, and Benjamin. As always, they are the ones who make it all make sense.

1

Fundamental Concepts and Issues

1.1 Introduction

A book about analogy and morphological change? That is so not what I was expecting. I never imaginated there'd ever be such a book. I guess I had another thing coming. Who'd of thunk it?

The short paragraph above contains at least four recognizable examples of some of the different kinds of innovations that we will be exploring in this book. *That is so not . . .* is an example of analogical change in syntax. Until recently, the intensifier *so* could only be used directly before an adjective or adverb. Now some speakers regularly use it in other syntactic contexts, such as before the negative particle *not*. This change can be attributed to the analogy of other intensifiers such as *really* (Kuha 2004). The next sentence contains the verb *imaginate*, which sounds very odd to many English speakers today but has been around since 1541. It means the same thing as the much more common and older verb *imagine* and may have been created by **backformation** from the noun *imagination*, on the analogical model of pairs like *speculation–speculate, dedication–dedicate*, etc. The fourth sentence contains an altered version of the familiar expression *to have another think coming*, meaning 'to be seriously mistaken about something'. For at least a century, English speakers/learners have sometimes mistaken the word *think* in this expression for *thing*. This kind of change is called **folk etymology**. It occurs when speakers identify one element in an expression with a different, often historically unrelated element. The word *of* (for *'ve*) in the final sentence of the paragraph could also be considered folk etymology. Finally, *thunk* is obviously an innovative past-participle form corresponding to standard *thought*. It is based on analogical models such as *sink–sank–sunk* or *stick–stuck*.

As the title indicates, this book is about two things. Analogy and morphological change are not two names for the same thing. Not all aspects of morphological change are analogical – at least not in the sense in which historical linguists most often use that term – and analogical change is by no means restricted to morphology, but analogy and morphology have always been intimately connected in historical linguistics, and this book will focus especially on the domain where they intersect. Beyond this, we will explore many aspects of the broader picture of morphological change and consider the role that analogy – in various senses of that term – plays in language history outside of morphology. First things first, though: What is analogical change (in morphology)? I will start with an expanded discussion of a fairly simple example before taking a stab at some definitions.

Until the late fourteenth century, the past tense and participle of the English verb *bake* were always formed in the same way as those of *take*, *shake* and *forsake*. If these forms had survived, the principle parts today would be *bake–book–baken* (rhyming with *shake–shook–shaken*). At some point, however, speakers started producing the form *baked* in parallel with the many English verbs that form their past tense and participle in this way: *fake–faked*, *like–liked*, *kiss–kissed*, etc., and before long this innovative form *baked* caught on and became established as the new normal.

This example illustrates several important general points about analogical change. First of all, there is no connection at all between the old forms *book* and *baken* and new form *baked*, aside from the fact that they express exactly the same meanings/functions. The first speakers to utter *baked* may well have never even heard the old forms. In fact, not knowing the old forms would presumably make a speaker more likely to produce the innovation. Secondly, the change does not apply to all lexical items that look like they could be potential candidates: *take*, *shake* and *forsake* are unaffected; a few other verbs that originally followed the same pattern, including *ache, fare, wade* and *wash* have changed in the same way as *bake*, but medieval texts reveal that they did not all change at the same time. The new form *fared* starts occuring as early as 1100, whereas the first instances of *waded* do not show up until around 1500. Other members of this class, such as *wake*, have changed in different ways (past tense now *woke* rather than *wook or *waked*), while *shave* has changed in the past tense in the same way as *bake*, but the participle *shaven* still occurs, especially in the expression *clean-shaven*. This kind of inconsistency is characteristic of much analogical change.

In later chapters, we will see that morphological change can entail much more than the regularization of individual words. Analogical changes of various types are extremely common in the histories of many languages. With a few examples under our belts, we can begin working toward an explicit understanding of what historical linguists mean when they attribute a change to 'analogy', but first we need to meet some important linguists who many readers may not be familiar with.

1.2 Essential historical background: Hermann Paul and the Neogrammarian period

One historical period that will figure prominently in this book is that of the **Neogrammarians**, roughly the last quarter of the nineteenth century. If you are not used to hearing of any linguist before Chomsky, or perhaps Bloomfield or Saussure, here is a brief history lesson.

The Neogrammarians first came to prominence in the 1870s and their approach to linguistics remained dominant for the next few decades, until structuralism and descriptivism rose to the forefront in the early part of the twentieth century. This was a time when 'linguistics' meant 'historical linguistics', but this did not mean that the scholars of the period were only interested in the issues that we associate today with the historical subfield. This becomes especially clear in the most important theoretical work of the period, Hermann Paul's *Prinzipien der Sprachgeschichte* (*Principles of Language History*), which appeared in several editions between 1880 and 1920. I will refer to this work often, sometimes simply as the *Prinzipien*.[1]

Paul saw all aspects of language in historical terms. He had relatively little interest in synchronic snapshots that tried to capture the state of a language at a single moment in time because he regarded language as something inherently dynamic, in constant flux, both at the level of the speech community and at that of each individual's mental system. He felt that only an approach that took this fluid character of language fully into account could be explanatory rather than merely descriptive. So in addition to what we think of today as historical linguistics, Paul and some of his contemporaries took a deep interest in the questions that we now associate with theoretical linguistics, psycholinguistics and sociolinguistics. Language acquisition, geographic and social variation, the nature of mental representations and processes – these are just a few of the topics that figure prominently in the *Prinzipien* and other theoretical work of the late nineteenth and early twentieth centuries.

After several decades when mainstream linguists tended to regard pre-structuralist thinking on these topics as quaint at best, a growing number in recent years have been moving closer to views that resemble Paul's in important ways. The increasing popularity of word-and-paradigm models of inflection (James Blevins 2004; Albright 2005; Ackerman and Malouf 2009); emergent grammar (Hopper 1987), usage-based and exemplar-based theories of grammar (Tomasello 2003; Bybee 2006; Goldberg 2006; Bod 2006); modeling of morphological processing and change in connectionist and similar associative networks (Rumelhart and McClelland 1986, 1987; Skousen 1989, 2009; Hare and Elman 1995) and 'evolutionary' accounts of synchronic patterns and universals (Bybee, Perkins and Pagliuca 1994; Juliette Blevins 2004) are among the major current trends that are broadly consistent with prominent nineteenth-century conceptions of the nature of language and grammar. (See Chapters 2, 7 and 8 for further discussion.)

Many linguists today have heard of the Neogrammarians only in connection with their 'regularity hypothesis' concerning the alleged exceptionlessness of (certain kinds of) sound change. But to their contemporaries, the Neogrammarians were known as 'analogists' because they made much greater and more systematic use of analogy in their historical accounts, and their most important theoretical work is dominated by this topic. Neogrammarians who made important contributions to the theory of analogy include August Leskien (1849–1916), Hermann Osthoff (1847–1909) and Karl Brugmann (1849–1919); important work on analogy from authors outside of the Neogrammarian circle includes Whitney 1867, Scherer 1868, Havet 1875, Misteli 1879–80, Henry 1883, Schuchardt 1885 and Wheeler 1887. But most important for our purposes is Paul (1846–1921). The theory of analogy that he first introduces in Paul 1877 and then develops further in the first (1880) and second (1886) editions of the *Prinzipien* is arguably still the most important treatment of this topic anywhere. It is impossible to make sense of ongoing debates about the nature of analogical change without engaging fully with Neogrammarian thinking on the topic, and above all with Paul's account. Lass (1997: 386) laments that 'we understand as much (or as little) about analogy as the Neogrammarians did'. On the one hand, I hope to convince the reader that Lass's assessment is unduly pessimistic, as linguists and other cognitive scientists have made important progress in this area in recent decades. On the other hand, I also hope readers will come to agree that understanding 'as much ... about analogy as the Neogrammarians did' is an accomplishment that any linguist today could feel pretty good about.

1.3 Preliminary (narrow) definitions

Paul offers no explicit definition of analogy, and never uses any term that could be translated as 'analogical change', but we can take his definitions of **analogical formation** (*Analogiebildung*) and **analogical innovation** (*analogische Neubildung/Neuschöpfung*) as a starting point. They can be roughly paraphrased as follows:

(1a) an **analogical formation** is a form (word, phrase, clause, sentence, etc.) produced by a speaker, writer, or signer on the basis of patterns discerned across other forms belonging to the same linguistic system.[2]
(1b) an **analogical innovation** is an analogical formation that deviates from current norms of usage.

In morphology, to say that a lexeme or wordform 'deviates from current norms of usage' can be understood to mean that speakers with whom the innovators are in communication – and in some cases even the innovators themselves (see §2.4.4) – would judge the form to be at best a possible but not an actual word in their language. The study of analogical change has always focused on cases where these speakers would use a different form to express the meanings/functions in question, although this has traditionally not been treated as a defining characteristic of analogical innovation/change (see §1.4.5).

The most important point to take away from these preliminary definitions is that for Paul, analogy is the basic principle underlying the normal productive operation of speakers' mental grammars (Becker 1990). It is not a type of change, and the vast majority of analogical formations are not innovations. As Paul sees it, the first step in accounting for an attested analogical innovation/change is to show how the new form could have arisen as a (by-)product of the normal operation of the innovator's mental grammar.

Much of the remainder of this chapter will be devoted to examining several ways in which these preliminary definitions and conceptions are controversial, problematic, or in need of clarification.

1.4 Conceptual and terminological fundamentals

1.4.1 The term 'analogy'

Like many scientific terms, 'analogy' and 'analogical' are familiar words in everyday use that are also used in various more or less technical senses in a number of specialized fields. Potential confusion for students of historical linguistics begins, on the one hand, with the use of 'analogy' throughout the cognitive sciences to refer to a very broad principle of cognition (Blevins and Blevins 2009), and, on the other hand, with the important distinction in grammatical theory between analogy and rules (see §8.6).

Historical linguists use 'analogy' both in a very general sense – for example, when Anttila insists that '"everything" in language is analogical' (1977: 12, 2003) or more specifically that 'all change is analogical' (1977: 20) – and in a range of closely related technical senses, exemplified by the definitions in §1.3 above. As far as the distinction between analogy and rules is concerned, many historical linguists who focus on morphology and morphophonology use the traditional terms 'analogy' and 'analogical change', regardless of whether they believe that analogy, as opposed to rules – or 'constraints' (§8.7) or what have you – has anything to do with the developments in question (Kiparsky 1978: 93 n. 2, 2012: 22 n. 9).

1.4.2 Analogy vs. analogical innovation/change

Since the mid-nineteenth century, many historical linguists – Neogrammarian and otherwise – have used 'analogy' – or sometimes 'false analogy' – primarily as a label for a type of innovation/change. Paul, however, pointed out that speakers could not possibly have even heard, let alone memorized, many of the (non-innovative) inflected, derived and compound words – not to mention phrases and sentences – that they utter, and that these must thus be products of exactly the same sort of 'analogy' that occasionally gives rise to innovations. Analogy, then, as Paul sees it, is nothing other than the productive/creative capacity inherent in speakers' mental morphological and syntactic systems, and analogical innovations – and, ultimately, associated changes in prevailing usage – are what results when analogy, in this sense, encounters the complexities, inconsistencies and indeterminacies of natural language. Thus, for Paul and his followers, analogy is neither a type of change nor a cause or a motivation for change. It is a cognitive-linguistic capacity that manifests itself constantly in language production and under certain circumstances can also play an essential role in one type of observable change.

In critiquing earlier work, Paul argues that the notion of analogy as first and foremost a type of change completely misses the fundamental nature of the phenomenon. In his view, progress in understanding analogical innovation and morphological and syntactic change depends above all on developing a comprehensive, psychologically informed theory of grammar that addresses two fundamental questions: (1) How do speakers use their grammars to produce and comprehend meaningful forms that they have never heard before?; and (2) How do learners, relying solely on exposure to utterances produced by other speakers and whatever innate abilities, knowledge and biases they bring to the table, construct a grammatical system that allows them to use their language productively and match the output of other speakers as closely as they do? Paul's approach harks back to earlier notions of analogy as paradigmatic regularity (Robins 1978: 6; Becker 1990). This 'synchronic' (Saussure 1995 [1916]: 228; Davies 1978: 42) conception of analogy is linked to Paul's narrow definition of analogical innovation, which excludes 'non-proportional' processes such as folk etymology and contamination. This narrow definition is problematic in a couple of important ways, and it is perhaps for this reason that a split develops among twentieth-century scholars. Historical linguists tend to adopt broader definitions of analogy and revert to defining it as a type of change (Sturtevant 1917; Lehmann 1962), whereas pre-generative theoretical work often follows Paul in treating analogy as the basic principle underlying productive language use (Saussure 1995 [1916]: 179, 226–8; Meillet 1995 [1918]: 47; Jespersen 1922; Bloomfield 1933: 275–7).

Chomsky's dismissal of analogy as 'vacuous' and 'an inappropriate concept' (1986: 32; see also 1964 [1959]: 575 n. 46) ushered in a period when the term was widely avoided by those working in grammatical theory – aside from a few reactionaries/visionaries – while historical linguists, even many such as Kiparsky and King who agreed with Chomsky's assessment, continued to use the term in their work to refer to a type of change.

1.4.3 Speaker-oriented approaches

Advocacy for a speaker-oriented approach to historical linguistics is widespread today (Weinreich et al. 1968; Milroy 1992, 1999). Perhaps a better term would be 'language-user-oriented'. Not only would this make it clear that there is no intention to exclude sign language and written language, but 'speaker-based' is sometimes used to refer specifically to an individual's role as a language producer, i.e. speaker-based as opposed to hearer-based or learner-based. That is not the intended sense of speaker-oriented here. It simply means that one strives to account for language change in terms of the concrete activity of people interacting with each other. This contrasts with a widespread approach that treats a language as a thing (a system) with a life of its own. One might refer to these two approaches as microlinguistics and macrolinguistics, in analogy with the familiar distinction in economics. The argument that real understanding of language change can only be achieved with a 'micro' approach that relates change to the cognitive and social activities of individuals apparently also has a parallel in economics (Lucas 1976). Readers interested in the case against speaker-oriented approaches to language change – which are rarely made explicit – should see Lass 1997.

The Neogrammarians learned speaker-orientation from some of their immediate predecessors (Whitney 1867; Scherer 1868), and – at least in their programmatic pronouncements – became passionate advocates (Robins 1978).[3] Osthoff and Brugmann (1878) open what is often referred to as the 'Neogrammarian manifesto' by arguing that previous linguistic research 'investigated *languages* quite zealously, but *the speaking human being* far too little' (iii, my translation, emphasis in original) and a few pages later they declare speaker-orientation along with uniformitarianism to be the twin pillars of their movement:

> These principles are based on the two-part, immediately self-evident notion, first, that language is not a thing that stands outside of and above the human being and leads a life of its own, but rather has its true existence only in the individual, and that all changes in language in its living reality (*sprachleben*)

can thus only emanate from the speaking individual, and secondly that people's physical and mental activity in acquiring the language inherited from their forebears and in the reproduction and reshaping of the sound images taken up into consciousness must be essentially the same at all historical times. (xii–xiii, my translation)

One significant thing missing from this statement is any mention of the importance of social interaction among speakers. Paul rectifies this in the *Prinzipien*, although critics of the Neogrammarians have even more to say about the crucial role of social interaction in language change (Schuchardt 1885; Hermann 1931).

Although the Neogrammarian 'mechanical' theory of sound change is arguably inconsistent with a true speaker orientation (Ross and Durie 1996), Paul's account of analogy is speaker-oriented in an important way that many of his contemporaries and successors have failed to appreciate, or – in the case of Bloomfield and his followers – explicitly rejected. This is so fundamental to Paul's understanding of analogy that I will refer to it here as Paul's doctrine:

(2) Paul's doctrine: Analogical innovations are not based on linguists' abstractions such as 'the grammar' of 'a language' but rather on the state of an innovator's mental grammar at the moment of innovation.

Paul points out that in some instances there is undoubtedly enough consistency across the mental grammars of the members of a speech community that the abstractions will suffice for practical purposes, but that this is by no means always the case. We can only make sense of certain analogical innovations by doing our best to reconstruct the innovator's mental grammar at the moment of innovation. In §4.4.2, we will see one significant instance in which Paul himself failed to apply this doctrine consistently.

1.4.4 Change vs. diachronic correspondence

Linguists often use 'change' to refer to correspondences among forms that may be separated by centuries or millennia, e.g. Old English *stān* and Modern English *stone* or Middle English *holp* and Modern English *helped*. For purposes of comparative reconstruction, diachronic correspondences that relate forms separated by hundreds of years may be just what one needs, but such correspondences often mask a complex sequence of smaller developments that may have taken a very circuitous route. Linguists who are serious about understanding how change actually happens often point to the fallacies that arise from treating diachronic correspondences as if they directly reflected individual changes. Where plentiful data allows us to examine the course of a change in fine-grained detail, the picture that emerges is often very different from what we would posit if we only had evidence of the 'before' and 'after' states (Andersen 1980).

1.4.5 Innovation vs. change

As indicated above, when linguists talk about language change, they generally mean developments that affect at least a large portion of a speech community.

Many contrast change, in this sense, with **innovation** in the speech or mental representations of individuals.

Views differ on whether historical linguistics should focus on innovation or change. A lot of important work on sound change greatly de-emphasizes the initial phonetic/phonological innovations in the speech of individuals and concentrates almost exclusively on how new pronunciations spread (Labov 1994). Croft (2000) argues that in grammatical change generally, the spread of new forms through speech communities is of greater importance and interest than how the innovations initially arise.

In the study of analogical change, there is a long tradition of focusing mainly on the individual innovations that give rise to the first occurrences of new forms. This focus can be justified in two ways. First of all, many historical linguists, Paul perhaps foremost among them, have become keenly interested in understanding language processing and acquisition for its own sake – quite independently of their relevance for language change. Individual innovations obviously constitute much more direct evidence of what is going on inside the heads of speakers/learners than do full-fledged changes. Analogical innovations are an important kind of evidence for cogntive processes and representations in modern experimental psycholinguistics.

Secondly, many scholars argue or assume that there is a fairly straightforward relationship between innovation and change. Paul's position (1886: 93–4) was that change is simply a matter of many individuals coming up with the same innovation at more or less the same time. Bloomfield (1933: 405) offers a slightly more sophisticated argument: that the same factors that favor the production of a new analogical form by a speaker who has never heard that form should also favor the acceptance and adoption of the new form by speakers who hear it from others, making accounts that, strictly speaking, only apply to initial innovations also relevant to the spread of those innovations through communities.

In much of this book, I will follow the traditional approach of focusing on initial analogical innovations and assuming a more or less straightforward extrapolation from innovation to change. In a number of places, however, I will discuss ways in which the adoption and societal spread of innovations needs to be investigated in its own right.

One other important issue regarding the distinction between innovation and change is especially relevant to analogy. An overt innovation can only involve a single form – since speakers only produce one form at a time – and most familiar textbook examples of analogical change involve just a single form: *holp* > *helped*; *kine* > *cows*; etc. One often reads that analogical change typically proceeds word by word, and some scholars even seem to treat this as a defining characteristic (Hock 1986). There are, however, many changes generally regarded as analogical that do not appear to proceed in this way at all. Even the simple regularization of an English verb usually appears to affect the past tense and the participle simultaneously (*holp* > *helped*; *holpen* > *helped*), and in languages with more complex inflectional systems, the shift of a lexical item from one inflectional class to another might affect dozens or even hundreds of forms. The effects of what is commonly regarded as a single analogical change can be even more far-reaching than this. Paul discusses the replacement of the Middle

High German third pl. pres. indic. verbal ending *-ent* by the *-en* of the subjunctive and the preterite. There was undoubtedly variation between the old and new endings while this change was going on, but I am not aware of any evidence that the change proceeded word by word. Paul (1886: 95–8) also discusses analogical changes involving 'living' morphophonological alternations (*Lautwechsel*), many of which most certainly do not proceed item by item. Classical generative work on analogical change focuses on this last point (see §6.4). This all raises questions about the view of analogical change as simply analogical innovation writ large.

1.4.6 Defining historical linguistics

Historical linguistics is commonly defined as 'the study of language change'. Some scholars do focus exclusively on changes and assume that if nothing changes, then there is nothing to account for. A large and growing number of scholars, however, recognize that lack of change can sometimes be just as remarkable and worthy of investigation as change (Milroy 1992; Nichols 2003). An obvious example from morphology is the apparent resistance to analogical change in certain highly irregular paradigms, such as English *good–better–best*; *have–has–had*; *bring–brought*; *child–children*, etc. In §5.2 we will examine some interesting types of analogical non-change. This all suggests that we should define historical linguistics as the study of language history rather than of (only) language change.

1.5 Clarifying the definition of analogical innovation/change

The following sections address a number of remaining issues that are crucial for a clearer understanding of what historical linguists mean by analogical innovation/change.

1.5.1 Narrow vs. broad definitions of analogical innovation

As mentioned above, Paul defines analogical innovations narrowly. He starts with a fundamental distinction between **production** and **reproduction**. A form (word, phrase, sentence, etc.) uttered by a speaker can be either: (1) a (perhaps imperfect) repetition of a form that she has heard from others and memorized (reproduction); or (2) a product of the speaker's own mental grammar that she may have never before encountered (production). If I utter a completely idiosyncratic past-tense form such as *went*, I must clearly be reproducing a form that I have heard from others. I would have no other basis for knowing or guessing that this is the past tense of *go*. If I utter a regular plural of a very uncommon noun, such as *edelweisses*, by contrast, it is very likely that I have never heard (or uttered or thought about) this form before; thus, it is probably a pure product of my capacity to form new regular plurals. Paul recognizes that production and reproduction often reinforce each other in non-innovative speech, and in later chapters of the *Prinzipien* he discusses various ways in which the two interact, but he identifies analogical innovations exclusively with production. This means that where such an innovation replaces a previously existing form, the latter plays no discernible role in the process.

Paul goes on to insist that a morphological formation is only truly analogical if it can be represented as the solution to a proportional equation of the form A : B = C : X, where, crucially, A, B and C are (sets of) complete wordforms belonging to the mental grammar of the innovator. This is the theory-specific (word-and-paradigm) part of Paul's account (see §3.4 and §8.8 below). Both the production–reproduction distinction and the insistence on proportional equations with surface wordforms as terms are definitional criteria for Paul, and do not entail any empirical claims. Paul recognizes and discusses various kinds of morphological and lexical innovations that do not meet these criteria, but he argues that they should not be classified as analogical.

Many of Paul's contemporaries and close associates, and most subsequent scholars, have operated with a broader understanding of analogy (Hock 2003: 444). The main issue is not Paul's theory-dependent 'proportional' criterion, but the more theory-neutral questions of: (1) whether it is really true that the old form never plays any role in analogical innovations generated by the innovator's mental grammar; and (2) the status of certain types of innovation in which reproduction clearly does play a major role, i.e. where the new form cannot be independent of the old.

With regard to the second question, consider an example of folk etymology, which is usually defined as a change in the phonological make-up of one word resulting from a perceived (but historically unfounded) relationship to another item. A well-known example is English *bridegroom*. The corresponding word in Old English was *brȳdguma*. The first element in this compound is clearly the word *bride* and has only been affected by regular sound changes. The puzzle is the source of the *r* in the second element in Modern English. The solution seems to involve speakers/learners innovatively identifying the second element with the historically unrelated English word *groom*. At some point, there must have been innovators who heard only forms like *bridegoom, without a second *r*, but nevertheless produced the new form *bridegroom*. One can imagine that they might have either misheard what others were saying or thought that the speakers were being sloppy and failing to pronounce an *r* that really should be there (see §2.3 and §4.2).

Is this an 'analogical' innovation? Paul and his followers say no. The new word *bridegroom* would only be analogical in Paul's sense if it were simply a new compound noun whose formal similarity to the earlier synonymous word *brȳdguma* was nothing but a remarkable coincidence. This narrow definition of analogy is coherent, and it is attractive because it makes for a very clear conceptual distinction between sound change and analogy. It is easy to see why sound laws governing phonetic development would be irrelevant to the production of new forms by innovators who have never even heard the old forms that they replace. But Paul's narrow definition has two consequences: Most obviously, folk etymology is clearly not sound change (in the Neogrammarian sense) or borrowing, so if it is not analogy either, then we cannot maintain the Neogrammarian claim that all change in the phonetic make-up of words can be attributed to sound change, analogy, or borrowing. This could easily be addressed, of course, simply by adding to the list: 'sound change, analogy, borrowing, folk etymology, contamination . . .'

The second consequence is more significant: Once we acknowledge that there are innovations such as *brȳdguma* > *bridegroom*, which are partly a matter of innovators reproducing a form they have heard from others but also partly a matter of influence from other forms that are (perceived to be) semantically or grammatically related to the affected form, how can we be sure that what looks like straightforward analogical innovation in Paul's sense does not also – at least in some cases – involve a similar interaction of production and reproduction? Is it possible, for example, that the innovators who launched *helped* on its road to eventual triumph over the older form *holp* actually had heard many tokens of *holp* from other speakers, and either misheard them or thought the speakers were trying to say *helped* but were, perhaps, simplying the final *pt* consonant cluster and altering the quality of the vowel under the influence of the following *l*? Whether or not you buy this particular story, it turns out that even Paul acknowledged a few cases where this kind of interaction between grammatical production and (imperfect) reproduction is clearly going on, and later scholars, such as Rogge (1925) and Hermann (1931), argue that it is more the rule than the exception in analogical change.

This requires a significant revision of Paul's account of analogy. We can no longer fix things simply by adding some more minor types of change to the list. Perhaps the most satisfactory solution would be to take a more holistic approach, in which the notion of analogical change as a distinct type of language change would dissolve. But the project in this book is to try to make as much sense as possible of the traditional notion of analogical change. This is best accomplished by recognizing at least one mechanism other than the productive operation of the speaker's mental grammar that can play a direct role in any analogical innovation. Following Oertel (1901), I will call this (family of) mechanism(s) 'associative interference' (see §2.3).

1.5.2 Toward a more adequate definition of analogical innovation/ change

The following points summarize several important issues raised in the preceding sections. They relate to the differences between the definitions below and those in (1) above:

1. Historical linguists use the terms 'analogy' and 'analogical' in a number of different senses. Most important for our purposes are: (1) a general sense that corresponds fairly closely to the familiar, non-technical meaning of the terms; and (2) a much more specific sense that is a legacy of the primary use of the terms by nineteenth-century linguists.
2. Overt language change, as opposed to innovation, is a complex phenomenon that: (1) involves the production/adoption of new forms by a significant number of individuals; and (2) may be more general/abstract that what is reflected in any single overt innovation.
3. Our final definition of analogical innovation/change is broader than Paul's,

as it is intended to encompass both 'proportional' and 'non-proportional' developments.

Here, then, are our revised definitions, with changes and additions in (3c) and (3e) italicized:

(3a) **analogy$_1$** [general sense] is the cognitive capacity to reason about relationships among elements in one domain based on knowledge or beliefs about another domain. Specifically, this includes the ability to make predictions/guesses about unknown properties of elements in one domain based on knowledge of one or more other elements in that domain and perceived parallels between those elements and sets of known elements in another domain.

(3b) **analogy$_2$** [specific sense] is the capacity of speakers to produce meaningful linguistic forms that they may have never before encountered, based on patterns they discern across other forms belonging to the same linguistic system.

(3c) an **analogical formation** is a form (word, phrase, clause, sentence, etc.) produced by a speaker on the basis of *analogy$_2$*.

(3d) **associative interference** is an influence of one form on the phonetic make-up of another with which it is (perceived to be) semantically or grammatically related.

(3e) an **analogical innovation** is an analogical formation *and/or a product of associative interference* that deviates from current norms of usage.

(3f) an **analogical change** is a difference over time in prevailing usage within (a significant portion of) a speech community that corresponds to an analogical innovation or a set of related innovations.

1.5.3 Some other definitions

Some historical linguists offer definitions that are close in spirit to the formulations in (3) above, but definitions that characterize analogy itself as a type of change are probably more common. Lehmann, for example, writes: '**Analogy** is a process by which morphs, combinations of morphs or linguistic patterns are modified, or new ones created, in accordance with those present in a language' (1962: 178; Hock and Joseph 2009: 151; Blevins and Blevins 2009: 4). Croft states directly that 'analogy is not a mechanism for innovation but a class of changes' (2000: 67). Other definitions relate more to analogy$_1$, and are thus not of much help in trying to figure out what historical linguists mean when they distinguish between analogical change and other kinds of change, e.g. 'analogy is a relation of similarity, that is, a diagram . . . In other words it is structural similarity' (Anttila 2003: 428). Deutscher's (2005: 62) definition: '*analogy*, is shorthand for the mind's craving for order, the instinctive need of speakers to find regularity in language' reflects a somewhat different take on analogy$_1$.

Joseph (1998: 362) defines analogy 'in a broad sense' as 'any change due to the influence of one form on another'. Similar definitions were prevalent in the nineteenth century and were the main target of Paul's and Saussure's insistence that (proportional) analogical innovations cannot be a matter of the influence of one form on another, since they are most likely to occur when the form that is supposedly being 'influenced' is not even present in the mind of the innovator. In terms of our definitions in (3), Joseph's formulation characterizes changes attributable to associative interference but would seem to exclude those resulting from analogical formation. Bloomfield identifies analogy with the pattern itself rather than with any process or mechanism: 'A grammatical pattern (sentence-type, construction, or substitution) is often called an *analogy*' (1933: 275, italics in original). Finally, some define analogy$_2$ in teleological terms, as when Hock writes: 'Its most common function is to make morphologically, syntactically, and/or semantically related forms more similar to each other in their phonetic (and morphological) structure' (1986: 167).

1.6 Analogical change as opposed to what?

If, as Anttila argues, analogy$_1$ encompasses just about all aspects of language and language change, what exactly are we excluding by basing our definitions of analogical innovation and change on analogy$_2$ and associative interference? What kinds of change – or what aspects of change – are *not* analogical, in this sense? I have defined analogical innovations as being: (1) actual, overt productions of innovative forms that are (2) based on other meaningful forms and (perceived) semantic or grammatical relationships among forms (3) within a single linguistic system. The first point distinguishes analogical innovations from covert reanalyses (§1.6.1); the second sets them apart from sound change (§1.6.2); the third distinguishes analogical change from the effects of language contact (§1.6.3) and from changes attributable to factors that lie outside of the grammatical system (§1.6.4).

1.6.1 Analogy vs. reanalysis

Much work on grammatically motivated change devotes the bulk of its attention to covert reanalysis, and reanalysis will be a major topic of Chapter 2, but for present purposes the crucial question concerns the relationship of reanalysis to analogy. We find at least three positions in the literature: (1) reanalysis and analogy are treated as two opposing/complementary aspects of grammatical change (Hopper and Traugott 2003; Saussure 1995 [1916]: 232–5); (2) reanalysis is subsumed under analogy (Wheeler 1887; Hermann 1931); (3) analogy is classified as a type of reanalysis (Traugott and Trousdale 2010; Kiparsky 2012). For reasons that I will explain in §2.4, I subscribe to the first of these three positions.

1.6.2 Analogy$_2$ and sound change

Mainstream historical linguists draw a fundamental distinction between analogy and sound change – the two main types of endogenous change that affect the phonetic shape of linguistic forms. Paul correlated this distinction with the more general one between **production** and **reproduction**, as explained in §1.5.1 above. His reasons for defining analogical innovations as narrowly as he did probably had a lot to do with his desire to make the distinction between sound change and analogy as clear as possible, but as we have seen, processes such as folk etymology and contamination do not fit into this narrow conception of analogical change.

The Neogrammarians did not believe that there is any sense in which sound change is analogical. In Chapter 6 we will see that dissenting opinions on this point date back to Neogrammarian times and have remained influential in recent decades.

1.6.3 Analogy$_2$ and language contact

Analogy$_2$ is traditionally understood to involve relations among forms that all belong to the same grammatical system, associated with a single variety or idiolect of a language. When speakers have (parts of) more than one grammatical system in their heads, these systems can influence each other in many ways. The term 'borrowing' is often reserved for the most straightforward kind of influence of one language or dialect on another, where a word or expression from one language is simply imported to express more or less the same meaning in another language. This is generally regarded as a source of overt innovations that is entirely distinct from analogy.

Contact influence can get much more complex than this. Certain kinds of contact phenomena, in particular (structural) hypercorrection,[4] clearly involve analogy$_1$, and they have enough in common with analogy$_2$ that mainstream historical linguists quite often classify them as a type of (proportional) analogical innovation/change (Campbell 2004: 113–14; Hock and Joseph 2009: 181–2). Structural hypercorrection occurs when speakers draw inferences about forms in one variety of a language based on patterns across corresponding forms in a related variety. Frequently, the potential for hypercorrection arises when individuals have first learned a dialect in which two originally distinct sounds have merged, and then start learning a different dialect where this merger has not occurred. The merger in Modern Standard German of MHG *î* and *ei* (as /ai/), for example, has not occurred in many dialects. Individuals who learn the standard first and then try to speak a dialect such as Viennese will notice that many words with /ai/ in the standard, such as *breit* 'broad' and *zwei* 'two', have /aː/ in Viennese. They may then extend this cross-variety correspondence to produce 'hypercorrect' dialect forms such as /draː/ for /drai/ 'three' and /waːt/ for /wait/ 'wide, far'. Paul says of this sort of hypercorrection that it 'is psychologically no different from what we have called analogical formation' (1886: 360, translation by Orrin Robinson). In keeping with his narrow definition, however, he stops short of saying that it *is* analogical formation.

Campbell (2004: 104; Anttila 1989: 104) points out that analogy$_2$ in general can be characterized as 'internal borrowing'. As he puts it: 'a language may "borrow" from some of its own patterns to change other patterns.' Similarly, Oertel (1901: 149–50) describes analogy as 'intra-individual imitation', 'an imitation of an individual by himself', explaining that 'analogical changes form the exact counterpart within the same individual to the "imitative" innovations within a social group.'

1.6.4 Changes attributable to extra-grammatical factors

A great deal of overt change would never be apparent merely from examining utterances divorced from their real-world contexts. The most obvious examples here involve semantic (semasiological) change. The form of an utterance does not necessarily provide any direct evidence for the meaning that an individual associates with a word, but the circumstances in which a word is uttered may reveal that a semantic change has taken place. A good example of the impact of extra-grammatical factors on a morphological system is the loss of the second person singular pronominal and verbal forms in English. Standard English speakers today are still familiar with the pronouns *thou, thee, thy, thine*, and with verbal forms such as (*thou*) *art* and (*thou*) *dost* from older literature and songs and from occasional current poetic or humorous use, but otherwise speakers now use the originally plural pronouns *you, your, yours* and the corresponding (morphologically unmarked) verb forms. This change occurred gradually in the Early Modern period as plural *you* was first introduced as a highly formal, polite form of singular address and then saw its use gradually extended until the originally normal ways to refer to a single addressee became so insulting that they were socially unusable. This is 'morphological change' in the sense that it has had a major impact on the morphological system, but it does not count as analogy$_2$ because the motivations and mechanisms behind it lie outside of that system (Itkonen 2005).

1.6.5 What about grammaticalization?

Some readers may be wondering where grammaticalization fits in here. To the extent that it refers to a type of change, grammaticalization is a complex development that can include elements of just about every basic type of change mentioned here, including analogical change (Hopper and Traugott 2003). The aspect of grammaticalization that is most relevant for morphological change, morphologization from syntax, is discussed in §2.5 below. Interestingly, this is the only type of change that Paul explicitly characterizes as 'non-analogical' (*nichtanalogisch*, 1886: 274).

Note, however, that what is often called 'grammaticalization theory' is not so much about a particular kind of change as it is a conception of the nature of language change in general. It typically emphasizes gradualness and the role of factors such as repetition, while de-emphasizing the significance of transmission to new learners. I address these issues further in Chapters 2 and 8.

1.7 Proportions and proportional equations

Almost all accounts of analogical change make use of proportional equations, and most readers have probably already encountered examples such as:

(4) *stone* : *stones* = *cow* : X; or *sting* : *stung* = *string* : X

Such equations are commonly regarded as a convenient, informal, more or less theory-neutral way to portray analogical innovations, implicitly expressing something like: 'Based on exposure to singular–plural pairs such as *stone–stones*, learners determine that one way to form plurals in English is by adding *-s* to the singular. They then apply this pattern to *cow*, yielding the innovative plural *cows* (replacing older *kine*).' Proportional equations undoubtedly owe their longevity to the fact that they can be read in this theory-neutral way.

For Paul – and for anyone who takes his theory of analogy seriously – proportional equations are anything but theory-neutral. Far from being a mere notational convenience, they embody his model of the mental grammar.[5] For much of the twentieth century, most linguists considered Paul's theory to be of purely historiographical interest at best. Today, however, as mentioned in §1.2 above, many scholars are again taking Paul's proportional model seriously and proposing new models that have a lot in common with it. I will address this issue in more depth in Chapter 8. For now, it is important for readers simply to be aware that the proportional model was developed as an integral part of a coherent theory of the acquisition, mental representation and productive use of a grammatical system. Using proportional equations only to portray analogical innovations, and for that matter using the term 'analogy' only to talk about change when one does not also use it for one's theory of grammar, creates the risk of losing sight of the inextricable connection between analogical innovations and the normal operation of speakers' mental grammars.

One final point about proportional equations: They are generally regarded as an implicit way of representing (only) overt analogical innovations, but they can also serve to imply an underlying reanalysis (Davies 1978: 55). Consider the example in (5) (Sturtevant 1947: 97–8; Anttila 1977: 20):

(5) *four* : *formation* = *two* : X, X = *twomation*

Twomation is of course an overt analogical innovation, but the interesting point here is that for most English speakers, unlike with more familiar textbook examples of proportional equations such as those in (4) above, there is no morphological relation between *four* and *formation*. The partial formal resemblance is purely coincidental, so the innovator has not merely extended an existing grammatical pattern; he has actually reanalyzed a coincidental formal relationship as a grammatical one, and then provided evidence for this reanalysis with the production of *twomation*. In this case, the proportional equation is thus being used to reflect two distinct innovations – the first covert, the second overt. These are in principle separable; a speaker could analyze *formation* as being morphologically related to *four* but go to her grave without ever producing an overt innovation to reveal the reanalysis. I will discuss several similar examples in §2.5 and suggest a classification of different types of reanalysis based on the structure of the proportional equation.

1.8 Why study analogy and morphological change?

If you have gotten this far (or have jumped to this point) and are still trying to decide whether to keep reading, here is a brief sales pitch.

If you are interested in grammatical theory, the notion of analogy – whether by that name or another – has once again become central in a number of important current frameworks, and studying the role that this notion has played in historical linguistics will, among other things, make it much easier to see where these current frameworks fit in a broader historical context. Major nineteenth- and early twentieth-century theoreticians such as Paul, Brugmann, Osthoff, Jespersen and Schuchardt are frequently cited in the recent literature, but one rarely finds any extensive discussion of their ideas.

Levelings, extensions and reconfigurations of morphophonological alternations provide a wealth of material for those interested in phonological theory, and our appreciation of the many ways in which prosodic structure is relevant to morphological change has grown dramatically over the past couple of decades.

Experimental psycholinguists and acquisition researchers of all stripes should not need much persuading. Analogical innovations have been a staple of the laboratory since at least Gleason 1958, and a great deal of the most interesting child-language data consists of such innovations. Looking at analogical innovation and change in a broader historical context can supply new, complementary kinds of evidence for cognitive processes and suggest new ways of thinking about individual innovation.

Sociolinguists may have the most to contribute to our understanding of morphological change. The traditional focus on narrowly cognitive aspects of grammatical change has meant a relative neglect of social aspects. That grammatical variants can bear social meaning, and that this may have an important influence on the course of change, is often noted in the literature, and there are of course variationist studies of morphological variables, but there is a great need for more systematic, theoretically sophisticated empirical studies in this area. Analogical change is also of great potential relevance to the study of language planning and standardization, since analogical innovations are often major targets of purist and prescriptivist condemnation.

Ironically, I think the hardest to win over might be historical linguists whose interests are concentrated in the traditional areas of sound change and comparative reconstruction. The Neogrammarian interest in analogy was initially driven by their determination to establish the utter exceptionlessness of regular sound change and to answer their critics, who argued that they were invoking analogy promiscuously to explain away every inconvenient development they came across. There have always been some historical linguists who, like Paul, develop a genuine fascination with analogical change for its own sake, but many others have always regarded it primarily as a nuisance that obscures the predictable developments attributable to sound change and makes it difficult or impossible to reconstruct many aspects of the proto-language.

In spite of all the efforts to develop coherent models and classification schemes, analogy is still widely considered a 'wastebasket' (Campbell 2004: 104), a 'terminological receptacle devoid of explanatory power' (King 1969: 127). In a sense, there is really nothing wrong with this attitude. It is fine to specialize in sound change and reconstruction, and once such specialists have established to their satisfaction that a phenomenon is not the kind of change they are interested in, it is natural to set it aside; but I hope to persuade at least a few readers that an insightful analysis of some of the developments they have been setting aside might contribute a great deal to our understanding of language history.

Finally, analogical change can be pretty entertaining. The OED characterizes several hundred coinages as 'humorous', 'jocular', or 'playful'. A large portion of these are analogical innovations of one type or another. Whether it is a simple proportional extension of an inflectional pattern, as in *lipsync–lipsanc–lipsunc*, a blend such as *brony* (coined to describe a 'bro' who is a fan of TV's *My Little Pony*), or a backformation, such as the verb *to buttle* from *butler* or the adjective *gruntled* from *disgruntled*, it is hard to deny that analogical innovations are, very often, kind of fun.

Notes

1. The sections that deal with analogy changed substantially between the first and the second edition (1886) and then remained largely the same after that, so references here are to the 1886 edition except where otherwise indicated.
2. Except in those instances where the phonetic aspect of speech is crucial, all references to 'speakers' in this book should be understood as a convenient abbreviation for 'speakers, writers and signers'.
3. Schuchardt points out, however, that the 'blinding sophistry' of the Neogrammarian doctrine of the exceptionlessness of sound laws 'is rooted in the earlier point of view that separated speech from human beings, that attributed to it an independent life . . .' (1885: 34, translation by Wilbur in Vennemann and Wilbur 1972: 64; see also Schürr 1925: 41).
4. This type of hypercorrection is sometimes referred to as 'structural' to distinguish it from the pattern of 'statistical' hypercorrection described by Labov (1966). For our purposes, it is even more important not to confuse either of these dialect-contact phenomena with Ohala's (1993) notion of phonological hypercorrection, which plays an important role in my account of folk etymology (§4.2).
5. Davies (1978) explains that proportional equations were introduced into linguistics by Havet (1875), and some of Havet's theoretical arguments are strikingly similar to Paul's. It is not clear whether Paul was familiar with Havet's work or arrived at his position independently. Something that very closely resembles a proportional equation can actually be found a few years earlier, in Whitney 1867: 85.

2

Basic Mechanisms of Morphological Change

2.1 Introduction

It has become fairly common to account for endogenous grammatical change in terms of two primary mechanisms, associated with two of the main things that language users do: (1) produce utterances that may include forms that they have never before encountered; (2) perceive and make sense of utterances produced by others, and of patterns across utterances. As we saw in Chapter 1, the first mechanism has long been referred to as analogy. The Neogrammarians did not use any single word consistently for the second mechanism. Saussure (1995 [1916]: 232) spoke of 'changes in interpretation' (*changements d'interprétation*); Jespersen proposed 'metanalysis' (1922: 173); many others have used the term 'reinterpretation'. The use of **reanalysis** in this sense started catching on in the 1970s, but at that point analogy was not the preferred term for the first mechanism (Haspelmath 1995: 24–5 n. 1). Timberlake (1977) distinguished between reanalysis and **actualization**. Andersen (1973, 1974, 1980), who has adopted Timberlake's terminology in more recent work, coined the terms **abductive** and **deductive innovations**. More recently, the term **(analogical) extension** has gained some currency (Harris and Campbell 1995; Haspelmath 1998; Deutscher 2001, 2002).

As far as I am aware, the first to propose the terminological pairing of reanalysis and analogy to refer to the two basic mechanisms of grammatical change were Hopper and Traugott (1993). I will follow their practice, with one clarification – that analogy in this context refers specifically to analogy$_2$ – and one slight modification: The *re-* in reanalysis is almost always understood to imply change. As explained in Chapter 1 with regards to analogy$_2$, nothing about the mechanisms themselves or their normal operation entails innovation or change (Andersen 2006). For this reason, I will call the basic mechanism **analysis**, reserving 'reanalysis' to refer specifically to the type of innovation to which analysis gives rise.

A defining criterion for distinguishing between analysis and analogy$_2$ is that the immediate effects of the former are **covert**, while the latter has immediate **overt** effects. Although advances in neuro-imaging techniques are rapidly opening up possibilities that were unimaginable a few decades ago (Jaeger et al.

1996), outside observers still generally cannot look into people's brains and see the internal representations they associate with forms and expressions. We can, however, directly observe the utterances they produce. (Occasionally, as fans of Amelia Bedelia know, an individual's behavior can also provide evidence for their interpretation of a linguistic expression.)

2.2 Defining (re)analysis

In textbook accounts of analogical change, 'reanalysis' is often used in a sense that is clearly narrower than what is intended here (Heine 1993: 116–19). Trask (1996: 103), for example, writes that '[i]n reanalysis, a word which historically has one particular morphological structure comes to be perceived by speakers as having a second, quite different structure.' Those who treat reanalysis as one of the two basic mechanisms of grammatical change often cite Langacker's (1977: 58) definition, 'change in the structure of an expression or class of expressions that does not involve any immediate or intrinsic modification of its surface manifestation' (Haspelmath 1998: 317; Hopper and Traugott 2003: 51). One point that is not made explicit in Langacker's definition, but is especially important for morphological change, is that covert reanalysis can involve either syntagmatic or paradigmatic structure (Kiparsky 1992: 57). One common kind of paradigmatic reanalysis involves the categories of lexical stems, as when English speakers started taking the stems of certain -*y* adjectives, such as *sleepy*, to be verbs rather than nouns, licensing the extension of this way of forming adjectives to unambiguously verbal bases, as in *runny* (§2.5.4). Another kind involves the motivations for paradigmatic distinctions, with morphologization from phonology (§2.5) and exaptation (§2.5.6) providing many examples.

The definitions below are intended to maintain a symmetry between the two complementary mechanisms of analogy$_2$ (§1.5.2) and analysis.

(6a) **analysis** is the capacity of hearers/learners to assign structural and semantic interpretations to linguistic expressions that they may have never before encountered.

(6b) *an* **analysis** is a structural and semantic interpretation assigned to an expression (word, phrase, clause, sentence, etc.) by a hearer/learner.

(6c) a **reanalysis** (a type of innovation) is an analysis that differs from those that previously were or would have been assigned to the expression in question.

It is often argued that **ambiguous** surface forms or patterns are an essential prerequisite for reanalysis (e.g. Timberlake 1977). Obviously, a form or pattern is normally consistent with the structure and meaning/function assigned to it by the individual who produced it, and a hearer/learner can only reanalyze it if it is also consistent with some alternative structure or meaning/function. We might say that reanalysis is licensed by ambiguous forms, while analogical innovation is licensed by missing forms. For discussion and clarification of the role of ambiguity in reanalysis, see Harris and Campbell (1995: 70–2).

2.3 Associative interference

In Chapter 1, I adopted Oertel's (1901) solution of recognizing associative interference as an additional phenomenon alongside analogical formation in order to account for 'non-proportional' developments and effects, i.e. overt innovations that are analogical in the sense that they are based on (perceived) semantic or grammatical relationships among forms, but that cannot be modeled as the solving of a proportional equation (or the application of a grammatical rule).

In order to account for the range of phenomena that Oertel and others attribute to associative interference, we need to recognize two additional mechanisms: (1) interference in production; (2) interference in perception (mishearing). As we will see in Chapter 4, these two interference mechanisms are directly associated with the two primary types of non-proportional analogical change: contamination and folk etymology, respectively. Beyond this, the interference mechanisms often play an important supporting role in proportional analogical change. Interference of both types can occur not only between existing forms, as they do in contamination and folk etymology, but also between an existing form and a potential proportional innovation. If a traditional irregular form is phonetically similar enough to the corresponding regular formation that the former could easily be misheard as the latter, this could greatly diminish the survival prospects of the irregular form. Similarly, in the course of speech planning, speakers presumably create mental representations of hypothetical regular counterparts to stored irregular forms; interference (contamination) between the former and the latter could help account for cases of partial regularization and partial leveling for which a proportional model is available but may not, by itself, provide a satisfactory explanation (see §5.1).

2.4 (Re)analysis, analogy$_2$ and grammatical change

As mentioned in §1.6.1, we find at least three positions in the literature regarding the ontological relationship between reanalysis and analogy: (1) some scholars treat them as two opposing/complementary aspects of grammatical change (Hopper and Traugott 2003); (2) others subsume reanalysis under analogy (Wheeler 1887; Hermann 1931); (3) still others classify analogy as a type of reanalysis (Traugott and Trousdale 2010; Kiparsky 2012).

With respect to the second of these three positions, there is no question that (re)analysis is often highly analogical in the sense that learners' analyses of expressions and patterns are guided by parallels they have encountered elsewhere in the language (Jeffers and Lehiste 1979; Fischer 2007; Traugott and Trousdale 2010; Garrett 2012). Similarly, analogy$_1$ plays an undeniable role in semantic change (Paul 1886: 80, 127, 130; Oertel 1901; Kroesch 1926). In fact, most (arguably all) grammatically or semantically motivated innovations are highly analogical in a general sense, but covert reanalyses are – by definition – opposed to analogical innovations in the technical sense of analogy$_2$.

Those who argue that the prevailing terminological confusion is reason enough for historical linguists to avoid the terms 'analogy' and 'analogical' altogether have a good point (Andersen 1980; Harris and Campbell 1995: 5), but the proposal to banish these terms has been around for some time, and the terms and the confusion are still very much with us. In this book, I try the alternative tack of retaining the terms but doing my best to be clear about what I mean by them.

The third position reflects a widespread view that closely identifies all changes in mental grammars with reanalysis. The assumption is that learners build their mental grammars based more or less exclusively on the utterances they hear from others, along with Universal Grammar. The underlying grammatical changes most directly associated with overt analogical innovations can be characterized as losses: loss of an irregular property of a lexical item; loss of a rule (King 1969: 46–51; Hock 1986: 267–70); loss of a condition on a rule (Harris and Campbell 1995: 101–15); loss of an 'adaptive rule' (Andersen 1973); etc. Many overt analogical innovations can plausibly be understood as essentially automatic consequences of such losses. A regular English past-tense form such as *glided* is simply the default that speakers assume in the absence of positive evidence for any particular form. In this sense, the only real innovation associated with the historical emergence of *glided* is the loss of the original irregular form *glode*. There is no separate grammatical innovation corresponding to the production of the default form *glided* because default forms need not (and in many theories do not) have representations in the mental grammar at all. The actual production of *glided* by speakers would then be of no consequence for the historical development of the language since, in the absence of any irregular alternative, this is the form that language users would assume even if they never encountered it.

It might seem like a stretch to attribute the simple loss of an irregular word-form to 'reanalysis', even if it does occur as learners construct their mental grammars based on the speech they hear from others, but when we consider more systematic types of 'rule generalization', there is an obvious sense in which learners might arrive at new hypotheses about conditions on rules by reanalyzing the ambiguous patterns they hear across relevant forms (Hopper and Traugott 2003: 68).

This view is by no means universally accepted. After providing some theoretical background in the next three subsections, I will return in §2.4.4 to the question of the relationship between analogical innovations and grammatical change under different conceptions of the nature of the mental grammar.

2.4.1 History, synchrony, diachrony, panchrony

Under Saussure's dichotomy between synchrony and diachrony, language use (speakers applying their mental grammars to produce and process utterances) is a strictly synchronic matter. Both before and since Saussure, however, many linguists have held a different view, according to which every speech act is a historical event and it is impossible for speakers to use their mental grammars without changing them. This is the 'dynamic' conception of grammar mentioned in §1.2 in connection with the Neogrammarians, and explored in somewhat more detail in §8.4 below.

This does not in any way call into question the crucial distinction between etymological and grammatical relations and the fallacies that linguists commit when they confuse the two, points which are emphasized not only by Saussure

(1995 [1916]: 135–8), but equally by Paul before him (1886: 29, 153, 200). But it does suggest that much of what we are used to thinking of as 'synchronic', specifically language use and acquisition, really belongs to language history, and that only a frozen snapshot of a grammatical system at a single moment in time is truly synchronic. It also means that 'historical' and 'diachronic' should not be used interchangeably.

Saussure briefly discusses the notion of a 'panchronic' (1995 [1916]: 134) perspective on language, by which he means essentially what other linguists call 'universals' and what Paul calls 'principles of language history'. All of the general forces, constraints, mechanisms and principles that we identify as being constantly at work in all languages – whether they are of a physical, social, cognitive, or specifically linguistic nature – are panchronic, in Saussure's sense, although many present-day linguists confusingly refer to them as 'synchronic'. The term 'panchronic' is also sometimes used in roughly the sense that I am using 'dynamic'.

2.4.2 'Language change is grammar change'?

Early proponents of a Chomskyan/generative approach to historical linguistics often emphasized a key point that set them apart from their immediate predecessors. As King put it: 'As historical linguistics is treated in generative grammar, grammar is enough: "sound change" is grammar change, "analogy" is grammar change, borrowing is grammar change' (1969: 128). Later scholars have sometimes summed up this position with the slogan 'language change is grammar change' (Bybee 2009: 351; Traugott and Trousdale 2010). This formulation is commonly taken to imply an approach to historical linguistics with the following characteristics:

1. most generally, the view that we should conceive of language change in terms of differences in speakers' mental grammars rather than differences in bodies of texts or utterances produced at different points in time;
2. that mental grammars only represent speakers' (core) competence;
3. that learners (children) are the primary agents of change in the sense that the interesting aspects of grammatical change are attributable to (child) language acquisition;
4. Chomskyans have often emphasized the importance of innate linguistic universals and downplayed the significance of surface forms and patterns to learners' construction of mental grammars (Kiparsky 1974: 260).

Some critics take an all-or-nothing attitude here, but the first characteristic, in particular, is entirely independent of the others. Chomsky and Halle point out that 'the conception of linguistic change as a change in the grammar is also implicit in the traditional views of sound change' (1968: 250), and indeed Paul, in particular, is quite insistent that we must think of language change in terms of differences in structured systems inside speakers' heads: '**The mental systems described above are the real carriers of historical development. The actual utterances have no development**' (1886: 25, my translation, emphasis in original). Paul conceived of the mental system as an elaborate network of representations that would reflect an individual's entire experience with language – and would be constantly updated to represent new experiences. Differences in frequency of use, for example, would be reflected in how strongly items are imprinted in memory (1886: 88; Bybee 1985, 2006).

The conception of grammatical change as differences over time in individuals' mental systems was widely rejected (or ignored) in the period of radical empiricism ushered in by Bloomfield. In the wake of the subsequent extreme rationalist reaction of Chomsky and his followers, many historical linguists have found their way back to something resembling Paul's position (see references in §1.2), i.e. embracing the general notion that we should conceive of language change in terms of differences in speakers' mental grammars, while (1) adopting a broad view of what is represented in mental grammars; (2) seeing acquisition as a lifelong process; and (3) understanding learners' construction of mental grammars as a matter of discerning and interpreting surface patterns, using maximally general cognitive abilities and strategies rather than relying on purported properties of Universal Grammar.

This book is primarily about change in morphological systems – the morphological components of grammars – and, like Paul and many others, I conceive of a morphological system as something that: (1) exists in the mind/brain of an individual, and (2) reflects all aspects of that individual's morphological knowledge and experience (Bybee 2006). This means, of course, that when we talk about a speech community we are actually talking about many morphological systems, one for each individual, and when we talk about morphological changes that have taken place between, for example, Middle English and Modern English, we are not really talking about change in 'a system', but rather about differences between the systems of individuals who lived at different times.

2.4.3 The role of transmission/acquisition in grammatical innovation

There is a long tradition of regarding the transmission of language to new learners as the primary locus of grammatical innovation. This was the prevailing view in pre-structuralist times (Paul 1886: 31); it was less in line with Saussurean and especially Bloomfieldian theoretical and methodological thinking, but then came roaring back with the advent of generative work on language change in the 1960s (Halle 1962: 64–5; King 1969: 78; Aitchison 2001: 201–2; Janda 2001). As Janda and Joseph (2003: 75) point out, many of the objections to this position may result from associating it with some of the more dubious aspects of the generative 'language change is grammar change' view outlined in the previous section. In particular, the equation 'learners = children', and the idea that children are thus the primary agents of change, has been the object of a great deal of well-founded criticism. 'Learners' in this book should always be understood to mean lifelong learners (Andersen 2006). We must be especially cautious about making too much of apparent parallels between historical change and analogical innovations in child speech. Children innovate in all kinds of ways in the early stages of acquisition. Much of this appears to be of little direct relevance to language change (Bybee and Slobin 1982b; Bybee 2009).

Most scholars accept that transmission plays a significant role in some aspects of language change. Quite a few do argue, however, that its importance has been overemphasized, resulting in an underappreciation of the role of other aspects of language use in driving change (Bolinger 1968: 93, 104; Haspelmath 1998; Bybee 2009). The argument for transmission playing a key role is especially strong in the common scenario where reanalyses are facilitated, or even necessitated, by the emergence of new surface ambiguities, often as a result of regular sound change – as in the following classic example, discussed by Osthoff (1878a), Saussure (1995 [1916]: 195) and Bloomfield (1933: 417), among others:

In Old High German (OHG), there were many noun + noun compounds such as *beta-hûs* 'prayer house'. The final *-a* on *beta* made this element unambiguously a noun stem. Later, this *-a* was lost by regular sound change. Learners could now just as easily interpret the first element in the compound *bet-hûs* (or later *bethaus*) as the stem of the verb *beten* 'to pray' rather than as the noun. We know that they did reanalyze it in this way because this was the basis for verb-stem + noun becoming a productive new pattern for compounding in German, as in Modern German *Esszimmer* 'dining room', literally 'eat-room'; *Fahrschule* 'driving school', *Schreibtisch* 'desk', literally 'write-table'.

If language were never passed on to new generations of learners, it would not be clear why the emergence of new surface ambiguities should have any consequences for grammatical structure. Even after forms with and without original final *-a* had become indistinguishable in speech, there is no obvious reason why speakers who had learned the language back when the *-a* was still present would lose their distinct mental representations. New learners who are exposed only to forms without *-a*, however, would have no access to these representations. Many cases of analogical change have a backstory similar to this.

2.4.4 The relationship of analogical innovation to grammatical change in static and dynamic models of mental grammar

We saw in the last subsection that the case for locating at least certain kinds of covert reanalysis in the transmission of language to new learners is quite strong. Linguists who assume a more or less strict synchrony–diachrony dichotomy and the associated 'static' model of the mental grammar attribute virtually all grammatical change to inter-generational or inter-lectal transmission, which means that overt analogical innovations, as direct reflexes of grammatical change, must also be consequences of transmission/acquisition. Langacker (1977: 58) sums up this position as follows: 'Reanalysis may lead to changes at the surface level ... but these surface changes can be viewed as the natural and expected result of functionally prior modifications in rules and underlying representations.' One popular view, developed by Kiparsky (1965, etc.), attributes (most) analogical innovations to 'imperfect learning'. In the simplest case, as we saw above, learners automatically produce previously unattested default forms because they have not (yet) acquired the corresponding traditional forms that block the default forms from surfacing in other speakers (see also Reiss 2006).

Proponents of 'dynamic' conceptions of grammar see the relationship between overt innovations and grammatical change differently. First of all, the production of an innovative form does not necessarily mean that the traditional form has not (yet) been acquired (Jespersen 1922: 163). Overt innovations frequently involve a little drama played out at the moment of production, with the traditional form and one or more analogical alternatives in competition (Yang 2002). These analogical alternatives are not necessarily defaults, and the traditional form does not automatically win just by showing up. Rather, the outcome is 'a question of dominance' (Paul 1886: 92, my translation), i.e. it is determined by the relative strength of the mental representation of the traditional form vs. that of the pattern(s) behind the potential innovation(s). Secondly, if the winning form is an innovation that previously had no representation in the innovator's mental grammar, one is now created, and otherwise the representation of the winning form is reinforced and thereby becomes slightly more likely to win out again on subsequent occasions. Thus, under this model, overt analogical innovations are not mere 'symptoms' (Saussure 1995 [1916]: 232) of underlying changes in the mental grammar; they are constitutive of such changes. Or we might say that the overt innovations and the corresponding changes in the mental representations of forms are two sides of the same coin.

All accounts of analogical change that make any pretense of being comprehensive acknowledge that imperfect learning is not the only source of overt analogical innovations. At least occasionally, speakers who have learned an established form might: (1) fail to access it at the moment of speaking; (2) produce an analogical slip of the tongue; (3) gradually forget low-frequency forms that they have not used for a long time; or (4) deliberately innovate for some kind of intended effect (e.g. humorous, shocking). In a static model, the overt innovations attributable to such 'performance' phenomena would not have any consequences for the speaker's mental grammar. Furthermore, an implicit assumption of many theories is that the last of these four factors – intentional, rule-bending creativity on the part of speakers – plays at most a minimal role in morphological change, that learners and speakers are generally striving to match the output of those around them as closely as possible.

An alternative view is that speakers' expressiveness and creativity is a major driving force in grammatical change (Coseriu 1970 [1969]: 211–12; Lehmann 1985; Haspelmath 1999). According to this view, individuals' objective in constructing mental grammars is not so much to enable themselves to produce output matching that of those around them as to give themselves a reference point that they can 'play on' (Sapir 1921: 148). They need to know what prevailing usage is not so that they can try to follow it slavishly, but so that they can deviate from it strategically and effectively. Speakers knowingly produce overt innovations that deviate from current norms of usage for communicative purposes – for example, to call attention to their point (or to themselves), or to try to be funny. Corresponding changes in mental grammars may then *follow* the overt innovations, as people gradually stop regarding the new forms as deviations and/or new learners fail to recognize them as such, and they become the new normal. As we will see in §7.6, this kind of development has important implications for the teleology of grammatical change.

The next step is to recognize that a speech community does not have one monolithic 'prevailing usage' but rather a multitude of 'styles' (Eckert 2012) that are constantly being renegotiated in every social interaction. This is far from being the whole story of morphological change, but it is an important and fascinating part of the story that deserves more attention than it generally receives. Although many overt innovations are undoubtedly produced unwittingly based strictly on the grammars constructed by the innovators, we know that some analogical innovations are produced intentionally – lexical blends being the most obvious example (§4.4.3), some instances of folk etymology being another (§4.2). Attempts at humor are frequently mentioned as a motivation for backformation (§3.6.3) and irregularizations. Osthoff (1879a: 36), for example, refers to innovative strong forms of historically weak German verbs, such as *geschonken* < *geschenkt* 'given (as a present)', *gemorken* < *gemerkt* 'noticed', *gewunken* < *gewinkt* 'winked', and *geschumpfen* < *geschimpft* 'scolded', as 'formations of jocular folk-speech' (*Bildungen des scherzenden Volksmundes*). There is even a 'Society for the Strengthening of Verbs' (*Gesellschaft zur Stärkung der Verben*; http://verben.texttheater.de/) dedicated to this form of morphological humor. American sitcoms also exploit the comedic potential of irregularizations, with forms such as *provode* for *provided* (*How I Met Your Mother*) and *hed* for *heeded* (*The Office*). A famous Boston joke is based on *scrod* being understood as the past participle of *screw*. There are also cases where an initial innovation appears to have been produced unwittingly, but then caught on and spread because imitators found it funny or expressive or useful (Kiparsky 1974: 264).

2.5 Types of morphological reanalysis

Kiparsky's (1992: 57) conception of the basic distinction between syntagmatic and paradigmatic reanalysis (see §2.2 above) corresponds at least roughly to Andersen's (1980) **innovations in segmentation** vs. **innovations in valuation**, and Hock's (1986: 200) **recutting** vs. **reinterpretation**, respectively. I will adopt the existing term **resegmentation** for the former and use its obvious counterpart **revaluation** for the latter. Resegmentation, which is the sole focus of many textbook accounts of morphological reanalysis, affects the location of grammatically significant boundaries, e.g. between stem and affix. We can identify at least three distinct subtypes, based on whether the reanalysis: (1) spawns a new formative, as in the reanalysis of *fork* as *four* + *-k* (Deutscher 2002: 483); (2) amalgamates previously separate formatives, as in German *-er* + *-ei* > *-erei* (Haspelmath 1995: 5); or (3) relocates a boundary without changing the number of formatives, as in Old English *forgifen* + *-ess* > *forgive* + *-ness* (see §2.5.3 below).

Revaluation, by contrast, typically affects the meaning or grammatical function or category of an element or of a paradigmatic pattern. A nominal stem might be reanalyzed as verbal, for example (as in the *beta-hûs* example discussed above), or a derivational affix might be reanalyzed as inflectional (as has happened with English *-ing*). Examples of each type will be discussed in more detail below.

Morphologization deserves special mention here as the type of reanalysis implicated in the birth of new morphology. The term most often refers to the revaluation of an originally phonological alternation as being morphologically conditioned (Joseph and Janda 1988). Such an alternation sometimes becomes a primary marker of a grammatical distinction, as has occured with ablaut in

Germanic strong verbs (*drive–drove*; *sing–sang*) and with umlaut in some English and German nouns (*tooth–teeth*; *Vater–Väter* 'father(s)'). In addition to morphologization from phonology, we can also speak of 'morphologization from syntax' when previously separate words in a syntactic construction fuse into one (Joseph 2003) – as in the case of the future tense in modern Romance languages, where what was once a construction consisting of an infinitive + an auxiliary gave rise to a new inflectional paradigm, e.g. French *porter* 'to carry' + *ai* '(I) have' > *porterai* '(I) will carry'. A great deal of inflectional and derivational morphology can be traced back to similar origins. This kind of development is discussed in great detail in the grammaticalization literature (Hopper and Traugott 2003).

One way of further classifying types of reanalysis is in terms of the relationship of what is reanalyzed to the subsequent analogical actualizations of that reanalysis. The traditional proportional equation provides a convenient schema here. Based on the four terms in an equation of the form A : B = C : D, where A and B (and C and D) belong to the same 'material group' (e.g. two inflectional forms of the same word), A and C (and B and D) belong to the same 'formal group' (e.g. the dative plural forms of two different nouns), and D is the traditional form that is replaced by the analogical innovation, we can distinguish between A-, B-, C- and D-reanalysis, as explained in the following subsections.

2.5.1 D-reanalysis

As just mentioned, the D form is the old form that is replaced by the solution to the proportional equation. Two kinds of D-reanalysis can open the door for an overt analogical innovation. Most obviously, the D form can be revaluated such that it is no longer regarded as related to C, or at least not in the same way as B is to A. This is the well-known type of development that Kuryłowicz (1966 [1945–9]) addressed with his Fourth Law of Analogy (Kiparsky 1974, 1992; Hock 1986: 223–7). Especially common in Germanic languages is the revaluation of an irregular past participle as a lexicalized adjective, opening the door for the analogical creation of a new, regular past participle. In cases such as *straight* (from *stretch*), *wrought* (from *work*), *sodden* (from *seethe*) and German *verwandt* 'related' (from *verwenden* 'use, apply'), *gediegen* 'dignified' (from *gedeihen* 'thrive'), the adjectives are probably no longer related to the verbs at all in most speakers' minds. In other cases, such as *molten* (from *melt*), it seems likely that many speakers still do regard the words as related.

The other important subtype is what we might call D→C reanalysis, whereby a form that was originally the output of a particular rule is reanalyzed as an input candidate for the same rule. This results in morphological double-marking (§4.4.2). Forms affected by D→C reanalysis are often but not always irregular, e.g. *bestest* and *worstest* vs. *drowned*.

The English adjective *near* has been affected by both types of D-reanalysis. *Near* was itself originally a comparative form. D→C reanalysis of *near* as a basic positive form licensed the creation of the new regular comparative *nearer*. The door for the new regular superlative form *nearest* was opened by D-reanalysis (lexicalization) of the old irregular superlative *next*.

The emergence of etymologically suppletive paradigms (Osthoff 1899;

Ronneberger-Sibold 1987, 1988) is essentially D-reanalysis in reverse: A form that was originally not related to the C form at all is reanalyzed as part of its paradigm. From the perspective of the verb *wend*, the original past form *went* has undergone ordinary D-reanalysis, opening the door for the new, regular form *wended*. From the perspective of the verb *go*, this development is a reverse D-reanalysis, whereby *went* has become the new past form, replacing earlier (equally suppletive) *yede/yode* (OE–ME *éode*). Similarly, *worse* and *worst* have always been suppletive comparative/superlative forms in English, but they once belonged primarily to the adjective *evil* and have since switched their allegiance to *bad*.

2.5.2 C-reanalysis

The best known examples of C-reanalysis are frequently discussed under the heading of backformation:

(7) *beans* : *bean* = *pease* : X, X = *pea*

Reanalysis of the C form in the equation, *pease*, is a prerequisite for the analogical innovation. Until they have reanalyzed the original mass noun *pease* as a plural, it would not make any sense to speakers to form a singular by dropping the final /z/. Campbell (2004: 116) claims that the backformation *chee* < *cheese* is common in child language. We can model this with the proportion in (8):

(8) *crackers* : *cracker* = *cheese* : X, X = *chee* (as in, *The host put out a big plate of crackers and cheese; we each took one cracker and one chee.*)

Presumably this innovation would never occur to many English speakers, and quite a few might be baffled when they hear it, because they have not analyzed *cheese* as a plural. An interesting hypothetical case to consider is *(panty) hose*, which not only has a final /z/ that would make it a candidate for reanalysis as a plural; we already treat it as a plural for agreement purposes: *These panty hose are dirty*, not **This panty hose is dirty*. Have speakers reanalyzed the /z/ as a plural ending? It is hard to say because semantically related nouns that (apparently) do have a plural ending, such as *pants*, *trousers*, *jeans*, *tights*, etc. are all – at least in my dialect – pluralia tantum. So the absence of singular *panty ho* does not prove that C-reanalysis has not occurred here.

In C-reanalysis, the item(s) or context(s) to which a rule is extended are the object of the reanalysis. Previously, these were not candidates for the rule because they did not have the right structure or status. C-reanalysis has no effect on the rule itself; what the rule does and the conditions on its application remain exactly as they were before. The only thing that changes is that one or more items that previously did not meet the conditions are reanalyzed in such a way that they do.

More examples of C-reanalysis in backformation can be found in §3.6.3. In languages like English, instances of C-reanalysis are somewhat harder to find outside of backformation simply because the base forms in most (inflectional and derivational) paradigms are morphologically simple, and there is thus no structure to reanalyze. However, one good example of C-reanalysis that does not involve backformation manifests itself in certain regularizations and irregularizations of verbs in Germanic languages. The weak inflectional pattern with a 'dental' suffix (English *-ed* and its cognates) in the past tense and participle is generally considered the default option for verbs of all shapes and sizes. Certain irregular patterns, however, display a strong analogical attraction for verbs with certain phonological characteristics (§8.7; Bybee and Moder 1983). Almost all English verbs ending in *-ing*, for example, are irregular, and all except *bring* form their participle with *-ung* and their past tense with *-ung* or *-ang*. Originally weak verbs such as *ring* and *string* prove that the attractive force of this pattern is real. However, the many verbs that are derived from homonymous nouns or adjectives by so-called **zero-derivation** or **conversion** systematically resist this attractive analogical force and remain regular (Kim et al. 1991):

(9) *I kinged* (not **kung*) *my opponent's checkers piece.*

There are several pairs of homonymous non-derived and denominal verbs where the former is irregular and the latter normally regular, e.g. *sling–slung* when the meaning is 'hurl' but usually *sling–slinged* in the sense of 'place in a sling'. This effect has been shown to work much the same way in German (Clahsen and Rothweiler 1993), and there is every reason to believe that the same is true of other West Germanic languages. To the extent that denominal status mandates regular and rules out irregular inflection, we would predict that an originally denominal verb would become a candidate for irregularization if reanalyzed as non-derived. Conversely, an originally irregular, non-derived verb would have to be regularized if it is reanalyzed as denominal.

There are a number of historical developments that appear to confirm these predictions, especially in German, Yiddish and Dutch. In most cases where an originally denominal verb has undergone irregularization in these languages, there appears to have no longer been a transparent semantic connection between the verb and any underlying noun or adjective when the irregularization occurred. German *weisen*, derived from *weise* 'wise', originally meant 'to make wise' but had come to mean 'to show' long before it underwent irregularization in the sixteenth c. (Pfeifer 1993; Fertig 2000: 113–14). As long as speakers analyzed *weisen* as being derived from the adjective *weise*, the regular, weak pattern (*weisen–weiste–geweist*) would have continued to be its only inflectional option. The historical irregularization to modern standard *weisen–wies–gewiesen* would thus constitute evidence that this verb had been reanalyzed as non-derived. This would be a C-reanalysis in that it turned a non-candidate into a candidate for an existing inflectional pattern. Similarly, the German verb *dingen* today shows variation between innovative strong and original weak forms. The relevant OHG meaning of the underlying noun *Ding* was '(Germanic) judicial assembly', and the derived verb meant to hold this assembly. Before any irregularization occurred, the noun had developed the basic meaning 'thing' and the semantics of the verb, which now means 'negotiate, hire', had gone off in a different direction, making it very unlikely that speakers continued to analyze the verb as derived from the noun. The Yiddish and Dutch cognates of *weisen* and *dingen* have also been irregularized.

Some Dutch dialects also show irregularization of *erven* 'to inherit' (Haeringen

1940: 250). Unlike in German, where the cognate *erben* is still transparently derived from *Erbe* 'inheritance' and remains invariably regular, the meaning of Dutch *erf* has been narrowed to 'piece of real estate (house + yard)', obscuring the semantic connection to the verb. German *preisen* 'to praise' is derived from *Preis*. The basic meaning of this noun (a loanword from Old French) was 'praise' in MHG, but it had shifted to 'price, prize' before the irregularization of the verb (Kluge 1975; Pfeifer 1993); German *schinden* 'to mistreat' is related to English 'to skin' (a borrowing from Old Norse); the underlying noun meaning 'skin' was lost in German before the verb was irregularized in MHG. Similarly, *weihen* 'to consecrate, ordain, make holy' was derived in proto-Germanic from the ancestor of OHG *wīh* 'holy'. The verb remained transparently deadjectival and invariably regular throughout the Middle Ages (Kühne 1999). Still weak in standard German today, it has been irregularized (participle: *gewiehen*) in many dialects following the loss of the adjective beginning in the sixteenth c. (Drosdowski et al. 1963; Pfeifer 1993; Jutz 1925: 298; Kranzmayer 1981: 281; Schatz 1897: 176; DWB); the Yiddish and Dutch cognates of German *schenken* 'to give (as a gift)' have been irregularized. The originally underlying adjective, reconstructed as Germanic *skanka-* 'tilted', was lost long ago. Irregularization of Yiddish *meldn* 'to declare, report' presumably also occurred only after the underlying noun (MHG *melde*) had been lost.

Clear evidence for the second prediction – that reanalysis of an originally non-derived verb as denominal sometimes forces regularization – is hard to come by simply because regularization of strong verbs is a relatively common and unremarkable phenomenon in the Germanic languages. This makes it hard to prove that derivational reanalysis was a contributing factor in any particular instance. Interestingly, however, there are a few cases where etymologists specifically mention this factor. The German noun *Reihe* 'row, series' was originally derived from the once strong verb *reihen* 'to thread, string beads'. Pfeifer (1993) cites reanalysis of the direction of this derivation as a possible reason for the regularization of the verb. Similarly, Kluge (1975) argues that the originally strong but now regularized verb *bleuen* 'to beat' came to be perceived as derived from the adjective *blau* 'blue', to which it is etymologically unrelated, and thus developed the sense 'to beat until (black and) blue'. Some regard the frequent spelling *bläuen* as orthographic evidence for this reanalysis. Finally, Drosdowski (1963) claims that the originally underived strong verb *(er)grimmen* 'to become angry', which underwent regularization beginning in the fourteenth c., was reanalyzed as derived from the adjective *grimm* 'angry' or the noun *Grimm* 'fury'.

Something analogous to C-reanalysis is very common in syntactic change. A classic example involves the argument structure of English verbs such as *like*, which formerly could be constructed with a dative experiencer, just like semantically similar verbs in other European languages such as French *plaire*, Spanish *gustar*, German *gefallen*. In other words, one could say *Me likes music*, where *music* is the grammatical subject, rather than *I like music*. According to the standard account, this change was facilitated by the fact that the distinction between nominative and dative case was not always marked morphologically even in Old English (and except in pronouns was rarely, if ever, marked in Middle English), which meant that many sentences containing such verbs were structurally ambiguous (Harris and Campbell 1995: 83–9). In *My friend likes poetry*, one cannot tell whether the grammatical subject is *my friend* or *poetry*. Structural reanalysis of such ambiguous instances was supposedly the precursor to overt change in sentences with disambiguating case-marked pronouns (*I* vs. *me*, *he* vs. *him*, etc.) and/or verbal agreement (*-s* for third sg. subjects only).

In all of these examples, we see the characteristic profile of C-reanalysis: There is no change in the rule itself; an existing rule simply comes to apply in cases where it previously did not apply. This characterization of C-reanalysis sounds very similar to the way many scholars would describe analogical change, and, as we have seen, covert reanalyses of this type are generally very closely linked to corresponding overt analogical innovations. I will consider some of the implications of this close connection between C-reanalysis and analogical innovation in §2.5.5 below.

2.5.3 B-reanalysis

We already saw one example of B-reanalysis in Chapter 1: *four* : *formation* = *two* : X, X = *twomation*. Here, it is the morphological structure of the B form, and specifically its relationship to the A form, that gets reanalyzed. B-reanalysis can result in the creation of a new rule where there was previously no rule at all, as a coincidental pattern is reanalyzed as being morphological. Since they are typically based on a single pair of forms, these rules usually do not get very far. They sometimes arise as spontaneous innovations in child speech and are kept alive, if at all, by parents proud of the linguistic ingenuity of their children. Examples include: *four* : *fork* = *three* : X, X = *threek* 'three-pronged fork' (Deutscher 2005: 174); *ear* : *irrigate* = *nose* : X, X = *nosigate* (Sturtevant 1947: 97–8; Anttila 1977: 19–20); *A* (a grade in school) : *ace* = *B* : X, X = *beece* (as in: *I don't think I aced that test, but I hope I at least beeced it*). The spawning of productive affixes from blends (e.g. *-(a)thon* < *marathon*) is a related phenomenon (§4.4.3).

More significant for morphological change are B-reanalyses that do not create rules out of coincidental patterns but rather change what existing rules do. This occurs frequently when the reanalysis affects the location of a boundary between stem and affix. A well-known example involves the Germanic suffix that became English *-ness*. The corresponding suffix in proto-Germanic was *-assu*. This suffix was frequently attached to stems ending in *-n*, and this *n* was subsequently reanalyzed as belonging to the suffix rather than the stem. In Old English, we find examples based on past participles, such as *forgifeness* 'forgiveness', which could still be analyzed as *forgifen* + *ess*, but also many instances based on adjectives, such as *gōdness* 'goodness' or *beorhtness* 'brightness', which provide unambiguous evidence of the reanalysis and the new productive rule of *-ness* suffixation (Krahe/Meid 1969: 159–62). Similar reanalyses give us the common Germanic suffix *-ling* – as in English *darling*, *sapling*, *nestling*, etc. – from attachment of *-ing* (OED *-ing*, suffix[3] 'one belonging to') to stems ending in *l*, as well as the German suffixes *-ner* and *-ler*, attributable to words where *-er* was attached to stems ending in *-n* or *-l* and then extended to give us new words such as *Rentner* 'pensioner' < *Rente* 'pension' and *Sportler* 'sportsman'. Of more limited consequence (so far, at least) are examples such as the resegmentation of *icicle*, originally *ice* + *ickle*, to yield the new formative *-sicle*, as in *popsicle, creamsicle, juicesicle*, etc.

Hyman (2003) discusses a fascinating case of B-reanalysis in Nyakyusa (Bantu). In this language, the coronal and velar root-final consonants *t, l, j, k* and *g* all neutralize to *s* when immediately followed by the causative suffix *-i̯-*, e.g. *-sat-* 'be in pain', *-sas-i̯-* 'give pain', *-sok-* 'go out', *-sos-i̯-* 'take out'. In the 'applicativized causative', where the applicative suffix *-is-/-es-* (from underlying *-il-/-el-*) is inserted between the root and the causative suffix, these verbs all have a root-final *-k*: *-sak-is-i̯-* 'give pain (applicative)', *-sok-es-i̯-* 'take out (applicative)'. Comparison with closely related languages indicates that this *-k* in the causative applicative is an analogical extension from verbs (such as *-sok-*) that have underlying root-final *-k* (see §3.6.2 below), and that the *s* in the applicative suffix *-is-/-es-* is not to be identified (historically) with the *s* that occurs root-finally when directly followed by the causative suffix. It would also be possible, however, for speakers to analyze a form such as *-sak-is-i̯-* as being derived from the causative *-sas-i̯-* by inserting *-ki-* before the root-final *s*. Evidence of such a reanalysis is provided by verbs with root-final *-p* and *-b*. These labial consonants become *f* rather than *s* when immediately followed by *-i̯-*, e.g. *-tup-* 'become thick', *-tuf-i̯-* 'make thick', *-olob-* 'become rich', *-olof-i̯-* 'make rich'. The corresponding applicativized causative forms are *-tuk-if-i̯-* and *-olok-ef-i̯-*. The *f*'s that appear to be part of the applicative suffix in these forms can only be explained by identifying them with the root-final *f*'s in *-tuf-i̯-* and *-olof-i̯-* and concluding that *-ki-/-ke-* has been reanalyzed as something like a productive applicative infix. (The picture is complicated a bit further, however, by verbs with root-final *-m*, such as *-lum-* 'bite' which forms the causative *-lum-i̯-* and the applicativized causative *-lum-ik-is-i̯-*.)

One type of B-reanalysis that is, according to Garrett (2001: 294), 'quite common cross-linguistically' occurs when 'prefixal reduplication that has become opaque is ... reinterpreted as infixation or internal vowel change (ablaut).' Garrett's own example involves the so-called 'intensive' in Yurok (an Algic language of Northern California). Most Yurok verbs form the intensive by infixing *-eg-* between the onset and the vowel of the first syllable in the stem; thus the verb meaning 'to pass' has the base form *la:y-* and the intensive *l-eg-a:y-*. Garrett argues that the intensive was originally formed by adding a reduplicant prefix *$C(C)e$-, consisting of a copy of the onset of the initial syllable of the stem plus the invariant vowel *e*. A regular $h > g$ sound change in intervocalic position, followed by analogical changes that re-introduced intervocalic *h* in other morphological contexts, made the reduplication opaque in verbs with stem-initial *h-*, so that when one looks at the base form and the intensive of a verb such as 'to make' – *hohkum-*, *-hegohkum-* – the most obvious analysis would be that the intensive is formed not by reduplication but rather by infixing *-eg-*. Garrett argues that this reanalysis of the ambiguous intensives of *h*-initial verbs was followed by an analogical extension of the *-eg-* infix to other verbs, replacing the original reduplication.

Morphologically complex words of foreign origin are particularly vulnerable to this kind of resegmentation for the same reason that they are so frequently affected by folk etymology: Their structure is opaque to speakers of the borrowing language. Thus, *helicopter* was originally formed (in French) from the Greek elements *helico-*, a bound stem corresponding to the noun *helix*, and *pter* < *pterón* 'wing' (as in *pterodactyl*). Resegmentation as *heli-* + *copter* is evidenced not only by the shortened noun *copter* itself, but also by the productive use of *heli-* in *heliport, helipad*, etc.

Shifts can occur across word boundaries as well, especially between a clitic and a host. The make-up of quite a few English nouns has been affected by reanalysis of the location of the boundary between a noun and a preceding determiner; *apron, adder, augur* and *aught/ought* 'zero' all originally had an initial *n-*. Resegmentation of sequences like *a napron* as *an apron* yielded the modern forms. The opposite development has given us the *n*-initial words: *nickname* < *eke-name*; *newt* < *ewt*; and *nonce* < *once*. In some cases, only a single word is affected by resegmentation across a word boundary, e.g: *druther(s)* < *(I')d rather* and *riding* 'administrative or electoral district' < OE *priding (ultimately < ON *þriðjung-r* 'third part') due to reanalysis of **North thriding,* *South thriding, etc.

An especially common kind of B-reanalysis is the coalescence of two whole affixes into one. The German diminutive suffixes *-chen* and *-lein* both arose in this way, from *-ch-* + *-īn* and *-(i)l-* + *-īn*, respectively. Often, two originally separate affixes will continue to occur separately in some words while behaving as a single affix in others. English *-istic* (of Greek origin) is an example. Even though *-ist* and *-ic* frequently occur separately, *-istic* must be a single suffix in a word such as *cannibalistic* because there is no word *cannibalist. Similar arguments lead us to posit the German suffixes *-igkeit* (< *-ig-* + *-heit/-keit*) and *-erei* (< *-er-* + *-ei*) and their Dutch cognates *-igheid* and *-erij* (Haspelmath 1995; Booij 2002). If we dig deeper, we find that many synchronically unanalyzable affixes originated in this way (Paul 1886: 204; Kiparsky 1992: 57). The superlative suffix *-est*, for example, is historically a combination of the ancestor of the *-er* comparative suffix (**-ōz-*/**-iz-* in proto-Germanic) followed by an originally separate **-to-*.

Perhaps the most famous example of B-reanalysis involves the Oceanic passive suffix **-(i)a*. In reconstructed Oceanic, this suffix could be added to consonant-final active stems such as *awhit 'embrace' and *hopuk 'catch', yielding the passive forms *awhitia and *hopukia. Regular loss of final consonants gives us the attested active forms *awhi* and *hopu*. The claim is that this sound change triggered a reanalysis of the morphemic structure of the passives: *awhit-ia > *awhi-tia; *hopuk-ia > *hopu-kia. Evidence for this reanalysis comes from apparent generalization of default passive allomorphs with particular suffix-initial consonants, for example *-tia* in Māori and *-ʔia* in Hawaiian (Hale 1973; Hock 1986: 200–2). In the Māori case, *awhit-ia > *awhi-tia would constitute B-reanalysis – reanalysis of outputs of the rule that forms passives from actives – yielding a new rule (suffixation of *-tia*) that is subsequently applied to other active forms to produce analogical innovations. The substance of the reanalysis would be somewhat different under the traditional account that regards the relevant consonants as 'thematic consonants' rather than as part of the passive suffix (Juliette Blevins 2008: 93–7; Albright 2008: 167) – much like the euphonic consonants that occur before the passive suffix in some Malagasy verbs (Rajemisa-Raolison 1971: 98).

2.5.4 A-reanalysis

The *beta-hûs* case discussed in §2.4.3 is a good example of A-reanalysis. Here, the change affects not what a rule does, as with B-reanalysis, but rather its domain or conditions of application. The A forms are those that an existing rule applies to. If properties of these forms are reanalyzed, then the rule can come to apply to a different set of inputs.

Examples of A-reanalysis are especially plentiful in derivational morphology. Affixes that could previously only be attached to nouns, for example, come to be used with verbs as well, because some of the original nominal bases are reanalyzed as verbal. In the older Germanic languages, the reflexes of the important proto-Germanic adjective-forming suffix *-ga- could only be attached to nouns and adjectives. The reflexes in Modern English (-*y*) and German and Dutch (-*ig*) can also be attached to verbal bases, e.g. English *runny*, German *wackelig* 'shaky' < *wackeln* 'to wobble', Dutch *nalatig* 'negligent' < *nalaten* 'to neglect'. This extension was apparently licensed by the reanalysis of bases that could be either nouns or verb stems, e.g. English *sleepy* (1225), German *gläubig* 'devout, trusting' (compare *Glaube* 'belief, faith' and *glauben* 'believe'). Similar developments have affected many other derivational suffixes in the Germanic languages, including English -*ish*/German -*isch*; English -*ly*/German -*lich*/Dutch -*elijk*; English -*some*/German -*sam*/Dutch -*zaam*. In the case of German -*bar*/Dutch -*baar* '-able', the shift to deverbal status has been much more thorough. This suffix is etymologically related to the verb *bear* and was originally attached to nouns, contributing the meaning '-bearing'. We still see this in a few words such as modern German *fruchtbar*/Dutch *vruchtbaar* 'fruitful (i.e. fruit-bearing)'. But in its primary modern use, this has become a highly productive deverbal suffix corresponding to English -*able*: it forms passive modal adjectives from transitive verbs, e.g. German *tragen* 'carry' > *tragbar* 'portable' (Paul 1886: 201–3; Booij 2002: 130–3).

An even more striking example is the English/German/Dutch agentive suffix -*er* (< proto-Germanic *-ārjo-z*). Originally, this suffix could only be attached to nouns to produce new nouns with the meaning 'person having something to do with X' (where X is the meaning of the base noun). This use can still be seen in Modern English words such as *hatter* and is highly productive with place names, e.g. English *New Yorker*; Dutch *Amsterdammer*; German *Pariser*, etc. In the older languages, we see this original use clearly in examples such as Gothic *bôkareis*/Old English *bócere* 'scribe', derived from the noun corresponding to Modern English *book*. As this example suggests, the construction was used especially to designate professions and occupations, and there was very often also a related denominal verb. In Gothic, for example, we find the basic noun *dôm-* 'judgment', the derived verb *dômjan* 'to judge' and the noun *dômareis* 'judge (i.e. person who judges)'. Nouns like *dômareis* were then reanalyzed as being derived from the verbs rather than directly from the basic nouns.

In some cases, what gets reanalyzed is the shared property of the entire set of A forms that defines them as the domain of a rule. The prefixation of *ge-* on past participles in German and Dutch provides a good example (Fertig 1998b). In both languages, this prefix does not occur on verbs that already begin with an unstressed derivational prefix, such as German *beginnen* 'begin' or *entkommen* 'escape'. The original conditioning of the rule seems to have been entirely morphological: the presence of a derivational prefix blocked the affixation of *ge-*. These prefixed items were once the only verbs in German or Dutch that did not have primary stress on the initial syllable, so speakers could also analyze the pattern prosodically: *ge-* is not prefixed to verbs with primary stress on a non-initial syllable. As long as the prefixed verbs were the only ones with this prosodic pattern, there was no way to tell whether speakers were analyzing the conditions on the rule as morphological or prosodic. Eventually, however, borrowing, conversion and onomotopeia introduced non-prefixed verbs with unstressed initial syllables, such as German *posaunen* 'proclaim loudly', *miauen* 'meow' and *studieren* 'study'. For some time, we see variation between participles with and without *ge-* for such verbs, apparently reflecting individual differences in speakers' analysis of the conditions on the rule. Eventually, standard German settled on the prosodic analysis, giving us prefixless participles: *posaunt, miaut, studiert*, whereas standard Dutch went with the morphological interpretation, resulting in *gestudeerd* and so on. The German development reflects an A-reanalysis, that is, a reanalysis of the set of inputs to the *ge-* prefixation rule. Before the reanalysis, this set is defined by a morphological property (the presence of a derivational prefix). After the reanalysis, it is defined by a prosodic property.

2.5.5 Summary of A-, B-, C- and D-reanalysis

This classification highlights the different kinds of possible relationships between covert reanalyses and associated overt analogical changes. The reanalysis can: (1) open the door for an overt innovation by affecting a traditional form that previously blocked a regular operation from applying to a particular item (D-reanalysis); (2) transform non-candidates into candidates for an existing rule (C-reanalysis); (3) create a rule where previously there was none or replace an existing rule with a new one by reanalyzing the relationship of outputs to corresponding inputs (B-reanalysis); or (4) reassess a property of (a subset of) the inputs, resulting in a change in the conditions under which a rule applies (A-reanalysis).

A- and B-reanalysis have in common that the objects of the reanalysis are items that already participate in the (perceived) rule, and the reanalyzed items are thus distinct from those to which the rule could be analogically extended – in contrast to C- and D-reanalysis. Only B-reanalysis actually changes what a rule does, whereas A-, C- and D-reanalysis only change the set of items to which an exisitng rule applies.

Hopper and Traugott (2003: 71) characterize reanalysis as 'rule change' and analogy as 'rule generalization' (see also Harris and Campbell 1995: 3). This suggests a narrower conception of reanalysis and a correspondingly broader conception of analogical change than what I am proposing. Specifically, their characterization of analogy as 'the attraction of extant forms to already existing constructions' (63–4) would seem to encompass what I am calling C-reanalysis. A similar view is apparently behind Haspelmath's (1998) position that the changes in argument structure affecting English verbs such as *like* (see §2.5.2 above) are entirely a matter of analogy rather than reanalysis.

Toward the end of their discussion, Hopper and Traugott consider an expanded conception of reanalysis, arguing that 'the sharpness of the distinction has been brought into question' and ultimately wondering 'whether everything is not reanalysis' (69). In my view, the distinction between reanalytic and analogical innovations depends precisely on the traditional understanding of analogical innovation and change as overt phenomena, rather than a type of change in mental grammar. We can and should distinguish between different types of reanalysis and recognize the especially close links that some types have to overt analogical innovations. The distinctions between A-, B-, C- and D-reanalysis are important in this context, as is Andersen's (2001c) contrast between usage-rule and base-grammar reanalysis. But we must not lose sight of the most basic distinction of all: that between covert and overt innovations, and the corresponding mechanisms of analysis and analogy$_2$.

Overt innovations are not, by themselves, changes in grammar. But regardless of one's theory of grammar, they are of importance for the story of grammatical change for at least one reason: Attested forms are the **explananda** of historical linguistics. Accounting for the forms that actually occur in written texts and observed utterances is what the field is all about. Since the nineteenth century, theoretically minded linguists have tended to regard covert reanalysis as inherently much more interesting than overt analogical changes. Even Paul devotes only about nine pages of the *Prinzipien* to the solving of proportional equations, compared to at least six entire chapters (VII, X, XI, XII, XIII and XVI) and parts of others dealing with various types of reanalysis. As we have seen, however, it is only under certain assumptions about the nature of the mental grammar that overt analogical innovations amount to nothing more than symptoms of underlying grammatical changes, and the number of linguists who question or reject those assumptions is very much on the rise.

2.5.6 Exaptation

Lass (1990, 1997: 316–24) suggests the term 'exaptation', which he takes from evolutionary biology, to refer to a potentially complex kind of revaluation of paradigmatic patterns whereby a system of formal grammatical distinctions takes on a grammatical function that has little or nothing to do with its original function. The occurrence of such repurposing in language development has long been recognized. Lass's characterization of the phenomenon in his (1990) title, 'How to Do Things with Junk', is reminiscent of Wheeler's (1887: 29) formulation: 'The mind proceeds with the best intentions to rescue these elements from their condition as mere phonetic rubbish and to assign them a use.' Exaptation is obviously related to morphologization from phonology (Osthoff 1879a: 33; Paul 1886: 178), although Lass and others generally reserve the term for cases where both the original and the new functions are morphological (Norde 2009: 115–18).

A simple example can be seen in the modern survival of two singular forms from the Old English demonstrative paradigm: *the* and *that*. The contrast between these two forms originally reflected a gender distinction; *that* (OE *þæt*) was an exclusively neuter form, while the predecessors of *the* were non-neuter. One would expect one of these forms to have been lost with the collapse of grammatical gender. They survived by being redeployed for the distinction between definite article (*the*) and demonstrative (*that*).

There are a couple of cases in Germanic where an originally derivational suffix acquired a new inflectional function after regular phonetic attrition at the ends of words resulted in a situation where the suffix only remained in certain forms in the paradigm. The derivational suffix *-*es*-/-*os*- was used in proto-Indo-European to form action nouns (Krahe/Meid 1969: 131–3). In West Germanic languages, this suffix was regularly lost in some forms of the inflectional paradigm, and where it survived it eventually took on the form -*er* (*s* > *r* is a regular conditioned sound change known as **rhotacism**). The only relic of this suffix in Modern English can be seen in the doubly-marked plural form *children*. It played a more important role in noun inflection in Old English, as it still does in modern German, where it functions as the plural ending for a fairly large class of nouns, e.g. *Kind–Kinder* 'child(ren)'; *Rind–Rinder* 'cattle'; *Mann–Männer* 'man–men'; *Lamm–Lämmer* 'lamb(s)', etc. The evolution of this morpheme from a derivational suffix to a plural marker involved a complex interaction of sound change, reanalysis (exaptation) and overt analogical changes (partial paradigm leveling and extension to new lexical items). A similar story can be told about the -*en* suffix, which survives in modern standard English only in *oxen* and *child*r*en*, but is one of the most important plural endings in modern German and Dutch and also marks a case distinction (nominative vs. non-nominative) in one class of German nouns. It was originally a derivational suffix with an individualizing function (Krahe/Meid 1969: 90–6).

This same -*en* suffix is the basis for the so-called 'weak' adjective declension in Germanic, which has been completely lost in Modern English but is still fully intact in German, as it was in Old English and all of the older Germanic languages. One of Lass's own examples of exaptation involves a recent repurposing of a reflex of this weak-adjective ending in Afrikaans. Exaptation involving the distinction between adjective forms with and without this suffix plays a much more extensive role early in the history of Germanic adjective inflection.

In Indo-European generally, adjectives are inflected for gender (masculine, feminine, neuter), number (singular, plural and sometimes dual) and case (typically at least nominative, accusative, dative and genitive, with various others depending on the language). Gender, number and case are not properties of the adjective itself, but rather of the noun phrase with which the adjective is associated; the adjective 'agrees' with the head noun it modifies. The inflectional ending on a particular adjective form depends not only on these agreement categories but also on the declension class to which the adjective belongs. In Indo-European, as reflected in Latin, Ancient Greek and Sanskrit, for example, declension class is an inherent property of an adjective lexeme. Generally, there is little need to discuss Indo-European adjective inflection separately from noun inflection because, as Table 2.1 shows for a Latin example, adjectives and nouns of a given declension class generally take the same endings, the only difference being that a noun has an inherent gender that never changes whereas an adjective must have forms for all three genders.

In Germanic, we find two major innovations to this system. First of all,

TABLE 2.1. Paradigm of the Latin first/second declension adjective *bonus* 'good' together with the nouns *amīcus* 'friend' (second decl.), *amīca* 'female friend' (first decl.), *dōnum* 'gift' (second decl.)

	singular			plural		
	M	F	N	M	F	N
nom.	bonus	bona	bonum	bonī	bonae	bona
	amīcus	amīca	dōnum	amīcī	amīcae	dōna
gen.	bonī	bonae	bonī	bonōrum	bonārum	bonōrum
	amīcī	amīcae	dōnī	amīcōrum	amīcārum	dōnōrum
dat.	bonō	bonae	bonō	bonīs	bonīs	bonīs
	amīcō	amīcae	dōnō	amīcīs	amīcīs	dōnīs
acc.	bonum	bonam	bonum	bonōs	bonās	bona
	amīcum	amīcam	dōnum	amīcōs	amīcās	dōna
abl.	bonō	bonā	bonō	bonīs	bonīs	bonīs
	amīcō	amīcā	dōnō	amīcīs	amīcīs	dōnīs

TABLE 2.2. Strong and weak declensions of the Gothic adjective *blind-* 'blind'

		strong			weak		
		M	N	F	M	N	F
sg.	nom	blinds	blind(ata)	blinda	blinda	blindō	blindō
	acc	blindana	blind(ata)	blinda	blindan	blindō	blindōn
	dat	blindamma		blindai	blindin		blindōn
	gen	blindis		blindaizōs	blindins		blindōns
pl.	nom	blindai	blinda	blindōs	blindans	blindōna	blindōns
	acc	blindans	blinda	blindōs	blindans	blindōna	blindōns
	dat	blindaim		blindaim	blindam		blindōm
	gen	blindaizē		blindaizō	blindanē		blindōnō

adjective inflection comes to reflect – in addition to gender, number and case – a new distinction that, like the agreement categories, is also dependent on syntactic context. This new distinction is traditionally called 'strong' vs. 'weak'. The strong and weak forms descend from distinct declension classes in Indo-European. Whereas each Germanic noun still inherently belongs to a single declension class (which may be either 'strong' or 'weak' in Germanic terms), there are no longer any lexical declension-class distinctions among Germanic adjectives. Instead, every Germanic adjective can take either strong or weak endings depending on how it is being used. The new paradigm is shown in Table 2.2 using Gothic forms. (The neuter is always the same as the masculine in the dative and genitive. In the strong neuter singular nom. and acc., there is variation between forms with and without the ending *-ata*.)

Originally, the function of this new distinction in Germanic involved definiteness (recall the original 'individualizing' function of the *-en* suffix in

TABLE 2.3. Comparison of Gothic strong noun and pronominal declensions

		strong	noun		demons.	pro-	noun
		M	N	F	M	N	F
sg.	nom	wulfs	barn	giba	sa	þata	sō
	acc	wulf	barn	giba	þana	þata	þō
	dat	wulfa		gibai	þamma		þizai
	gen	wulfis		gibōs	þis		þizōs
pl.	nom	wulfōs	barna	gibōs	þai	þō	þōs
	acc	wulfans	barna	gibōs	þans	þō	þōs
	dat	wulfam		gibōm	þaim		þaim
	gen	wulfē		gibō	þizē		þizō
		'wolf'	'child'	'gift'			

Indo-European): strong = indefinite, *blinds guma* '*a* blind man'; weak = definite, *blinda guma* '*the* blind man').

The other Germanic innovation, which may not be entirely separable from the first one, is that many of the endings on the strong forms of adjectives do not correspond to strong noun forms, as they had in Indo-European. Instead, they correspond largely to pronominal forms, as can be seen by comparing the strong forms in Table 2.2 with the two sides of Table 2.3.

Together, these two innovations completely transform the inflection of adjectives in Germanic. In present-day German, which preserves the Germanic system remarkably well, there has been yet another major innovation: Adjectives are only inflected when they are used attributively. Predicate adjectives have an invariant form corresponding to the bare stem, as shown in (10).

(10) *der alte Mann*   *ein alter Mann*   *der Mann ist alt*
      'The old man'   'an old man'   'the man is old'

This new inflectional distinction between attributive and predicate adjectives is yet another example of exaptation: It redeploys the variation between the original 'strong' adjective forms (which happened to develop a null ending in the nominative) and the innovative pronominal-based forms to mark the predicative vs. attributive distinction.

In Modern English, of course, adjective inflection has been lost entirely, and modern Dutch only retains the barest traces of the old system. These latter changes must be attributed largely to regular sound change, specifically to the (more or less) regular loss of unstressed word-final vowels, regardless of any grammatical function that they may have been serving. The other changes described above, however, are largely attributable to reanalysis – primarily exaptation – and analogy$_2$.

2.6 Chapter summary

Morphologically-motivated change can be largely accounted for in terms of the twin mechanisms of analysis and analogy$_2$. The former gives rise to covert innovations (reanalyses), the latter to overt (analogical) innovations. In order to account for changes that necessarily involve not only morphological but also phonetic/phonological factors, I introduce the additional mechanisms of associative interference in perception and production.

In proposing a classification that distinguishes between resegmentation and revaluation as well as between A-, B-, C- and D-reanalysis, I argue that many familiar definitions of reanalysis are overly narrow.

3

Types of Analogical Change, Part 1: Introduction and Proportional Change

3.1 Introduction

A well-motivated classification scheme for analogical change has been a high priority for many linguists since early Neogrammarian times. Osthoff (1879a) regarded this as essential for countering the arguments of those who saw analogy as little more than an ad hoc trick to account for anything that looked like an exception to a regular sound change. Even if analogical change is often sporadic and somewhat unpredictable, a well-motivated typology could show that it is more systematic than critics claimed.

Important classificatory work has continued right down to the present, alongside the increased interest in identifying and explicitly modeling constraints on analogical change (Chapter 7). The highly original typology in Andersen 1980 is especially noteworthy in this regard. Textbook classification schemes, by contrast, often appear rather haphazard. The main goals of this chapter are to try to clear up some of the terminological and conceptual confusion surrounding existing typologies of analogical change and to take at least some small steps in the direction of a classification that 'correspond[s] to the natural divisions of its subject matter' (Andersen 1974: 18).

3.2 Outcome-based vs. motivation-based classifications

Wheeler's (1887: 3) criticism that the classifications of analogical change proposed by the major Neogrammarian theoreticians 'describe only the results of the action of analogy, instead of referring back to the activities of the mind' applies equally to the classification schemes found in many recent textbooks and handbooks. A good example is paradigm leveling. This is typically defined as the elimination of morphophonological or allomorphic stem alternations across a paradigm, as when, for example, *old–elder–eldest* is (largely) replaced by *old–older–oldest*. If we take this definition literally, then any instance of elimination of a stem alternation would count as leveling, even if the leveling is a result of regular sound change (§5.1). This is at odds with our usual understanding of what analogical change is all about. We classify a change as analogical based on its motivation, not its outcome, and it makes sense then to base our classifcations of different types of analogical change on motivations as well.

3.3 Terminology and terminological confusion

Virtually every label that has ever been used to designate a type of analogical change has been used differently by different scholars, starting, as we saw in Chapter 1, with the term analogy itself. In the sections that follow, I will try to point out some of the main terminological discrepancies in the literature that are likely to give rise to misunderstandings, but it is impossible to be exhaustive here. Readers should always be aware of the possibility that an author is using a familar term in an unfamiliar way.

3.4 Proportional vs. non-proportional analogy

Many recent accounts draw a fundamental distinction between proportional and non-proportional analogy, with the latter category including – at least – contamination and folk etymology. The controversial status of a number of other types of change with respect to this distinction will be discussed below. Kiparsky asserts that the proportional-vs.-non-proportional dichotomy reflects 'the traditional view' (1992: 56), but this is somewhat misleading. First of all, the term 'non-proportional analogy' appears to date back only to Anttila 1972. Secondly, as we saw in Chapter 1, Paul's position, which was adopted by Saussure, Bloomfield and many others, and thus arguably has some claim on the designation 'traditional view', was that 'proportional' and 'analogical' meant the same thing, so that 'non-proportional analogy' would be an oxymoron.

Some early scholars with more inclusive definitions of analogy do make a distinction similar to proportional-vs.-non-proportional. Osthoff (1879b) distinguishes 'proportional analogy' (*proportionale analogie*) from 'simple form transfer' (*schlichte formübertragung*), although the latter category does not encompass everything that current work generally includes under the non-proportional heading. Oertel's distinction between 'analogical creation' and 'associative interference' (1901: 154–5), adopted also by Sturtevant (1917: 37, 42), is much closer to proportional-vs.-non-proportional.

There are at least two substantive questions here: First of all, do the so-called 'non-proportional' phenomena have anything in common that would justify classifying them together and treating proportional-vs.-non-proportional as a fundamental binary split among types of analogical change? Kiparsky clearly believes that the traditional answer is yes. One of his criticisms of traditional approaches is that 'non-proportional analogy ... subsumes an assortment of phenomena without unified analysis' (1992: 56), and he contrasts this with the 'optimization approach' which 'brings many "non-proportional" analogical changes out of their theoretical limbo' (57). Some scholars who define analogy narrowly as excluding non-proportional processes do lump the latter together under a label such as 'adaptation' (Bloomfield 1933) or 'contamination' (Pope 1952), but others do not suggest that these processes have anything in common, and many who operate with a more inclusive definition of analogy either reject the idea of setting proportional developments apart from the rest (Wheeler 1887: 6; Andersen 1980; Campbell 2004: 104–5), or they treat proportional changes as one of several types of analogical development, with no indication that the other types should be grouped together (Lehmann 1962). Moreover, the use of the term 'non-proportional' does not necessarily imply that one regards these processes as having anything in common (Mayerthaler 1980: 82).

A fundamental proportional-vs.-non-proportional distinction is thus perhaps not as 'traditional' as Kiparsky suggests, but it might nevertheless be useful and well motivated. I will consider this possibility in connection with the second substantive question: whether all – or any – of the non-proportional phenomena stand in a 'principled relationship to proportional analogy' (Kiparsky 1992: 56). This is the question behind the debate over narrow (that is, strictly proportional) vs. broad definitions of analogical change.

There is considerable confusion over exactly what is at stake here. The first source of confusion is the word 'proportion(al)' itself. As mentioned in §1.5.1, the real essence of Paul's narrow definition of analogical innovations has nothing to do with proportions per se. In theory-neutral terms, his basic point is that analogical innovations are straightforward products of a speaker's mental grammar. In his version of word-and-paradigm morphology, this can be modeled nicely with proportional equations in which the terms must all be complete surface wordforms. In a theoretical framework that posits abstract underlying stems or morpheme-concatenating rules, such proportional equations would obviously not be an appropriate model of the mental morphological system. One could instead use something more like Paul's syntactic (syntagmatic) proportions (1886: 87–91), or paradigmatic proportions that allow abstract elements such as lexical stems as terms, or some completely different kind of rule formalism. Paul and his contemporaries were well aware of this issue, and some of Paul's closest Neogrammarian associates disagreed with his strict word-and-paradigm model (Osthoff 1879b). Saussure (1995 [1916]: 228–30) suggested that languages might actually differ on this point. As Davies (1978: 48–9) shows, Paul himself flirted with a somewhat more abstract theory of morphology in the first edition of the *Prinzipien* (1880: 64), but completely dropped that line of thinking in subsequent editions.

The take-home lesson here should be: Do not get too hung up on the word 'proportional'. The question of the correctness of Paul's word-and-paradigm theory, and thus of his proportional model, is independent of the question of whether analogical innovations in morphology should be defined narrowly to refer only to forms generated by the innovator's mental morphological system.

The second source of confusion is that many linguists wrongly assume that the narrow definition of analogy embodies an empirical claim. It is in fact a purely definitional issue. No advocate of a narrow definition disputes that non-proportional phenomena occur. Paul devotes a whole chapter of the *Prinzipien* to 'contamination' (1886: 132–9), a term that he coined, and also has an insightful discussion of folk etymology (1886: 180–3). He even admits that there are some changes that would seem to support a more abstract model of morphology (1886: 95). Narrow, 'proportional' definitions of analogical change do not entail or imply any predictions about what kinds of morphological developments are possible or not possible. They merely state that only certain kinds of innovations should be classified as analogical.

So what is at stake here? Is this just a terminological issue? Not entirely. As mentioned in Chapter 1, the Neogrammarians' central claim was that all change in the phonetic make-up of linguistic forms could be attributed to (exceptionless) sound change, analogy, or borrowing. Although they soon recognized that they had to qualify this claim in the realm of sound change – certain kinds of change, such as metathesis and dissimilation, are often lexically sporadic – most Neogrammarians clung to the idea of a single analogical category of developments that could be opposed to sound change and borrowing. Paul's narrow view of analogical innovation was thus unappealing to many of his associates and followers. After all, what is your slogan going to be if you adopt Paul's view: 'All change in the phonetic make-up of linguistic forms is attributable to sound change, borrowing, analogy, folk etymology, contamination, or perhaps some other factor that we have not identified yet'?

Paul, on the other hand, recognized that broad definitions of analogy raise more serious issues for Neogrammarian doctrine than the risk of having to give up a catchy slogan. As explained in Chapter 1, a product of proportional analogy is completely independent of the form that it replaces. The Neogrammarians were thus on solid ground when they responded to their critics who argued that (proportional) analogical innovations presented a serious problem for the hypothesis of exceptionless phonetic change: Phonetic laws clearly have no jurisdiction over developments that involve the replacement of one word with another.

Things become much murkier, however, when we consider non-proportional processes such as folk etymology and contamination. To take a slightly more complex example than *bridegroom*, discussed in §1.5.1, consider the set of English words ending in *-most*, such as *foremost, utmost* and *northmost*. When we examine the Old English forms of these words, we see that the *-most* element originally had nothing to do with the word *most*. It was actually made up of an old superlative element *-m-* combined with the familiar superlative suffix *-est*. This means that the modern forms of these words should be **foremest, *northmest*, etc., with a reduced schwa in the final unstressed syllable just like other superlatives in *-est*. In fast, casual speech, we undoubtedly do pronounce it in more or less this way, but the careful pronunciation has /oʊ/. At some point, learners analyzed these words as compounds with final element *-most*. Apparently, they assumed the pronunciations with reduced vowels that they heard from others were fast-speech tokens of intended *-most*. They might have matched this reduced pronunciation exactly in their own fast speech, but when they had occasion to pronounce these words carefully, they produced the innovative forms with /oʊ/.

Is this sound change or analogy? We can now expand on the answer given in Chapter 1. Such developments clearly have something important in common with analogical change, in that perceived morphological relationships among wordforms play a crucial role, but they are also like sound change in that they involve speakers' imperfect attempts to reproduce forms they have heard from others. The problem with broad definitions of analogical change is not that they recognize that proportional and non-proportional innovations have something in common; the problem is rather with the fundamental opposition between analogy and sound change. Non-proportional processes are hybrids, combining defining characteristics of both sound change and analogy. We can capture this by replacing the conventional hierarchical classification that first draws a fundamental distinction between sound change and analogical change, and then further subdivides the latter into proportional and non-proportional, with one that treats the two basic types as overlapping. Changes in linguistic forms can be motivated by: (1) aspects of speech production or perception; (2) grammatical or semantic relations among forms; or (3) both. (1) is canonical sound change; (2) is proportional change; and (3) is so-called non-proportional analogical change.

Paul's narrow definition of analogy based on the production–reproduction distinction obviously excludes folk etymology and contamination, but Paul also excludes one other type of formation, even though it meets his criterion of involving only 'production': Sometimes an inflectional formative is extended to a new lexical or grammatical context even though there does not seem to be any well-formed proportional equation to license this extension. A possible example might be the extension of the *-st* second sg. ending to the pres. indic. of the modal verbs in German.[1] The OHG forms in (11) show that most of the modal verbs originally had a distinctive *-t* ending in the second sg.

(11) *darf-t* 'you (sg.) need'; *scal-t* 'you (sg.) ought'; *mah-t* 'you (sg.) can'

The innovative *-st* ending arguably comes (mainly) from the non-modal verbs, but as shown in (12) using forms of the regular verb *machen* 'make, do', if we try to formulate a proportion to account for this development, we always get the wrong solution or no solution.

(12) *mache* (1st sg.) : *machst* = *darf* : X; X = ??; *macht* (3rd sg.) : *machst* = *darf* : X; X = ??; *machen* (1st/3rd pl., inf.) : *machst* = *dürfen* : X; X = *dürfst

Of course one possibility is that we are truly dealing with something other than pure production in this case. The new form *darfst* could be analyzed, for example, as a product of contamination between the mental representations of the old form *darft* and a proportional solution such as *dürfst*. This is not the way Paul saw it, however. He suggests instead that such innovations are matters of pure production but are nevertheless not, strictly speaking, analogical because of the impossibility of accounting for them in terms of a proportional equation. Paul sees these as cases where 'an inflectional ending [is] perceived as essentially the normal ending for an inflectional form. Then it can be transferred to other words even without the support of words constructed in the same way' (1886: 95, my translation).

There is an obvious alternative to Paul's conclusion that such innovations cannot be classified as analogical, but it is an alternative that Paul's strict word-and-paradigm theory forces him to reject. Osthoff (1879b: 142; Kuryłowicz 1977: 21–2) had already pointed out that all innovations attributable entirely to production as opposed to reproduction can be captured in proportional equations if we allow the terms of the proportions to be grammatical abstractions (such as lexical stems) rather than complete wordforms. It is easy to see how this would work with our example: *mach-* : *machst* = *darf(-)* : X; X = *darfst*. A similar solution could be based on Paul's own account of syntactic analogy, where productive grammatical patterns do not depend on paradigmatic support. Paul's syntactic proportions are syntagmatic rather than paradigmatic (see §6.2 below). Syntagmatic proportions could work for the extension of *-st* to the modals (and for the morphological examples that Paul himself discusses in this context), but again this would require us to allow the terms in each proportion to be grammatical abstractions (in this case abstract affixes as well as bound stems): *mach-* : *-st* = *bring-* : *-st* = *schreib-* : *-st* = *kann(-)* : X; X = *-st*. Paul refuses to consider this solution. For him, productive morphological relations are paradigmatic and differ fundamentally in this respect from productive syntactic relations. Abstract roots, stems and affixes that never occur by themselves have no reality in a speaker's mental grammar. One could argue, however, that what Paul has discovered in these cases where an inflectional affix 'can be transferred to other words even without the support of words constructed in the same way' is that morphology at least occasionally does work like syntax after all, and perhaps that speakers occasionally do store and use mental representations of grammatical abstractions. If we allow stems and affixes to be terms in proportions, then the proportional vs. non-proportional distinction corresponds exactly to Oertel's and Sturtevant's between 'analogical creation', which Sturtevant defines as 'a new creation on the basis of a known relationship' and 'associative interference', defined as 'a modification of something old' (1917: 42).

3.5 Morphological vs. morphophonological change

Analogical change can affect both the morphological markers of grammatical categories and alternations that are partially or entirely phonologically conditioned. Most scholars see the other distinctions discussed below as cutting across this one. Leveling and extension, for example, can involve either morphology or morphophonology (Hock 1986). Kiparsky (1965), however, launched an important tradition of generative work on analogical change that focuses primarily on (morpho)phonological alternations. Since then, leveling and extension have sometimes been defined exclusively in terms of such alternations (Kiparsky 1968: 201; Campbell 2004: 108; Blevins and Blevins 2009: 6). Analogical change involving purely phonologically conditioned alternations has some special characteristics and will be discussed in §6.4.

3.6 A critical overview of traditional subtypes of proportional change

There is little consistency in the subtypes of proportional analogical change proposed by different linguists, and many of the distinctions in the literature are rather arbitrary. Here is a brief overview of some of the most common labels.

3.6.1 Four-part analogy

Most linguists who use the term 'four-part analogy' treat it as a synonym for proportional analogy (McMahon 1994: 72; Trask 1996: 106; Hale and Reiss 2008: 237). Hock, however, characterizes it as 'the most systematic sub-type of proportional analogy' (1986: 171), distinguishing it from 'processes such as backformation and hypercorrection' (Hock and Joseph 2009: 157). Hock's motivation for positing this subtype seems to be closely related to his efforts to account for differences in how 'systematic' analogical changes are (Hock 2003). It is convenient for him to have a name for the normal instances of proportional analogy, rather than constantly having to repeat something like 'proportional analogy other than backformation and hypercorrection' (see §1.6.3 above for the relevant sense of hypercorrection). The examples of analogical extension in the next section are all instances of four-part analogy in Hock's sense.

3.6.2 Extension

We have already encountered the term 'extension' in a couple of contexts. This term is a particularly confusing one because it is widely used in at least three closely related but subtly different ways. In Chapter 2, we saw that a number of scholars use it broadly to refer to everything that I am calling (proportional) analogical innovation/change (Harris and Campbell 1994; Haspelmath 1998; Deutscher 2001). At least since Kiparsky 1968, however, many scholars have drawn a fundamental distinction between '(analogical) **extension**' and '(paradigm) **leveling**'. Finally, as mentioned above (§3.5), a minority of scholars use these two opposing terms to refer only to changes in morphophonological alternations (Kiparsky 1968: 201; Campbell 2004: 108; Blevins and Blevins 2009: 6). At least for purely descriptive purposes, 'extension' is undeniably a useful term in this last narrow sense. Much more widespread in the literature on analogical change, however, is the use of 'extension' to refer to any development whereby some paradigmatic formal distinction – whether morphological or morphophonological – comes to apply to items or in contexts where it previously did not apply (Mayerthaler 1980: 82; Anttila 1989: 104; McMahon 1994: 70–4; Haspelmath and Sims 2010: 127), so that the extension-vs.-leveling opposition corresponds exactly to that drawn by some Neogrammarians between 'formal leveling' (*formale Ausgleichung*) and 'material leveling' (*stoffliche Ausgleichung*), respectively (Brugmann 1876: 318–19 n. 33; Paul 1879: 7; Osthoff 1879a: 25, 1879b: 143). Whether this sense of 'extension' is distinct from Harris and Campbell's broad sense depends on the status of (paradigm) leveling. Is it just a type of extension (extension of a non-alternating pattern) or is it really something different? This is a very old and still unresolved question that I will discuss below in §5.1, but it is relevant here because if leveling is a type of extension, then the latter term, as it is most often used, becomes essentially just a synonym for '(proportional) analogical innovation/change'.

Sapir (1921: 188) gives no explicit clarification of exactly what he means by 'leveling' and 'extension', but he seems to use both terms to refer to the same developments, suggesting that he views this as a difference not between two types of change but rather between two ways of looking at the same changes, a view that one also finds in some Neogrammarian work. In any (proportional) analogical change, a formal distinction of some kind is leveled (eliminated) while a pattern is extended. Thus, in the *kine* > *cows* example, the difference in plural marking between *cow* and most other English nouns is leveled while the pattern of marking the plural with -*s* is extended. The leveling of the *s–r* ([z]–[r]) alternation in Old English *frēosan–froren* (> *freeze–frozen*) is an extension of the non-alternating pattern found in most verbs of this class. At least at a purely descriptive level, the difference between these two types of developments is thus not a matter of whether a distinction is being leveled or a pattern is being extended, but rather of whether the leveling is (only) interparadigmatic ('formal leveling', aka 'extension') or (also) intraparadigmatic ('material' or 'paradigm leveling').

Examples of analogical extension – in the sense that contrasts it with leveling but does not restrict it to morphophonological alternations – fill the pages of language histories. The exponent that is extended is most often an affix (or a paradigmatic set of affixes). I have already mentioned several popular examples in other contexts, such as the English -*s* plural coming to be used with items that previously marked the plural in other ways: *eyen* > *eyes*; *hande* > *hands*; the Latin case/number endings of the second declension being extended to nouns that originally belonged to the fourth declension: gen. sg. *senatūs* > *senatī*; or the extension of the German third pl. verbal ending -*en* from the subjunctive and preterite into the present indicative, replacing earlier -*ent*.

Another example, this one involving an infix, comes from the Yurok language of Northern California. As mentioned above in §2.5.3, most verbs in Yurok form the so-called 'intensive' by infixing -*eg*- between the onset and the vowel of the first syllable in the stem (*laːy-*, *l-eg-aːy-* 'to pass'). Some verbs, however, mark the intensive by changing the vowel in the first stem syllable to *iː*, e.g. *lekoː(t-)*, *liːkoː(t-)* 'to stab'. Garrett (2001: 269–71) explains that this vowel alternation surely arose through a regular sound change: *ege* > *iː*. We would thus expect to find this way of forming the intensive in all verbs with *e* as the vowel of the first stem syllable. Garrett attributes cases that violate this expectation, such as *t-eg-ewomeł* (for expected *tiːwomeł), intensive of *tewomeł* 'to be glad', to an analogical extension restoring the dominant -*eg*- pattern.

In derivational morphology, historical linguists talk about analogical extension where synchronic morphologists see productivity (Bauer 2001; Haspelmath and Sims 2010: 127). With the most highly productive derivational patterns, it hardly seems like an innovation when someone extends the pattern to a new item. Once an adjective like *scuzzy* (OED 1969) has entered the language, the derived noun *scuzziness* seems inevitable. The idea that the simple extension of a derivational pattern to a new word constitutes a type of innovation/change should raise fewer eyebrows:

1. with somewhat less productive patterns. New nouns formed with suffixes such as -*dom*, e.g. *stardom* (1865), *officialdom* (1894), *fandom* (1903) and *consumerdom* (not yet in the OED), feel like real additions to the lexicon, in a way that nouns like *scuzziness* do not (Paul 1897; Aronoff 1976).
2. where the new formation comes to replace an existing word. This is more like extension in inflectional morphology, where an analogical innovation almost always replaces an existing form since there are rarely any empty cells in inflectional paradigms. Replacement in derivational morphology is usually not as straightforward as it is in inflection because distinct

derivational formations rarely mean exactly the same thing. Deadjectival nouns in *-ity* and *-ness* often exist side by side, for example, with more or less subtle differences in meaning, e.g. *absurdness–absurdity*.

The fact that the mere application of a (somewhat) productive derivational rule can, by itself, constitute an innovation illustrates one of the main differences between derivational morphology on the one hand, and inflection and syntax on the other. The distinction between 'possible words' and 'actual words' (Haspelmath and Sims 2010: 71) has no counterpart in syntax or inflection, and no one considers the mere application of an inflectional or syntactic rule, where nothing previously blocked it, to constitute an innovation, even if the wordform or phrase in question had never before been uttered. Thus, proportional extension in inflection or syntax virtually always involves either: (1) the appearance of a form that was previously blocked by a synonymous alternative; or (2) a reanalysis that either creates a new rule or makes new applications of an existing rule possible.

Extension of stem alternations

The most widely cited example of the extension of a stem alternation[2] involves umlaut noun plurals in German. Umlaut originally arose in the Germanic languages as an assimilatory fronting of stressed vowels where there was a high front vowel (*i*) or a palatal glide (*j*) in a following unstressed syllable. The alternation developed phonologically in this way in several classes of nouns in German, and has subsequently been extended analogically to quite a few nouns that did not meet the original phonological conditions. Examples that still generally had no plural umlaut in Middle High German (eleventh to fourteenth century) but do have it in the modern standard language include: MHG *koch–koche* 'cook(s)' > Mod. Stand. Germ. *Koch–Köche*; *vrosch–vrosche* 'frog(s)' > *Frosch–Frösche*; *wolf–wolve* 'wolf/ves' > *Wolf–Wölfe*; *boum–boume* 'tree(s)' > *Baum–Bäume*; *vogel–vogele* 'bird(s)' > *Vogel–Vögel* (Paul 1989: 190). Other nouns had already been affected by this extension before MHG times. In Yiddish and in some modern German dialects, plural umlaut has been extended to even more items, e.g. Yiddish *tog–teg*, Imst (Tirol) dialect *tɔːg–taːg* 'day(s)' (Sapir 1921: 190–1; Weinreich 1977 [1968]; Wurzel 1984: 168; Jacobs 2005: 163–6).

A few other examples of extensions of stem alternations are:

1. English *scarf–scarfs* > *scarf–scarves*; *dwarf–dwarfs* > *dwarf–dwarves*. Some speakers extend the parallel /θ/–/ð/ alternation to a number or items, such as *myth* (/θ/)–*myths* (/ðz/).
2. In the Germanic languages, there have always been a number of verbs with the same vowel in the present and the past participle, as in English *give–given*; *grow–grown*; *slay–slain*, etc. Some verbs that originally had the same vowel in these two forms have acquired vowel alternations extended from other strong verb patterns, e.g. Old English *tredan–treden* > Modern English *tread–trodden*; *sp(r)ecan–gesp(r)ecan* > *speak–spoken*; *wefan–wefen* > *weave–woven*; OHG *laufan–gilaufan* > Yiddish *loyfn–gelofn* 'run'.
3. In Nyamwezi (Bantu), *l* and *g* both become *j* before *j*. Roots ending in *-g*

have a *-g-*, *-j-*, *-g-* alternation that arose by regular sound change between the basic root, the causative and the applicativized causative respectively, for example *-og-* 'bathe (intr.)'; *-oj-į-* 'bathe (trans.)'; *-og-éj-į-* 'bathe (trans. applicative)'. Roots ending in *-l* would be expected to show an *-l-*, *-j-*, *-l-* alternation, but instead we find *-l-*, *-j-*, *-g-*, e.g. *-gul-* 'buy'; *-guj-į-* 'sell'; *-gug-ij-į-* 'sell (applicative). The only conceivable explanation for the *-g-* in the applicativized causatives of such verbs is extension of this part of the alternation from verbs with the *-g-*, *-j-*, *-g-* pattern (Hyman 2003).

4. Garrett (2008) discusses several extensions of stem alternations between the present and the aorist of verbs in Ancient Greek. One set of verbs with root-final *-k*, for example, developed an alternation by regular sound change between *-k-s-* in the aorist (where *-s-* is an aorist suffix) and *-tt-* in the present, for example *e-tarak-s-* (aorist)–*taratt-o-* (present) 'disturb'. This alternation was extended to another set of verbs that originally had root-final *-g*, which was devoiced to *-k* before the aorist suffix *-s-* and would normally have become *-zd* in the present (before a *-y-* suffix that was lost prehistorically). Instead of expected present forms such as **prazd-o-* 'do' corresponding to aorist *e-prak-s-*, the actually attested present form is analogical *pratt-o-*. Note that in this case, the extended alternation replaces a different alternation, rather than a non-alternating pattern: *-k-s-*∼*-zd-* > *-k-s-*∼*-tt-*.

3.6.3 Backformation

The rationale for treating backformation as a distinct type of analogical change is based on the view that morphological rules are inherently directional, that English words such as *beauty* and *beautiful*, for example, do not stand in a symmetrical relationship with each other that would allow a speaker to derive either one based on knowledge of the other. Instead, the rule relating them takes *beauty* as input and yields *beautiful* as output. Some linguists have argued that the very occurrence of backformations is evidence that morphological rules are bidirectional (or non-directional), but saying that *beautiful* is derived from *beauty* by a directional rule does not entail that a speaker who knows only *beautiful* could never come up with *beauty*. It simply means that a speaker who did this would be doing something different from one who derives *beautiful* from *beauty*. Whereas the latter is a straightforward application of a rule – a purely deductive matter – the former is inferential. It is like the difference between seeing someone cut their finger and predicting that it is going to bleed, and seeing someone's finger bleeding and inferring that they must have cut it: humans can reason in both directions, but the type of reasoning involved is different in the two cases.

If we accept the idea that backformation amounts to innovators guessing at the input to a rule based on its output, how can we tell the difference between this and straightforward rule application? Presumably, derivational backformation should be rarer and somehow odder. In this regard, the widespread textbook practice of classifying backformation along with contamination and folk etymology under a heading like 'non-systematic processes' (Hock 1986: 189) or 'sporadic analogy'

(McMahon 1994: 74–6; Campbell 2004: 113–20) and citing only a handful of standard examples is potentially misleading. Backformation, at least in English, is anything but rare. While it may not be possible to find comparable numbers of examples from most other languages, we should keep in mind that we only know about many of the English cases because the history of the English lexicon is so extraordinarily well documented, in particular in the OED and now the MED. Unlike many other types of analogical change, derivational backformation usually leaves no paper trail (or papyrus/parchment/inscription trail) in the form of easily recognizable older forms that have been replaced by corresponding younger forms. In most of the examples listed below – and the many other similar examples that I have collected – we would have no hint that we might be dealing with backformation without extensive, accurate evidence for the dates and circumstances of the earliest attestations of English words.

A popular example of derivational backformation is the verb *orientate* (1848) from *orientation* (1839), which according to the OED has become more common than *orient* (1728) in British English, but still strikes many American ears as 'incorrect'. Similar examples include *applicate* 'apply', *computate* 'compute' and *degradate* 'degrade'.

Among the hundreds of Latinate verbs in English that have corresponding nouns ending in *-ion* and/or agent nouns in *-or*, the OED reveals that there are quite a few cases where a derived form is attested before – often long before – the verbal base. Relative dates do not by themselves prove backformation for loanwords, since the verb and the derived forms could have simply been borrowed separately, but there are quite a few instances where there is no plausible source for the verb other than backformation, including: *automate* (1954) < *automation* (1874); *televise* (1927) < *television* (1907); *gradate* (1753) < *gradation* (1538); *manipulate* (1827) < *manipulation* (1728); *locomote* (1834) < *locomotion* (1646); *extradite* (1864) < *extradition* (1852); *aviate* (1887) < *aviation* (1866); *emote* (1900) < *emotion* (1562); *speciate* (1964) < *speciation* (1906); *demarcate* (1816) < *demarcation* (1728).

Sometimes there is a differentiation in meaning or usage between an original base and a much later backformation: *persevere* (1380) vs. *perseverate* (1912); *remedy* (1414) vs. *remediate* (1837); *value* (1482) vs. *valuate* (1873); *destroy* (1230) vs. *destruct* (1958, most familiar in the compound *self-destruct* (1969)). The verb *analyze* (1587) is probably a back-formation from *analysis* (1580) on the model of pairs like *paralyze–paralysis*. Other clear examples include *reminisce* (1829) < *reminiscence* (1589); *injure* (1597) < *injury* (1382); and *surveil* (1960) < *surveillance* (1802).

The verb *laze* (1592) < *lazy* (1549) is a popular example of backformation, but adjectives in *-y* are much more often derived from nouns than from verbs, so it should come as no surprise that the corresponding type of backformation is also quite common: *drear* (1593) < *dreary* (Old English); *must* (1602) < *musty* (1492); *greed* (1609) < *greedy* (Old English); *gloom* (1645) < *gloomy* (1593); *smut* (1664) < *smutty* (1597); *haze* (1706) < *hazy* (1625); *dinge* (1846) < *dingy* (1736); *stinge* (1914) < *stingy* (1615); *priss* (1923) < *prissy* (1894); *snoot* (1941) < *snooty* (1919); *raunch* (1952) < *raunchy* (1937); *sleaze* (1967) < *sleazy* (1644); *glitz* (1977) < *glitzy* (1966); *ditz* (1984) < *ditzy* (1976); *tack* (1986) < *tacky*

(1862). Similar examples from German include *Trauer* 'sadness, mourning' < *traurig* 'sad' and several compound nouns in *-sinn* from corresponding adjectives in *-sinnig*, such as *Blödsinn* 'nonsense, rubbish' (1774) < *blödsinnig* 'idiotic' (1617). There will undoubtedly be more such backformations in English in the future, as there is no shortage of remaining candidate adjectives: *pretty, fancy, dizzy, queasy, pesky, tidy, flimsy, randy, petty, puny, tardy, woozy, grody* and so on.

In inflectional morphology, it is common to speak of backformation at least where there is a relatively clear directionality to the relationships among forms (§7.4), as when speakers who know a noun in the plural guess at the singular. This has happened with a few items in some German dialects where plural is marked only by umlaut of the stem vowel, which in these dialects is accompanied by unrounding of front rounded vowels, so that a plural form with a front vowel could correspond either to a singular with the same vowel or to one with the corresponding back vowel. Thus, in these dialects we find the innovative sg. *Fusch* 'fish' replacing earlier *Fisch* based on the plural *Fisch* and the analogy of nouns such as *Busch–Bisch* 'bush(es)', (Standard German *Busch–Büsche*). This example is striking in that it involves the extension of a morphophonemic alternation. More commonly, inflectional backformation leads to the leveling of alternations, as when English *stave* replaced earlier *staff* and *glove* replaced *gluff* as the singulars of *staves* and *gloves*, respectively.

Similarly, innovative present-tense verb forms can result from backformation from the past tense or participle. This explains the final *d* in the English verb *to lend*. The ME form *lende* was the past tense of *lēnen*, but *lende* would also be the expected past form if the present were *lenden*. For speakers who had only heard the verb in the past and had to guess at the present, the preponderance of evidence from other ME verbs such as *benden, renden, senden, wenden* suggested that *lenden* was more likely to be the right guess. Similar developments are responsible for the final *-t* in the verb *hoist*. Reanalysis of an ambiguous participle resulted in just the opposite development in sixteenth-century *blenne* for *blend*, nonstandard *upbray* < *upbraid* and perhaps *chill* (< ME infinitive *childen*?).

The present-tense forms of *sigh* are probably attributable to backformation from the ME past form *sihte* (where the *h* represents the palatal or velar fricative still reflected orthographically as <gh> in *sigh*). The forms that occur in OE and early ME texts would lead us to expect the present-tense form to be something like **sich* /sɪtʃ/, with the same consonant alternation as in *teach–taught*. Speakers guessing at the present tense based on the past, however, apparently assumed non-alternation and came up with /sɪç/, of which the present-day pronunciation /saɪ/ is a continuation by regular sound change (OED). Other English verbs with present forms attributable to backformation from the past tense or participle include *strew, find* and perhaps *quit, shit, stall, wet* and *sweat*.

In Malagasy, the root form *goboka* has arisen alongside original *hoboka* 'hollow', apparently through backformation from the 'active' verb form *mangoboka*, with the common change of root-initial *h* > *g* following the prefix *man-*. A proportional model for the leveling of the *g-* into the unprefixed root can be found in items that have always had non-alternating *g-*, such as *geja–mangeja* 'grasp, squeeze' (Rajaona 2004: 128–9).

Backformation following C-reanalysis

In the cases discussed so far, the status of the forms that serve as the pivots for the backformations do not change: *orientation* and *imagination* are deverbal nouns before and after the backformation, just as *lende* and *sihte* remain past-tense verb forms. The label backformation is often also applied to more complex developments where the innovators first reanalyze the pivot form (C-reanalysis) as being something that it was originally not (§2.5.2). This is similar to the morphological reanalysis behind folk etymology (§4.2), but whereas folk etymology results in an overt change in the reanalyzed form itself, the overt change here involves the (proportional) invention of a new, related form. A well-known example from derivational morphology is the verb *lase* (1962) from *laser* (1960), which was originally an acronym of *light amplification (by the) stimulated emission (of) radiation*. The *-er* was thus not originally a suffix at all.

Textbook accounts often treat the C-reanalysis and the overt backformation as two aspects of a single change, but in fact the latter does not follow automatically from the former. Speakers might analyze the *-er* in *laser* as the instrument suffix but still learn, as an arbitrary lexical fact about their language, that the verb *to lase* happens not to exist, and English has many verbs that have been created by simple backformation – with no reanalysis – from *-er* or *-or* agent or instrument nouns: *swindle, legislate, loaf, spectate, tweeze, curate, escalate* and probably *scavenge, peddle* and *edit*.

C-reanalysis followed by backformation is also widely attested in inflectional morphology. Several English nouns that happened to end in /s/ or /z/ have been reanalyzed as plurals, setting the stage for the backformation of a singular. The old mass noun *pease* is still known to many from the nursery rhyme 'Pease porridge hot, pease porridge cold . . .' but has otherwise been reanalyzed as a plural, giving rise to the new singular *pea*. The history of *cherry* and *asset* is similar, as is that of *burial, riddle, shay* ('horse-drawn carriage') and *eave*, except that the original *s*-final singulars *buriels* (< OE *byrgels*), *ridels* (< OE *(h)rædels*), *chaise* (French loanword) and *eaves* (< OE *efes*) were not mass nouns.

Similarly, reanalyzing an adjective or adverb that happens to end in *-ing* or /t/, /d/, or /ɨd/ as a participle can set the stage for the backformation of a new verb. The adjective/adverb *groveling* was originally formed by adding the directional adverbial suffix *-ling(s)* to the now obsolete noun *groof/gruve* 'prone position'. The disappearance of the noun and the rarity of the suffix *-ling(s)* undoubtedly both enhanced the likelihood that speakers would reanalyze the word as the *-ing* form of a verb *grovel* (1605). The verb *suckle* (1408) may have arisen in much the same way from the noun *suckling* (< *suck* + *ling*). Similarly, *husht* was originally an interjection commanding silence, like *sh!*. It came to be used also as an adjective meaning 'silent', which speakers then analyzed as a past participle, resulting in the modern spelling *hushed* and the backformation of the verb *hush* (1546).

A type of backformation that is of considerable theoretical interest involves the creation of English verbs from compounds of which the second element is a deverbal noun or a participial adjective, usually with the suffix *-er, -ing* or *-ed*, and the first element corresponds to a complement of the verb from which the second element is derived. The creation of such compounds has apparently been highly productive throughout the history of English, and there are hundreds of familiar lexicalized items in the language today, e.g. *lawnmower, troublemaker, ground-breaking, tongue-tied*.

Generally, the verbs corresponding directly to such compounds strike speakers as odd or impossible:

(13) ??Her recent work really ground-breaks.

There are dozens of cases, however, where such verbs have been created through backformation. A few are now in widespread use, including *partake* (=*part-take*) (1546); *kidnap* (1682); *sight-see* (1824); *bargain-hunt* (1937); *babysit* (1946); *bartend* (1948); *nit-pick* (1956); *people-watch* (1967); *trouble-shoot* (1978); *ass-kiss* (1984); *gay-bash* (1987).

Backformed verbs characterized in the OED as 'humorous', 'playful' or 'jocular' (see §2.4.4) include *buttle* (1867 < *butler*); *burgle* (1872; Chapman et al. 1989: 66); *elocute* (1884); *referend* (1899 < *referendum*); and *enthuse* (1827). There are also a number of well-known backformations introduced into the language by popular humorist authors that continue to be used for comic effect, including *couth* (1896, Max Beerbohm) < *uncouth*, *ept* (1938, E.B. White) < *inept*, and *gruntled* (1938, P.G. Wodehouse) < *disgruntled*. Hockett (1958: 426) mentions *kempt* < *unkempt* along with *couth* as examples of 'feeble attempts at humor'.

3.6.4 Regularization and irregularization

Traditional accounts often speak of **regularization** and **irregularization**, although these notions usually play no major role in classification schemes. The examples we have already seen of the extension of the *-s* plural for nouns (*eyen* > *eyes*) and the *-ed* past/participle for verbs (*holp(en)* > *helped*) are obvious cases of regularization. In languages other than English, it is not always so clear what the 'regular' pattern is. For verbs, things are just about as straightforward in other Germanic languages as they are in English, and we find many similar historical regularizations, e.g. German *buk* 'baked' > *backte*. Noun plurals in German, however, are a different story. German plural suffixes include *-e*, *-er*, *-(e)n* and *-s*, but quite a few nouns take no suffix at all; umlaut of the stem vowel occurs in some plurals, by itself or in combination with a suffix. It is not immediately obvious that any of these patterns should be considered the (only) regular one. This has been a hotly debated topic in the dual-mechanism literature (§8.6.1), where it is argued that the *-s* plural is the German default (Marcus et al. 1995; Clahsen 1999; Pinker 1999). This would be significant because only a small minority of German nouns form their plural in this way. Regular (or default) status for an inflectional pattern is often considered to be a matter of relative type frequency – the regular inflectional class is the one with the largest number of lexical items in it. Dual-mechanism advocates regard the German *-s* plural as proof that this is not always the case.

Analogical developments that can be described as irregularizations are considerably more common than textbook overviews generally indicate (Nübling

2000). English verbs that have shifted partially or entirely out of the regular *-ed* class – at least in some major varieties – include *strive, dive, wear, stick, dig, ring, string, show, prove, sneak, catch, kneel* (§5.3.1), *make, fit, bet, quit, plead, hurt* and *cost*, although this raises the question of whether *-ed* should really be considered the regular pattern for verbs of all phonetic shapes (see §8.7).

In addition to regularizations of irregular items and irregularizations of regular items, there are many analogical changes that could be described as lateral with respect to (ir)regularity, i.e. shifts from one irregular pattern to another. Irregularizations and lateral shifts can be grouped together as non-regularizing analogical changes. I explore the significance of the distinction between regularizing and non-regularizing analogical change further in §8.6.1.

3.6.5 Item-by-item vs. across-the-board change

This is generally not recognized as an important distinction by the Neogrammarians, but is central to the generativist critique of traditional accounts of analogical change (see §8.4), and figures prominently in some textbooks (Hock 1986; McMahon 1994). Generativists point out that Paul's conception of analogical change works well enough for the familiar textbook examples of item-by-item regularization and inflectional-class shift, but that many important kinds of analogical change involve 'sweeping' extensions of patterns to entire classes of candidate forms. In these cases, the new forms produced by speakers are arguably best understood as manifestations of a single change in the grammar (Kiparsky 1972, 1974; King 1969).

According to Kiparsky (1974: 262), 'the difference between sporadic and across-the-board analogy seems to reduce simply to the difference between the effect of simplifying a general (phonological or syntactic) rule, or a morphological or lexical rule applying only to designated lexical items.' The identification of 'general rule' with phonology and syntax as opposed to morphology is highly questionable. Morphological rules can also be completely general, and when they are, analogical changes involving them show the expected across-the-board behavior (for example, the extension of the third pl. ending *-en* to the pres. indic. in German). Similarly (as Kiparsky recognizes) phonological alternations and syntactic rules can be lexically idiosyncratic, and associated analogical changes then proceed word by word, as one would expect.

Notes

1. I call this a 'possible example' because there was at least one modal verb, MHG *turren*, cognate and synonymous with English *dare*, that happened to develop an *-st* second sg. ending by regular sound change, and this could have served as a proportional model for extension of this ending to the other modals.
2. Hock, who uses '(rule) extension' in a somewhat different sense, calls this kind of change 'morphophonemic proportional analogy' (1986: 187), which he classifies as a subtype of four-part analogy.

4

Types of Analogical Change, Part 2: Non-Proportional Change

4.1 Introduction

The term 'non-proportional' has become established in the recent literature. I put it in scare quotes initially to remind the reader that 'proportions' are not really the issue (see §3.4). Non-proportional overt innovations are those that are entirely attributable to associative interference rather than to the innovator's productive morphological system. Two criteria allow us – at least in principle – to distinguish clearly between the two main types of non-proportional analogy, namely folk etymology and contamination. Firstly, folk etymology is based on associative interference in perception/analysis, whereas contamination involves interference in production, and secondly, folk etymology involves morphemic elements, whereas contamination operates at a submorphemic level based on a close semantic relationship.

4.2 Folk etymology

Lehmann argues that folk etymology is '[p]ossibly of greater amusement than significance in the development of languages' (1962: 187). Many scholars would concur, but as Coates points out, the reason it seems so insignificant may be precisely because 'willingness to ascribe a form to folk-etymology varies directly with ... the risibility of the product. Funny forms are the best folk-etymologies' (1987: 326; McMahon 1994: 183–4; Palmer 1882).

The basis of every folk etymology is a morphological or lexical reanalysis that innovatively identifies part of one form with another form. The elements in question are historically distinct, often completely unrelated, but the innovator analyzes them – sincerely or facetiously – as being the same item. This kind of reanalysis goes on all the time, as when children think *the right to bear arms* concerns the forelimbs of grizzlies. In many such cases, the original forms themselves provide no clue that the innovative interpretation is historically incorrect, and thus the reanalysis has no overt consequences. Many English speakers, for example, undoubtedly think that the second element in the words *godhead* and *maidenhead* is the word *head* when in fact it is historically a dialect variant of the suffix *-hood*. Many German speakers assume that words such as *Vormund* 'guardian' and *unmündig* 'under-age' contain the word *(der) Mund* 'mouth', when in fact the element in question is an unrelated obsolete word *(die) Mund* 'hand, protection'. The German adjectives *trübselig* 'gloomy' and *armselig* 'wretched, meager' look like they have something to do with *Seele* 'soul', but the *-sel-* part of these words is actually an umlauted form of the derivational suffix *-sal*.

In languages like English, where homophones are often distinguished orthographically, we find many cases where the reanalysis is revealed in spelling: *right* (for *rite*) *of passage*; *playwrite* for *playwright*; *copywrite* for *copyright*; *free reign* for *free rein*; *anchors away* for *aweigh*; *wet* (for *whet*) *one's appetite*; *tow* (for *toe*) *the line*; *nerve-wracking* for *-racking*; *bellweather* and *bellwhether* for *bellwether*. German examples include *Landsknecht* for *Lanzknecht* (*Land* 'country', *Lanz* 'lance', *Knecht* 'servant, page') and *Verließ* for *Verlies* 'dungeon', where the actual morphological connection is to the verb *verlieren* (older *verliesen*) 'lose', but the innovative spelling reveals a perceived connection to unrelated *verlassen* (preterite *verließ*) 'abandon'.

Paul calls such instances of innovative morphological or lexical identification that have no overt (phonetic) consequences 'the simplest type of so-called folk etymology' (1886: 180, my translation). The same kind of reanalysis can also set the stage for all sorts of proportional analogical change, and such developments are sometimes also referred to as folk etymology (Campbell 2004: 114–16). Much more commonly, however, folk etymology is understood in a narrow, technical sense to refer only to cases where this type of reanalysis leads to an overt change in the phonetic make-up of the form that is the object of the folk-etymological reanalysis (Bloomfield 1933: 417, 423–4; Hock 1986: 202–3). Paul calls this 'the more complicated type of folk etymology' (1886: 182, my translation). From here on, I will always distinguish folk etymology in this narrow sense from folk-etymological reanalysis.

In all of the examples in the last paragraph, the two forms involved in the innovative identification (*rite* and *right*, *reign* and *rein*, etc.) are phonetically identical. Reanalysis of phonetically identical items as being the same item does not lead to any overt change in either of the items. Thus, folk etymology, as defined here, always involves elements that are – before the change – phonetically *similar* but not *identical*. Folk etymology makes them identical.

The instances of folk etymology discussed in Chapter 1 (§1.1 *have another thing coming* and *could/would/should of*; §1.5.1 *bridegroom*) and Chapter 2 (§2.3, *-most*) were all (largely) attributable to mishearing or phonological reanalysis. These contrast with examples that (clearly or presumably) involve deliberate modifications of forms (Paul 1886: 182), which are especially common with loanwords. The semantic basis for the alteration is often fanciful at best. In many cases, the ultimate forms may have arisen gradually as the word was passed from bilinguals to monolinguals to other monolinguals, with new distortions arising at every step. For example, the OED reports the early spellings *Cacarootch* (1624) and *Kakaroch* (1665) for *cockroach* < Spanish *cucaracha*. Other well-known English examples include *woodchuck* (1674) < Algonquian *otchock*, *mandrake* < Latin *mandragora*, based on what Sturtevant calls 'a ridiculous connection with "man" and "drake"' (1917: 40) and *chaise lounge* < French *chaise longue*. German examples include *Hängematte* 'hammock' (literally *hang-mat*) < *hamaca* (a word borrowed by Christopher Columbus from Carib into Spanish), as well as the custom of wishing people *einen guten Rutsch ins neue Jahr*, literally 'a good slide into the new year', whereby *Rutsch* probably comes from Hebrew/Yiddish *Rosh (Hashanah)*. Trask (1996: 36) cites the Basque word *zainhoria* 'carrot', which is borrowed from Spanish *zanahoria* (ultimately of Arabic origin). The *zana-* > *zain-* change is attributable to association of the two parts of the word with Basque *zain* 'root' and *hori* 'yellow'.

An inability to reproduce the foreign sound sequences may be a factor in many such developments, but there are also cases where speakers are clearly not doing their best to reproduce the string as they perceive it; rather they assimilate it to familiar words that it vaguely resembles, and if the result is mildly humorous, so much the better: *donkey shine* < German *Danke schön*; *grassy ass* < Spanish *gracias*, etc.

Such cases are to be distinguished from unintentional folk etymology attributable to mishearing or phonological renanalysis (Paul 1882: 183). My younger son thought it was odd that his preschool teachers promised a *clean Play-Doh board* to kids who finished their whole lunch; it was only years later that he realized it was actually a *clean plate award*. Generations of children have wondered why *Olive, the other reindeer*, used to laugh at Rudolph and call him names. Similar examples from song lyrics, prayers, nursery rhymes, etc. are legion, and this phenomenon is by no means limited to young children. I know adults who have wondered why people would express such dismay over living in a *doggy-dog world* (< *dog-eat-dog world*).

Some fiction writers make extensive use of folk etymologies. David Foster Wallace's *Infinite Jest* is packed with examples such as *Sir Osis of Thuliver* < *cirrhosis of the liver*. The radio pseudonym of his central character, *Madame Psychosis*, is an allusion to a famous folk etymology from Joyce's *Ulysses*: *met him pike hoses* < *metempsychosis* (Scott Patrick Kerrigan, pers. comm.).

As I have mentioned, unintentional folk etymology can be attributed either to mishearing of the affected form or to a phonological reanalysis – which we can think of informally as a hearer's guess at how the speaker would have pronounced the form if s/he had been enunciating more carefully. This phonological reanalysis may be either hypercorrective or hypocorrective, in Ohala's (1993) sense.[1] These three mechanisms of folk etymology – mishearing, hypercorrective reanalysis and hypocorrective reanalysis – correspond pretty closely to Juliette Blevins's (2004) trio of CHANGE, CHANCE and CHOICE respectively, underlining the parallels between this kind of non-proportional analogical change and regular sound change.

In hypocorrection, a language user hears a surface string that includes phenomena such as casual-speech neutralizations and assimilations, and takes these aspects of the string at face value, or at least closer to face value than other speakers had taken them. Non-standard English *upmost* for *utmost* is a good example. Speakers who know that the form is *utmost* undoubtedly often produce *p* for the first *t* in casual speech due to phonetic assimilation to the following *m*. Normally, learners might hear just enough careful pronunciations of the word to learn that it is really *utmost*, but the folk-etymological assocation with *up* could bias them to take the casual realizations more at face value than they would otherwise. Similarly, German *Seehund* 'sea lion' (literally 'sea dog') arose through folk etymology from earlier *Seelhund* 'seal (dog)'. Before the change, speakers undoubtedly often pronounced the *l* in the coda of the first syllable barely or not at all in fast speech. The plausible semantic association with *See* 'sea' would have made learners more inclined to take these *l*-less pronunciations at face value. Another German example is *Einöde* 'middle of nowhere' < MHG *einœte*, where the *t* > *d* change is due to identification of the second element with the unrelated noun *Öde* 'barrenness, wasteland'. In this case, that identification also affected the semantics and the gender (neut. > fem.) of *Einöde* (Kluge 1975). Further English examples of apparently hypocorrective folk etymology include *land lover* < *landlubber*; *winfall* < *windfall*; *(on) tenderhooks* < *tenterhooks*.

In hypercorrection, by contrast, the hearer/learner guesses that the canonical realization of the form is *more* different from what they are hearing than it actually is. They might wrongly attribute features of a segment to fast-speech assimilation, for example, or assume that a reduced vowel would have some particular quality or that missing segments would be present in more careful pronunciations. English *hangnail* comes from Old English *angnægl*. After the word *ang*- 'compressed, tight, painful' was lost from the language, speakers could make a new connection with *hang* by interpreting *h*-less tokens as reflecting deletion of *h* in casual speech. Related examples include *hand-iron* < *andiron* and *Leghorn* < the Italian placename *Legorno*. (Alternatively, these changes could have originated in 'aitch-dropping' dialects and then spread through the written language.) Other English examples of hypercorrective folk etymology include *headlong* < *headling*; *avail* < *vail*; *gridiron* < *gridire*; *tummy egg* for *tummy ache*. The -*r* in *lobster* (OE *lopystre*) < Latin *locusta* can also be ascribed to folk-etymological hypercorrection (identification with the suffix -*ster*, OE -*ystre*). A more complex example, where both elements of an original compound have been reanalyzed and the semantics have also been affected, is *livelihood* < OE *liflad* = *life* + OE *lād* 'course, journey'.

The compound *middle earth* (re-popularized but by no means invented by Tolkien) can be traced back to early Middle English *middelærde* and OE *midangeard* and *midanærd*. Comparison with related words in other older Germanic languages, such as Old Saxon *middilgard*, Old High German *mittilagart* and Old Norse *miðgarðr* suggests that the second element originally corresponded to the Modern English word *yard*. We then see two successive folk-etymological identifications of this element, first with the Old English word *eard* '(native) land, home', then later with *earth*.

German examples of hypercorrective folk etymology include: (1) *Ohnmacht* 'unconsciousness' < Early Modern German *ōmacht*, where the insertion of the *n* is due to association of the first element – historically an old prefix meaning 'away' – with the preposition *ohne* 'without'; (2) *zu guter Letzt* < *zu guter Letz(e)* 'lastly, last but not least', where the accretion of -*t* is due to association with *letzt*- 'last', which is only very indirectly related to the noun *Letze* 'end, parting'.

The type of change that Hock calls **recomposition** (1986: 199–200; Hock and Joseph 2009: 167–9) can be regarded as essentially hypercorrective folk etymology that 'gets it right' – at least to the extent that its product is not completely independent of the earlier, less transparent form, as it presumably is in cases such as *housewife* vs. *hussy*. The fact that we say *churchyard* rather than *churchard, which would show the normal phonetic reduction of the second, more weakly stressed element of the compound (as in *orchard*), and the widespread pronunciation of *forehead* as /fɔrhɛd/ rather than reduced /fɔrɪd/ can be ascribed to speakers analyzing these compounds just as they do in cases of folk etymology, the only difference being that here their analysis is historically accurate.

Cases of folk etymology that are probably most plausibly attributed to mishearing include: *I'd just assume* < *I'd just as soon* (Jillian Pugliese, pers. comm.); *take for granite* < *take for granted* (Derry Moore, pers. comm.); *hone in on* < *home in on*.

The elements identified with each other in folk-etymological reanalysis can be morphologically related. The second element in English *bedridden* (< OE *bedrída*) was originally a derived agent noun, i.e. the original meaning was 'bed-rider'.

Unintentional folk etymology thus typically involves subtle phonetic differences that may be difficult to hear and/or not maintained (consistently) in casual speech. Phonological dialect variation can also play a crucial role. Someone who grew up with the low-back merger before nasals is presumably much more likely to think there is a jam band called *Dawn of the Buffalo* –the actual name being *Donna the Buffalo* (Paul Roberge, pers. comm.). Similarly, any North American whose dialect taps *t* and *d* but lacks Canadian raising would be especially likely to wonder, with Jim in an episode of *The Office*, why someone would *cut off her nose to spiderface*. In dialects with categorical tapping, some common reanalyses, such as *sweetish fish* for *Swedish fish* have no phonetic consequences at all. Similarly, the change in standard German from early modern *Freithof* to current *Friedhof* 'cemetery' (< MHG *vrīthof* 'enclosed plot', with the change being due to identification of the first element with unrelated *Friede* 'peace') may have originated in dialects with open-syllable lengthening (MHG *vride* > *frīde*) but no diphthongization of MHG *ī*. This folk-etymological reanalysis would have had no phonetic consequences in such dialects and could then have spread to other regions through the written language (Kluge 1975).

Occasionally, we find instances where folk-etymological associations appear to have blocked an otherwise expected sound change. English *handiwork* goes back to Old English *hand-geweorc*. The prefix *ge-* (pronounced /jə-/) was normally lost during Middle English times, so we would expect the modern form to be *handwork*. The retention of the medial vowel seems to be attributable to folk-etymological identification with the adjective *handy*.

4.3 Confusion of similar-sounding words

Folk etymology is usually understood to involve the identification of historically distinct elements in a particular context, such as within a (perceived) compound or an idiomatic expression. It also happens, however, that speakers simply confuse similar-sounding words independent of context. Whether or not this should be regarded as a type of analogical change is perhaps debatable – to some extent it depends on whether we look at the developments from an onomasiological or a semasiological perspective – but it bears some resemblance to both folk etymology and contamination, and when textbooks discuss it at all, they usually do so in this context (Aitchison 2001: 213).

Most like folk etymology are cases such as German *Spieß*. Most German speakers today probably feel that there is a single word *Spieß* that means both 'spear' and 'skewer, spit (for roasting)'. Historically, these are two distinct words. The 'spear'-word goes back to MHG *spieʒ* < OHG *spioʒ*, while the 'spit'-word was *spiʒ* in MHG. After regular monophthongization, the only difference between them was that the vowel of the former was long and that of the latter short. The subsequent change is usually characterized as the lengthening of the vowel in the 'spit'-word under the influence of the 'spear'-word. Another way to put it is that learners failed to notice that the two words were (consistently) different.

A similar example is the English verb *bid*. Formally, this verb descends from OE *biddan*, but semantically it has become completely conflated with an originally distinct verb, OE *béodan*, which would have the form *beed in Modern English if it had survived. (Compare the modern German cognates *bitten* and *bieten*.) In fact, the main sense in which the verb *bid* is still used by speakers of standard English today, 'to make an offer to buy something (as at an auction)' comes from *béodan* rather than *biddan*.

4.4 Contamination and blends

The word *smog*, formed by combining the *sm-* from *smoke* and the *-og* from *fog*, is a favorite example of a blend. A popular example of contamination is the change from Latin *gravis* 'heavy' to Vulgar Latin *grevis*, which is attributed to the influence of *levis* 'light'.

The terms **contamination** and **blending** were introduced by different scholars (Hermann Paul and Henry Sweet, respectively) in the late nineteenth century to refer to roughly the same range of phenomena. Many historical linguists, if they use both terms at all, have continued to use them more or less interchangeably (Anttila 1989: 76; Campbell 2004: 118–19), whereas most morphologists use blend(ing) to refer only to the type of deliberate creation of new lexical items illustrated by *smog*. Hock (1986) draws a somewhat different distinction between the two. Aitchison (2001: 213) does not mention contamination, and speaks of blends only in reference to the occasional, unintentional amalgamation of adjacent words: *foreigncy* < *foreign currency*. Pope (1952: 294–5) uses 'Contamination (Blending)' as a cover term for all non-proportional analogy, and characterizes folk etymology as a 'special form of contamination'.

I treat blend(ing) as a subtype of contamination, as explained below.

4.4.1 Contamination

Contamination yields new forms that combine phonetic elements of two semantically or grammatically related forms. Unlike folk etymology, it is speaker-based rather than hearer/learner-based, in the sense that its motivation lies in speech planning and/or production rather than in perception or phonological analysis (Andersen 1980: 16–17, 38–9). The input words to a (non-blend) contamination are always very closely related semantically, typically either as near-synonyms or antonyms. Some phonetic similarity is often present but not necessary. This contrasts with folk etymology, which requires a high degree of phonetic similarity but can occur with the barest hint of a semantic connection ('How much wood would a woodchuck chuck . . .?'). As clear as the distinction between folk etymology and contamination is conceptually, there are cases where it is virtually impossible in practice to determine which one is behind an innovation. Not surprisingly, given the definitions, these problematic cases arise wherever the input items are closely related in both form *and* meaning, and especially where the affected item can be (re)analyzed as morphologically related to the affecting item. A classic example is English *femelle* > *female* under the influence of the etymologically unrelated word *male*. This is widely offered as a prime example of contamination, but what speaks against analyzing it in exactly the same way as *bridegoom > *bridegroom*? The same question can be asked about French *anormal* (< earlier *anomal* < Greek *anōmalos*, whence English *anomalous*), where the *r* is due to the influence of *normal* (< Latin *normālis*). Folk etymology often affects (perceived) compounds, but – contrary to what some accounts suggest (Hock and Joseph 2009: 169) – it makes no sense to treat this as a defining characteristic if the same mechanisms are at work in developments that do not involve compounds. In truth, it appears highly likely that the mechanisms behind (production-based) contamination and (perception/analysis-based) folk etymology often operate in concert, making it not only impossible but also inappropriate to try to exhaustively assign all developments to one category or the other (Coates 1987; McMahon 1994: 183–4). This point may also be relevant to some changes in idiomatic expressions that are usually characterized as contamination, e.g. *for the life of God* < *for the life of me* + *for the love of God*.

The situation is somewhat clearer where there is no relevant portion of the affected and affecting items that speakers/learners would be likely to regard as a shared morpheme. Pronunciation of English *covert* (originally a variant of *covered*) has changed to rhyme with its antonym *overt*; the shortening of the vowel in the first syllable of *sorry* may be due to association with etymologically unrelated *sorrow* (OED); the initial *h-* in German *heischen* 'demand' (cognate with English *ask* < Germanic *aiskōn) is commonly ascribed to the influence of *heißen* 'be called, command' (Kluge 1975). English *nauther* became *neither* under the influence of *either*; *pæder* and *hwæder* became *þider* and *hwider* (whence modern *thither* and *whither*) due to the influence of *hider* (modern *hither*) (Wheeler 1887: 20); the *p* in *purse* (< Latin *bursa*) may be due to the influence of the Old English synonym *pusa*. Mutual contamination may have occurred in Old French *citeain* > Anglo-Norman *citesain* (borrowed into English as *citizen*) and Anglo-Norman *deinzein* > English *denizen*, whereby *citizen* owes its *z* to the influence of *denizen*, and *denizen* may owe its medial syllable to the influence of *citizen*.

There are numerous examples of contamination in idiomatic phrases. One that I have noticed a lot recently is *on accident* < *by accident* under the influence of *on purpose*.

Paul's initial conception of contamination (1886) involved influence attributable exclusively to paradigmatic (semantic) relations between forms, but he later (1920) recognized that lexical contamination often involves items that are not only semantically related but also frequently occur in close proximity in utterances. The importance of these syntagmatic relationships is emphasized in almost all modern accounts of contamination (Campbell 2004: 118–20 being the only exception that I am aware of). The most frequently cited examples involve adjacent numerals, which often influence each other's phonetic make-up: English *eleven* < Proto-Gmc. *ainlif under the influence of *ten*; Latin *novem* 'nine' instead of expected *noven under the influence of *decem* 'ten'; Greek dialectal *hoktō* < *oktō* 'eight' under the influence of *hepta* 'seven' (Osthoff 1878b; Trask 1996: 111–12; Hock and Joseph 2009: 163). Similar effects are attested in a number of languages among days of the week and months of the year, e.g. post-classical Latin *October* < *Octōber* under the influence of *November* and *December*.

Such contamination attributable to syntagmatic proximity of the affecting and affected items is often characterized as distant assimilation. Some scholars characterize contamination as a kind of assimilation even when it is purely paradigmatically motivated. Anttila calls it 'assimilation . . . toward another word in the semantic field' (1989: 76). Andersen (1980: 16–17) explicitly distinguishes such 'paradigmatic assimilation' from the more familiar 'syntagmatic assimilation'. As an unambiguous example of the latter, he mentions the influence of one word on another within a formulaic expression, such as French *au fur et à mesure* 'as, in due course' < Old French *au feur et mesure* (Wackernagel 1926: 49–50). Contamination involving antonyms, such as Late Latin *sinexter* < *sinister* 'left' under the influence of *dexter* 'right' or Vulgar Latin *grevis* < *gravis* 'heavy' under the influence of *levis* 'light', could be both paradigmatically and syntagmatically motivated, since antonyms frequently co-occur in close proximity within an utterance, especially in questions: *Is that thing heavy or light? Should I turn right or left?* Wundt's view of paradigm leveling as a type of assimilation should also be mentioned in this context (Paul 1920: 116n 1).

Contaminations appear to occur fairly often as slips of the tongue, but most of them gain no foothold and have no lasting impact on the language. Examples are occasionally recorded for posterity when they make their way into a written text or happen to be uttered by a prominent person, as with Shakespeare's *glaze* < *glare* + *gaze* or Sarah Palin's *refudiate* < *refute* + *repudiate* (July 2010).

Recognized instances of (non-blend) lexical contamination are not numerous. One encounters the same handful of examples again and again in the literature, but this may be at least partly a consequence of the inherent methodological difficulty of establishing contamination as the source of a new word. The OED suggests contamination-like accounts of a number of words with unclear or phonetically problematic etymologies: *scratch* (1474) < *scrat*, n.[1] + *cratch*, v.; *lag* (1525) < *lack* + *flag*; French *coussin* (the source of English *cushion* (1374)) < *coissin* + *coute* 'quilt'; the verb *jolt* from (the largely obsolete verbs) *jot* v.[1] + *jowl* v.[1]; the noun *tag* (1402) < earlier *dag* + *tack*; *twirl* (1598) < *tirl/trill* + *whirl*; the verb *glance* (1489) < Old French *glaichier* + *guenc(h)ir*. The *t* in *falter* (1386) may be due to 'the influence of approximately synonymous verbs like *balter*, *totter, welter*'; *graze* in the sense 'touch lightly/abrade the skin in passing' may come from earlier *glace* under the influence of *grate* '*rub*'; *boisterous* (1483) is explained as a variant of earlier *boistous* 'modified by some obscure analogy'. We also find intriguing etymological notes such as the following (s.v. *askance, adv.2*): 'There is a whole group of words of more or less obscure origin in *ask-*, containing *askance, askant, askew, askie, askile, askoye, askoyne* . . . which are more or less closely connected in sense, and seem to have influenced one another in form.' The literature on phonaesthesia is also clearly relevant in this context (Samuels 1972; Ohala et al. 1994). It is thus possible that our current theories and methodologies simply prevent us from doing justice to the importance of contamination in language history.

4.4.2 Double marking of grammatical categories

It has long been customary to regard the emergence of double marking of morphological categories as a major type of contamination (Paul 1886: 132–3), unconscious blending (Hock and Joseph 2009: 162) or simply non-proportional analogy (Anttila 1989: 92). Paul's examples include double marking of the German genitive in proper names such as *Fritzens* and *Mariens*, where the regular genitive ending *-s* is added to forms of *Fritz* and *Maria* that already contained the genitive ending *-(e)n*, and the double prefixation of *g(e)-* in the participle form *gegessen* 'eaten' from *essen* 'eat'. Modern textbooks provide English examples such as *ki* (or *kye*) > *kine* (which preceded the later proportional replacement of *kine* by *cows*), *childer* > *children* or non-standard *feet* > *feets, came* > *camed*. A more systematic example occurs in many Upper German dialects, where the regular subjunctive suffix *-əd* is frequently attached to strong verb forms that are already marked as subjunctive by a vowel alternation (ablaut+umlaut), as in *naməd* '(I/he/she) would take' from *nemən* 'take' (Schirmunski 1962: 512).

When we apply 'Paul's doctrine' ((2) in §1.4.3) and try to figure out what is most likely going on in the minds of the innovators who first produce these forms, one very plausible scenario is that they have not (yet) realized that the forms they are hearing were already marked for the grammatical category in question. An individual might have heard the form *kye*, or *feet*, or *childer*, for example, only in situations where the plural meaning was not obvious. Words with irregular plurals tend to be words that occur more often in the plural than in the singular (Tiersma 1982), and in the absence of recognizable formal clues to tip them off that the forms are plurals, the innovators could have interpreted them as singulars and then formed plurals in accordance with the regular pattern, i.e. in accordance with a proportional equation. In the attested double plural *bollixes*, the spelling with *x* confirms that *bollocks* was analyzed as a singular (OED, s.v. *bollock, n.* and *adj.*).

Under this account, these innovations would not be instances of non-proportional analogy, but rather of D→C reanalysis (§2.5.1) followed by proportional analogy (Becker 1990: 24). The appearance that something non-proportional is going on arises in cases like *child–children* from the fact that speakers ultimately combine the new plural and the old singular into a single paradigm, but this does not change the fact that the initial source of an innovative form like *children* could well have been a strictly proportional development in the speech of individuals who were interpreting *childer* as a singular. This is significant because these are often cited as cases that 'simply do not fit the proportional schema in any way' (Kiparsky 1974: 260).

4.4.3 Blends and related phenomena

I classify blends as a subtype of contamination. Exactly where to draw the line is tricky, but a prototypical blend has the following properties: (1) it is lexical, i.e. both the input forms and the product are words (rather than phrases or bound morphemes); (2) it is a deliberate creation; (3) the input words both (or all) contribute to the meaning of the blend. The third property can be decisive for distinguishing blends from non-blend contamination in the majority of cases where the input words to the blend have clearly distinct meanings. The gray area between blending and non-blend contamination is inhabited largely by fusions of near-synonyms, such as *insinuendo* (1885) < *insinuation* + *innuendo*; *begincement* < *beginning* + *commencement* (Wheeler 1887); and perhaps *irregardless* (1912) < *regardless* + *irrespective*, and German *Gemäldnis* < *Bildnis* 'likeness, portrait' and *Gemälde* 'painting', although no sub-morphemic elements are involved in these last two examples. It is also often precisely in these cases involving near-synonyms that we cannot be sure whether the formation was intentional. Equally important and problematic is the line between blending and 'normal' word-formation (derivation and compounding), which I will address below (see also Gries 2004).

In addition to *smog* (1905), favorite examples of lexical blends in English include: *brunch* (1896) < *breakfast* + *lunch*; and *motel* (1925) < *motor* + *hotel*. Blends resemble compounds in the ways they combine the meanings of their components, but the formal portions of the input words that make up a prototypical blend do not otherwise behave as morphemes or participate in morphological operations. The vast majority of lexical blends are based on exactly two input words. A rare example of a three-part blend is *turducken* < *turkey* + *duck* + *chicken*. Most researchers state or imply that the end of a blend must correspond to the end of one of the input words. This means, in particular, that combinations of the initial portions of two (or more) words, as in *moped* < *mo(tor)* + *ped(al)* or *sci-fi*, are usually not classified as blends, although some accounts do include these (e.g. Trask 1996: 34). Some sources define blends as formations that combine the beginning of one word with the end of another (Bauer 2004: 22; Booij 2007: 20). This is true of the vast majority of blends but would exclude classic examples like Lewis Carroll's *chortle* and *slithy*, as well as recent examples like *Jafaican* (see below for details).

Outside of linguistics, lexical blends are often referred to as **portmanteau** words. Linguists sometimes use 'portmanteau' in this way as well (e.g. Piñeros 2004), but more often reserve it for unsegmentable morphs that express more than one meaning or grammatical function. This phenomenon is also known as cumulative exponence (see §7.3.4). Bauer (2003: 19) offers English *was* as an example of a portmanteau in this sense; in addition to the lexical meaning 'be', it expresses the grammatical meanings PAST TENSE and SINGULAR. Similarly, English *-s'* expresses both PLURAL and POSSESSIVE (*the employees' spouses*). The French preposition + definite article combinations *au* 'to the (masc.)' and *du* 'of/from the (masc.)' are also frequently cited. Historically, many portmanteaus develop from contractions, like the German preposition + article combination *zur* = *zu* 'to' + *der* 'the (fem. dat. sg.)', which can still be morphologically segmented: *zu* + *r*. Such contractions often look like blends in that they combine the beginning of one word with the end of another, but they arise from sequences of adjacent words, whereas the input words to blends do not typically occur next to each other in speech.

Classic examples like *smog* (*sm-og*) and *brunch* (*br-unch*) have: (1) no overlapping portions consisting of segments that could come from either element, and (2) a first element that only contributes the initial syllable onset. Blends with these properties are fairly rare. Other English examples include *spork* (1909) < *spoon* + *fork*; *bit* (1948) < *binary* + *digit*; and *blerd* < *black* + *nerd*. A well-known German example is *jein* 'yes and no' < *ja* 'yes' + nein 'no'. A number of other words could be analyzed as having this structure, but overlap makes it impossible to say where the contribution of the first element ends and that of the second begins. The classic example *motel* (1925) < *motor* + *hotel* is of this type, as are *prissy* (1894) < (?) *prim* + *sissy*; *Chunnel* (1914) < *Channel* + *tunnel*; *scuzzy* (1965) < (?) *scummy* + *fuzzy*; *glamp(ing)* < *glamour* + *camp(ing)*; and German *Grusical* 'horror musical' < *Grusel* 'horror' + the English loanword *Musical*.

Most blends, however, at least in English, consist of (often overlapping) parts that look like they could be morphemes even though they happen not to be. As we will see, this means that they are subject to reanalysis as morphemes. Examples with no overlap include *ginormous* (1948) < *gigantic* + *enormous* and *Chrismukkah* < *Christmas* + *Hannukah*; with various kinds of overlap: *celebutante* (1939) < *celebrity* + *debutante*; *cafetorium* < *cafeteria* + *auditorium*; *stagflation* (1965) < *stagnation* + *inflation*. Much rarer are cases where part of one input word replaces a middle portion of the other, as in Lewis Carroll's famous *chortle* (1871), apparently from *chuckle* + *snort*. Here too, overlap can occur, as in *slithy* (1855) < *slimy* + *lithe*. As these examples show, most blends have the same prosodic structure as the longer of the two input words.

In the majority of English items commonly classified as blends, one or both of the input items is present in its entirety, with some overlap of phonologically similar or identical portions. By far the most common pattern involves a shorter word superimposed on the beginning or, much less often, the middle or the end of a longer word. The shorter word can often be said to replace the first syllable or trochaic foot of the longer word, although more often than not the phonological similarity between the two means that only one or two segments can unambiguously be attributed to either word: *funtastic* < *fun* + *fantastic*; *blacksploitation* (1972) < *black* + *exploitation*; *adultescent* (1996) < *adult* + *adolescent*; *stalkerazzi* < *stalker* + *paparazzi*; *sexpionage* < *sex* + *espionage*; and perhaps *bodacious* (1845), if the OED is right that this is a variant of *boldacious* < *bold* + *audacious*. In one especially productive pattern, the only non-coinciding part of the two elements is their initial consonant (cluster), which means that the blend rhymes with its second element: *brainiac* (1958) < *brain* + *maniac*; *mockumentary* (1965)

< *mock* + *documentary*; *gaydar* (1988) < *gay* + *radar*; *sext(ing)* < *sex* + *text(ing)*; *broem/broetry* < *bro* + *poem/poetry*; *manty hose* < *man* + *panty hose*.

German *Ostalgie* 'nostalgia for the former East Germany' < *Ost* 'east' + *Nostalgie* 'nostalgia', is similar, except that superimposing *Ost* onto the first syllable of *Nostalgie* entails deleting the initial consonant of the latter, so that the blend is actually shorter than either of its elements (compare *emocracy* < *emo(tion)* + *democracy*). A few other blends that rhyme with their second element have a truncated first element: *frenemy* (1953) < *friend* + *enemy*; *Bollywood* (1976) < *Bombay* + *Hollywood*; *glocal* (1983) < *global* + *local*. Examples with no phonological similarity between the replacing and replaced parts are less common: *gerrymander* (1812) < *Gerry* (person's last name) + *salamander*; *breathalyzer* (1960) < *breath* + *analyzer*.

In *Jafaican* < *fake* + *Jamaican*, the shorter word replaces a middle portion of the longer word, and in *prostitot* < *prostitute* + *tot* (Jonathan Faulhaber, pers. comm.); *prostiteen*; *prostidude*, it replaces a final portion.

Where the longer word begins with a vowel – or a consonant that can be preceded by another consonant to form a cluster – both input words can be present in their entirety, with overlap of identical segments. From a strictly formal perspective, most of these blends could be analyzed as compounds with **haplology** (the deletion of segments, often an entire syllable, in close proximity to similar or identical segments): *slanguage* (1879) < *slang* + *language*; *guesstimate* (1936) < *guess* + *estimate*; *palimony* (1977) < *pal* + *alimony*; *hacktivist* (1995) / *hacktivism* (1998) < *hack(er)* + *activist/-ism*; *sexploitation* (1924) < *sex* + *exploitation*; *bromance* < *bro* + *romance*; *backronym* < *back* + *acronym*; *toe-besity* < *toe* + *obesity*. German examples include *Kurlaub* 'spa vacation' < *Kur* 'treatment at a spa' + *Urlaub* 'vacation' and *Teuro* < *teuer* 'expensive' + *Euro* 'euro (currency)'.

A prosodically different type of blend combines two polysyllabic words with the overlap limited such that the blend contains more syllables than either of the input words. If the last part of the first word is identical to the first part of the second, both words can be present in their entirety: *anecdotage* (1835) < *anecdote* + *dotage*; *barococo* < *baroque* + *rococo*; *cyburglar* < *cyber* + *burglar*, and (an important one for linguists) *morphonology* (1933) < *morpho-* + *phonology*, an internationalism first coined in French (1929). In other cases, the overlapping syllables are not identical: *Exercycle* (1936) < *exercise* + *bicycle*; *Californication* < *California* + *fornication*; *prostituition* < *prostitute* + *tuition*. The pattern of overlap is more complex in cases such as *fantabulous* < *fantastic* + *fabulous*.

Blends of these types can give rise to productive series, and at some point one could argue that a new morpheme has been spawned, so that subsequent creations should no longer be considered blends. There are generally prosodic constraints on these creations, which is not uncommon for productive wordformation, but in some cases there also appears to be a rhyming restriction, which clearly sets these patterns apart from any canonical kind of word formation. Thus, *netiquette* (1982) < *net(work)* + *etiquette* seems to have been the initial model for *sweatiquette*, *petiquette*, *debtiquette*, and so on. Similarly, *staycation* < *stay* + *vacation* has led to *daycation*, *gaycation*, *awaycation*, etc.

These examples look very much like well-known cases of morpheme-spawning such as *-(a)thon*, originally from *marathon* and now found not only in established words such as *walkathon* (1930), *telethon* (1949) and *swimathon* (1968), but also in countless more or less ephemeral coinages. It is a challenge to come up with a possible *-(a)thon* formation that is not already well attested on the Internet: *eatathon, barfathon, reflectathon, cheeseathon, dumbathon* and so on; *-(o/a)holic*, spawned from *alcoholic*, is similar: *sugarholic* (1965) and *workaholic* (1968) were perhaps rightly considered blends when they were first coined, but soon we had *golfaholic* (1971), *chocoholic* (1972) and *footballaholic* (1974), and today the productivity seems to be unlimited: *sushiholic, sneakerholic*, and so on.

Other elements that are at least well on their way to becoming affixes include *-tainment* from *entertainment*, where we have *infotainment* (1980); *edutainment* (1983); *irritainment* (1993); *torturetainment*; etc., and *-preneur* from *entrepreneur*, with *infopreneur* (1985); *technopreneur* (1987); *edupreneur*; etc. The element *-zine* < *magazine* has also become productive since its initial use in *prozine* (1942) and *fanzine* (1949). This case is somewhat different, however, in that *zine* (1965) has also established itself as a word, and subsequent coinages such as *e-zine* (1994) and *girlzine* could thus be analyzed as straightforward compounds.

These examples further illustrate the role of prosodic constraints in blending and related phenomena. Both *-(a)thon* and *-(o/a)holic* have an optional initial unstressed vowel that occurs if and only if the base does not already end (and cannot be truncated so that it ends) in an unstressed vowel; *-tainment* does not have this feature, and as a result, only formations on bases that already end in a sequence of a stressed followed by an unstressed syllable (a syllabic trochee) seem to be fully felicitous. Monosyllabic bases sound less good: *?booktainment; ?worktainment; ?sextainment*; and bases consisting of an unstressed followed by a stressed syllable are even worse: *??designtainment*.

The oldest blend listed above only dates back to 1812 (*gerrymander*). A number of scholars cite *dum(b)found* (1653) < *dumb* + *confound* (e.g. Jeffers and Lehiste 1979: 131), but it is questionable whether this meets the usual definition of a blend. Although it was undoubtedly created by replacing the first part of *confound* with *dumb*, and it combines the meaning of the two input words, it seems likely that speakers analyzed *confound* morphologically as *con+found*, in which case *dumbfound* would be not a blend but an instance of the kind of paradigmatic word formation discussed in §8.8, which is sometimes confused with blending, as when Cable (2002: 135–6) lists *slumlord* and *transceiver* as blends. A much older example of this type is *Ormulum*, the title that the twelfth-century monk Orm gave to his work of poetic exegesis, based on a combination of his own name with Latin *speculum* 'mirror', a word widely used in the titles of non-fiction works of the time.

It is thus possible that blending, as defined here, is a modern phenomenon, but as with (non-blend) contamination, the OED tentatively suggests possible blend-like sources for a number of older words, including: *blot* (1386) < *spot* + 'some words in *bl-*'; *blotch* (1669) < *blot* + *patch* (compare *splotch* 1601); the verb *stodge* (1674, base of the adjective *stodgy*) < *stuff* + *podge*; *struggle* (1386) < *strive* (1225) + *tuggle/toggle* (1250); and perhaps *spunk* (1540) < *spark* (OE) + *funk* (1330) (see also Millward 1996: 206, 290, 331–4; Algeo and Pyles 2004: 262–3).

Blends are an especially natural fit for certain types of human activity, such as the creation of new hybrid plants and animals. The world of dog breeding provides at least one linguistically interesting example: The medial -*d*- in *labradoodle* < *labrador* + *poodle* seems to have been resegmented as belonging to the second element, so that names of other crosses with poodles also end in -*doodle*: *goldendoodle*, *Aussiedoodle*, and so on. Many language varieties are also regarded as hybrids by speakers, who often coin blends to refer to them, e.g. *Spanglish* < *Spanish* + *English*; *Urdish* < *Urdu* + *English*; *Denglisch* < *Deutsch* 'German' + *Englisch*; *Franglais* < *Français* 'French' + *Anglais* 'English'. Equally international are blends of proper names, such as *Brangelina* < *Brad* (Pitt) + *Angelina* (Jolie); or *Merkozy* < (German chancellor Angela) *Merkel* + (former French president Nicolas) *Sarkozy*.

Blends are often treated as a marginal phenomenon (Haspelmath and Sims 2010: 40). Aronoff discusses them under the heading 'oddities' and considers them 'words which have no recognizable internal structure or constituents'; they are 'opaque, and hence uncommon' (1976: 20). Recent developments suggest that Aronoff may have had the relationship between opacity and frequency backwards here. Blends may have been rather opaque in 1976 precisely because they were still relatively uncommon. Today, at least in English, blends (of certain types) can hardly be called uncommon, and we generally seem to have little trouble parsing and processing them. As we will see in §7.3.8, this issue of the relationship between the frequency of a morphological pattern and its transparency/opacity has implications for some fundamental theoretical issues of great relevance to morphological change.

To the extent that some types of blending have become productive and predictable morphological operations in present-day English, it is no longer accurate to classify them as non-proportional. They amount to a kind of compounding with the two elements overlapping in accordance with well-defined constraints. Within Paul's proportional theory, they could thus be handled by an extension of the (syntagmatic) proportional equations that he proposes for syntax (see §6.2 below). Blending as a type of word formation would fit even more easily into certain other theories of morphology. Insights and analytical tools from Prosodic Morphology (McCarthy and Prince 1995) have made it clear that (most) blends absolutely do have 'recognizable internal structure'. They are a type of non-concatenative morphology. Instead of combining two words in a linear string, as in compounding, blends superimpose one word onto the prosodic structure of another (Piñeros 1998, 2004).

Note

1. It is important not to confuse Ohala's phonological 'hypercorrection' with the other senses in which this term is used in sociolinguistics (see §1.6.3 and §3.6.1).

5

Types of Analogical Change, Part 3: Problems and Puzzles

5.1 A problem child for classification schemes: paradigm leveling

Although the Neogrammarians used the term **leveling** (Ger. *Ausgleichung*) for all types of (proportional) analogical change, '(analogical) leveling' is now usually understood to refer specifically to the elimination or reduction of stem alternations, i.e. what the Neogrammarians called 'material' as opposed to 'formal' leveling. Also known now as 'paradigm leveling', it presents special problems for analogical theory.

Occasionally, a linguist takes the familiar informal definition of leveling as 'the elimination of a stem alternation within a paradigm' literally and applies the term even to cases where regular sound change results in the elimination of an alternation (e.g. German *suchen–suchte* < West Gmc. **sōkjan–sōhta*). Generally, however, it is at least tacitly understood that the development must be morphologically motivated in order to count as leveling (Hock 1986: 206; Fertig 1999a).

As mentioned above, quite a few linguists classify regularizations that include but are not limited to the elimination of a stem alternation as 'levelings'. Thus, Blevins and Blevins (2009: 6) offer *cleave–clove* > *cleave–cleaved* as an example of leveling and state more generally that 'the regularization of any historically strong [English] verb' constitutes a leveling. Similar examples can be found in Bybee 2001: 116 and Campbell 2004: 106. Garrett characterizes all regularizations of English verbs as 'transfers with the effect of leveling' (2008: 129).

This contrasts with the more common practice of restricting 'leveling' to changes that consist *only* of the (partial or complete) elimination of a stem alternation (e.g. Jeffers and Lehiste 1979: 55–7; Andersen 1980; Hock 1986: 168–82; Dresher 2000). Leveling in this sense coincides with regularization only in those cases where the stem alternation that is eliminated was the only irregularity before the change. Thus *old–elder–eldest* > *old–older–oldest* would be an instance of both leveling and regularization, but *cleave–clove* > *cleave–cleaved* would not be leveling, because in addition to the elimination of the stem alternation, the new past-tense form shows the extension of the regular *-ed* suffix. The significance of these definitional issues for some of the substantive questions surrounding leveling will become clear below.[1]

Even under this restricted definition, many cases of leveling are regularizations, since the stem alternation that they eliminate was the only irregular inflectional feature of the item(s) in question. The elimination of the consonant alternation in Middle English *day–dawes* turned *day* into a perfectly regular English noun. Similarly, in Middle High German, a very large number of weak verbs had a vowel alternation known as *Rückumlaut* whereby the infinitive and present-tense forms had an umlauted vowel while the past indicative had the corresponding non-umlauted vowel. This alternation survives in modern standard German in a handful of verbs such *brennen–brannte* 'burn'. Its elimination leaves dozens of other verbs completely regular, e.g. *scherfen–scharfte* > *schärfen–schärfte* 'sharpen'; *küssen–kusste* > *küssen–küsste* 'kiss'; *tröumen–troumte* > *träumen–träumte* 'dream'.

The controversy that makes paradigm leveling a classificatory problem child concerns the question of whether it is proportional – in other words, whether it simply amounts to the extension of a pattern that happens to be non-alternating, or whether it must instead be attributed to some kind of general bias that favors non-alternating stems independently of any specific model. In the latter case, there would truly be an important distinction between leveling and extension. A number of recent works have been quite unequivocal in arguing that leveling is proportional. As Garrett (2008: 142) puts it: 'pure leveling does not exist and . . . the emergence of paradigm uniformity is always the imposition of an existing (uniform) pattern on a non-uniform paradigm.' A very similar view is expressed by Hill (2007; see also Albright 2005). Paul also eventually came to this conclusion (1920: 116 n. 1) but had earlier accepted the standard Neogrammarian distinction between material and formal leveling (1880; Hock 2003: 444, 458 n. 9, 459 n. 11). We find a parallel change of heart in Sturtevant (1917: 43–4, 1947). Kiparsky (1992: 58) gives us a clear and concise statement of the opposing position: 'LEVELING . . . is "non-proportional" because it does not require a non-alternating model paradigm'. Jeffers and Lehiste (1979) also come down clearly on this side of the debate. The majority of those who express opinions on this question are more cautious, arguing that leveling is largely or partially or probably or sometimes proportional (Osthoff 1879a: 42–4; Wheeler 1887: 31; Bybee 1980; Hock 1986: 179–82; Fertig 1999a; Reiss 2006).

Those who argue that leveling is not (entirely) proportional recognize that regularization, whether of the *clove* > *cleaved* or of the *daw(e)s* > *days* type, is always amenable to a proportional account. Any empirical case for either position in this debate must thus focus on non-regularizing leveling. **Partial leveling** can refer either to the elimination of a stem alternation between some forms in a paradigm, but not across the entire paradigm (e.g. *speak–spake–spoken* > *speak–spoke–spoken*), or to cases where one aspect of a stem alternation is eliminated while another aspect is retained, i.e. where stem alternants become more similar to each other without becoming identical. Hyman (2003) describes a systematic case of the former type in a number of Bantu languages where 'frication' of root-final consonants that arose in proto-Bantu as a sound change triggered by an immediately following *i* occurs not only (as expected) in forms where the causative suffix *-i̯- is attached directly to the root, but also in 'applicativized causative' forms where the applicative suffix -is-/-es- (underlying -il-/-el-) is inserted between the root and the causative suffix, e.g. Bemba -leep- 'be long', -leef-i̯- 'lengthen', -leef-es-i̯- 'lengthen (applicative)'.

Partial levelings of this type often result in a closer correspondence between stem alternations and morphosyntactic distinctions. An often cited example (e.g. Lahiri 2000: 7) is the umlaut alternation in Old English nouns such as fōt 'foot'. Originally, the non-umlauted back vowel ō occurred in the nominative/accusative and genitive singular and in the genitive and dative plural, while ē occurred in the dative singular and the nominative/accusative plural. Analogical restructuring yielded a Late Old English paradigm with the stem alternant fōt- throughout the singular and its umlauted counterpart fēt- throughout the plural. Andersen (1980: 25–6) discusses a number of somewhat similar developments in Slavic, one of which involves the paradigm of the numeral 'two' in Russian dialects and in Belarusian. Standard Russian preserves the older pattern where palatalization is limited to the nominative feminine form dvjé, whereas the innovative varieties have palatalization in all case forms of the feminine, so that it becomes a consistent marker of the gender distinction, e.g. genitive/locative: masc./neut. dvúx vs. fem. dvjúx.

There are several instances of partial leveling of the latter type involving consonant alternations in strong verbs in Germanic languages. These levelings are partial because the ablaut alternation in the vowels of these verbs is retained. An English example occurs in the verbs *swear* and *swell*, where the regular loss of *w* between a consonant and a back vowel (compare *sword* and *two*, where the lost *w* is retained orthographically) must have resulted in past/participle forms such as *sore/sorn* and *sol/soln* in Middle English. The *w* was then replaced in these forms after the *wo* sequence became phonologically possible again. Similarly, the English palatalization of *k* before front vowels resulted in an alternation between initial *ch* and *k* in a few strong verbs. This alternation was leveled in favor of /k/ in *carve* (before it was regularized) and in favor of *ch* in *chine* (before it became obsolete). Both *ch~k* and another consonant alternation to be discussed momentarily were leveled in *choose*.

A more consequential instance of this type is the elimination of the stem-final consonant alternations that arose in Germanic strong verbs as a result of Verner's Law. The only clear inflectional remnant of the Verner's-Law alternation in Modern English is *was–were*. This same *s–r* alternation has been eliminated in a couple of other verbs that still had it in Old English: *frēosan–froren* > *freeze–frozen*; *cēosan–coren* > *choose–chosen*. (In Old English, there were also strong verbs with Verner's-Law alternations between þ and d and between Ø (< earlier h) and g. A lexicalized remnant of the former can be seen in *seethe–sodden*. The other verbs that had this alternation are obsolete. The Ø–g alternation was eliminated by regular vocalization of postvocalic g.) The *s–r* alternation has also been leveled in modern German, though there it is the *r* that spreads (e.g. *frieren–gefroren* 'freeze'; *war–waren*, cognate with *was–were*). Other Verner's-Law alternations are still retained in some verbs in German. Can these developments be accounted for in proportional terms? There were several verbs in OE with the same ablaut pattern as *freeze* whose root-final consonants were not subject to

Verner's Law. Only one of these, *cleave–cloven*, has survived (marginally) into present-day English, but there were a number of others in Middle English when the leveling in *freeze* and *choose* began (Garrett 2008: 131).

One of several vowel alternations in the present indicative of German strong verbs is illustrated by the example *helfen–hilfst* 'help', where some forms have a short mid vowel /ɛ/ while others have a high vowel /ɪ/. Open-syllable lengthening gave rise to a new vowel alternation in the present indicative of many German verbs since vowel-initial inflectional endings such as *-en* created an open stem syllable while the consonantal endings *-t* and *-st* closed the syllable. Thus, at one point a long vowel in infinitive and first/third plural forms such as *leben* 'live' alternated with a short vowel in the forms *lebst* and *lebt*. This length alternation has been leveled in modern standard German in all verbs that had no other vowel alternation in the present indicative. In verbs with the *e–i* alternation, the length alternation has been retained in some cases, such as *nehmen* (with a long mid vowel) vs. *nimmt* (with a short high vowel) 'take'. Other verbs have leveled the length alternation while retaining the height alternation, e.g. *lesen* /leːzən/–*liest* /liːst/ 'read'; the second and third sg. of *geben* 'give' show variation in the length of the vowel. There is no apparent model for the new alternation between long /eː/ and /iː/, although it could conceivably be modeled on the parallel alternation between short vowels in verbs such as *helfen–hilfst*: /hɛlfən/ : /hɪlfst/ :: /leːzən/ : X, X=/liːst/).

It seems that one can almost always find proportional models for non-regularizing leveling if one looks hard enough. In some cases, however, there are legitimate questions about the plausibility of an account based exclusively on these models. Those who argue that leveling is at least partly non-proportional often assume this can only mean that some kind of universal preference for non-alternation is at work. Some relate this preference to the more general one-form-one-function principle discussed in §7.3.4 (Vennemann 1972b, 1993; Anttila 1977; Mayerthaler 1981; Hock 1986: 168). Others propose a more specific constraint favoring stem-uniformity within a paradigm (Kiparsky 1971; Kenstowicz 1996; McCarthy 2005). Recent work has made it clear, however, that any bias in favor of non-alternation could also be an entirely system-dependent matter (see §7.3.8). In addition to the specific patterns on which morphological rules (or proportional equations) are based, we know that speakers/learners also draw higher-order generalizations about their languages: whether prefixes or suffixes predominate, for example. Rather than assuming that all individuals are predisposed from the outset to prefer non-alternating stems, we could postulate that learners just figure out at some point that non-alternation is the norm in their language. This suggestion raises two important questions: (1) How does the realization that non-alternation predominates give rise to non-proportional leveling effects? (2) Non-alternation appears to predominate in the vast majority of the world's languages. How do we account for this without a universal constraint?

The second question will be addressed in §7.3.8. A counterpart to the first question would actually arise even if we attributed non-proportional leveling effects to a universal constraint. One possible answer to this question involves the mechanisms of associative interference in perception and production that were introduced in Chapter 2, where we saw how the latter can reinforce proportional change. Recall how interference in perception works in folk etymology: Speakers/learners are biased to mishear a portion of one form as phonetically identical – or to reanalyze it as phonologically identical – to another form because they mistakenly take them to be the same element. In paradigm leveling, the two stem alternants actually are the same element. Here, it is the expectation of non-alternation, based on the fact that learners have figured out that that is the dominant pattern in their language, that could bias them to mishear or misanalyze the stem portions of two forms as identical. Mishearing could play an important role wherever the phonetic differences between stem alternants are subtle or not consistently maintained in casual speech. Phonological reanalysis could take the form of a 'rephoneticization' of a previously phonologized neutralization (after the phonological rule in question no longer applies automatically). Learners might correctly hear, for example, that the vowel in *li(e)st* is shorter than that in *lesen*, but assume that this is just a low-level phonetic shortening before the final voiceless consonant cluster and that speakers were really 'shooting for' a long vowel, or they might notice the absence of a *w* in *swore* or *swollen* but assume that it is just getting swallowed up phonetically in casual speech.

Among the many linguists who attribute at least some leveling to a universal constraint or preference, there is a wide range of views on the nature of this constraint. Optimality theory models the mental grammar as a ranked set of violable constraints on the well-formedness of surface forms. The set includes both markedness constraints, many of which deal with universal phonotactic preferences, and 'correspondence' or 'faithfulness' constraints, which capture a preference for related forms to be similar or identical in certain specified ways. Correspondence constraints can refer either to relations between a surface form (output) and an abstract, underlying representation (input), or to relations among surface forms ('output-to-output correspondence', abbreviated OOC) (Kenstowicz 1996; Benua 1997; Raffelsiefen 2000; Burzio 2005; McCarthy 2005). The existence and the ranking of OOC constraints can be invoked to account for paradigm leveling in at least three ways:

1. The mere existence of OOC constraints, regardless of their ranking, can account for learners' tendency to assume non-alternation in the absence of any clear evidence one way or the other, giving rise to the 'overapplication' (McCarthy 2005) of phonotactic constraints within paradigms, as in the Bemba example from Hyman (2003) cited above. Another example would be Latin rhotacism ($s > r$), which involved a constraint against intervocalic *s*, originally giving rise to *s–r* alternations, as in *honōs–honōris*, 'honor' (masc. and gen. sg.). While this phonotactic constraint was still active (i.e. ranked above any relevant OOC constraint), speakers leveled the alternation in many paradigms by overapplying the constraint against *s* and thus extending *r* to all forms: *honor–honōris*.
2. Ranking of an OOC constraint above a relevant phonotactic constraint can account for cases where an alternation that might be expected on phonotactic grounds does not occur, as in the much-cited American-English example of the untapped /t/ in *militaristic* vs. tapped [ɾ] in *capitalistic*,

which is attributed to the influence of the respective base forms: *capital* (with [ɾ]) vs. *military* (with /tʰ/) (Steriade 2000).
3. Leveling by 'rule-loss' (King 1969), i.e. cases where a once-active phonotactic constraint ceases to apply within paradigms, can be modeled as the historical re-ranking of an OOC constraint above a relevant phonotactic constraint. A classic example is the loss of final devoicing in Yiddish, e.g. Middle High German *liet* 'song' (gen. sg. *liedes*) > Yiddish *lid* (pl. *lider*). The restoration of the *w* in *swore* and *swollen* would also fall into this category. Rule loss can obviously be modeled equally well in terms of conventional (input-to-output) correspondence constraints.

Others see the preference for non-alternation as an extra-grammatical matter, an ever-present cognitive 'pressure to level paradigms' (Albright 2005: 18), which might result from non-alternating paradigms being easier to process, thus influencing speakers' 'selective adoption' of variants (Kiparsky 1992: 59, 1978). Yet another possibility is a universal acquisition strategy such as Clark's (1987) 'Principle of Contrast', which posits that learners initially assume that any difference in form corresponds to a difference in function/meaning (Saussure 1995 [1916]: 224; Carstairs-McCarthy 2010). This assumption could lead learners to: (1) fail to recognize some stem alternants as belonging to the same paradigm, and thus replace them with analogical creations (see §2.5.1); (2) invent semantic distinctions to correspond to formal distinctions; and (3) fail to notice (and thus to reproduce) small phonetic differences between elements with the same function/meaning, resulting in (non-proportional) paradigm leveling.

Regardless of how plausible such mechanisms might sound, the question remains whether the evidence really justifies positing a universal preference for non-alternating stems (Garrett 2008). I address this question in §7.3.8.

5.2 Analogical non-change

As mentioned in §1.4.6, stasis over time can be just as interesting a historical phenomenon as change (Janda and Joseph 2003: 83, 86). Although accounts of analogy rarely call attention to the fact, there are a number of examples in the literature where the mechanisms of morphological change are invoked to account for an absence of overt change, i.e. for the survival of an element, construction or distinction. Saussure (1995 [1916]: 236–7) reminds us that analogy$_2$ is just as much responsible for the lack of change in the inflection of most forms that have always belonged to dominant, regular classes as it is for change in other, primarily irregular items. English speakers, for example, form the plural of dozens of nouns, such as *stone, eel, oath, comb, stool*, etc. essentially the same way they were formed in Old English, not because each of these plurals has been transmitted perfectly across all the generations, but rather primarily because analogy$_2$ yields exactly the same results as if the forms had been transmitted perfectly. These nouns all belonged to the dominant class that formed their plurals with *-as* in Old English, so even if English speakers never memorize any of them and always rely on analogy$_2$ to recreate them, they continue to come up with the same forms that were used in the past.

Less obviously, we often find that a covert change results in overt non-change (Wackernagel 1926: 47; Harris and Campbell 1995: 22). Or conversely, we could say that it is sometimes precisely the absence of overt change that provides evidence of a covert change. Some of the types of reanalysis discussed in Chapter 2 fit this description. The morphologization of a phonological alternation (§2.5), for example, can result in the survival of an alternation that would otherwise have been lost. As we have seen, this kind of reanalysis only rarely leads to overt analogical change, i.e. to the extension of the morphologized alternation, as has happened with verbal ablaut in Germanic or the umlaut plurals in German. Much more often the morphologization results in non-change: The evidence that the alternation has been morphologized is the fact that it does not disappear with the demise of its original phonological motivation.

The same is often true of exaptation (§2.5.6). Lass (1990) explains that the formal distinction between the Indo-European aorist and perfect is preserved in Germanic only because it takes on a completely new function. Similarly, in the example of German adjective inflection, we saw that the original nominal strong adjective forms (with Ø-ending) have survived in the nominative in German, in spite of general replacement by forms adopted from the pronominal paradigm, because these endingless forms were redeployed for exclusively predicative use.

A different kind of non-change can be seen in the vowel-length alternation in the past tense of Dutch strong verbs that originally belonged to Classes IV and V (Fertig 2005). Verbs of these classes had an alternation in West Germanic between a short vowel in the preterite singular and the corresponding long vowel in the other preterite forms. These verbs still have the same alternation in modern Dutch, for example /nɑm/ (sg.)–/naːmen/ (pl.) 'took', in spite of general leveling of vowel alternations within the preterite. Now, however, this ancient length alternation looks just like the general modern Dutch alternation between short vowels in closed syllables and long vowels in open syllables, as in a noun such as /bɑt/ (sg.)–/baːden/ (pl.) 'bath(s)'. When an alternation seems to owe its survival to a morphological-to-phonological change in its motivation, we essentially have the mirror image of morphologization, and this may be a good example of the allegedly rare type of reanalysis known as demorphologization (Joseph and Janda 1988).

5.3 Phantom analogy

I propose the term 'phantom analogy' to characterize cited examples of analogical change that never actually happened. This is a remarkably common phenomenon and underscores the importance of meticulous empirical research. Sometimes, an author's case for a theoretical point evaporates once we unveil the phantoms. More often, there are other, valid examples of the point that the phantom was supposed to illustrate. Nevertheless, we often discover that the evidence for a claim is not quite as strong or quite as straightforward as it initially appeared to be.

I start with the example of the alleged leveling in German of the stem-final consonant alternation in the OHG verb *kiosan* (cognate and synonymous with English *choose*) simply because it has been repeated so often (Hock 1986: 45,

168, 213–14; McMahon 1994: 74; Trask 1996: 110; Hock and Joseph 2009: 153). The alleged development is:

(14) OHG *kiosan–kōs–kuron–gikoran* > Mod. Ger. *küren–kor–gekoren*

The problem is that the (extremely rare) modern form *küren* is probably not a reflex of OHG *kiosan* but rather a distinct, originally weak denominal verb derived from the noun *Kür* 'decision' (which is itself a deverbal derivative from *kiosan*). In eighteenth- and nineteenth-century texts, we find regular past tense and participle forms of this verb such as *kührte* and *gekührt* (DWB, s.v. *KUREN, küren*). Modern German dictionaries and grammars still consider the (also extremely rare) unleveled form *kiesen* to be the normal present tense corresponding to *kor* and *gekoren*. I have seen no evidence that significant numbers of German speakers regard *küren–kor–gekoren* as the principle parts of a single verb, but to the extent that some do, I would argue that this is best analyzed as a matter of suppletion rather than paradigm leveling. The present forms of the originally distinct but largely synonymous verb *küren* sound like they should belong to the same verb as *kor* and *gekoren*, especially considering the exact parallel in the common verb *lügen–log–gelogen* 'to lie', and it is thus natural that some speakers might have reanalyzed *küren–kor–gekoren* as forms of a single lexical item. The formation of a new paradigm out of lexical scraps is a relatively rare and, in my opinion, extremely interesting kind of morphological change, and in that sense it is a shame that so many textbooks present this as an example of plain old paradigm leveling. One does not have to look far for a valid example of the points that *küren–kor–gekoren* is supposed to illustrate. German *frieren–fror–gefroren*, cognate and synonymous with English *freeze–froze–frozen*, is just as straightforward as it looks.

The *d* > *ð* change in English *father* (<OE *fæder*) is a popular example of contamination. (The parallel case of *mother* is cited less often in this context, for reasons that are not entirely clear to me.) The claim is that, by regular sound change, this word should have -*d*- rather than -*ð*- both in Old English (as it apparently did) and in Modern English (as it clearly does not). The -*ð*- in Modern English is thus attributed to contamination from the semantically related word *brother*, which has had -*ð*- throughout the history of English (Lehmann 1962: 177; Jeffers and Lehiste 1979: 57–8; McMahon 1994: 74–5).

The problem here is that *father* and *mother* are by no means the only words with OE -*d*- before *r* that show this *d* > *ð* change. It also occurs in *together, gather, weather, whither, hither, thither, slither*. There may be some legitimate differences of opinion here, but on balance, this certainly looks like regular sound change – with dialect borrowing perhaps accounting for apparent exceptions such as *ladder*. The OED agrees:

> The modern English -*ther* /ðə(r)/ for Old English -*der*, -*dor* in *father* and *mother* is often wrongly said to be due to the analogy of *brother*, or to Scandinavian influence; it is really the result of a phonetic law common to the great majority of English dialects (OED s.v. *father*, n.).

A phantom change that may be more consequential for our thinking about the likelihood of analogical extension of different kinds of patterns involves a stem-vowel alternation in the present indicative forms of certain German verbs. In the dominant variety of MHG, strong verbs of classes IIIb, IV and V showed an alternation between *i* in the three pres. indic. sg. forms (first, second and third person) and *ë* in all other present forms (infinitive, pres. ptc., subjunctive, and plural indicative). The indicative forms of the representative verb *gëben* 'give' are shown in (15).

(15)   sg   pl
     1st   *gibe*   *gëben*
     2nd   *gibest*   *gëbet*
     3rd   *gibet*   *gëbent*

In Modern Standard German, this alternation remains intact except for the fact that *e* (< *ë*) now also occurs in the first sg. pres. indic., as shown in (16).

(16)   sg   pl
     1st   *gebe*   *geben*
     2nd   *gibst*   *gebt*
     3rd   *gibt*   *geben*

This change is widely assumed to reflect an extension of a pattern of alternation that was already present in certain strong verbs of classes VI and VII (Augst 1975: 250; Gerth 1987: 111, 146–7; Hempen 1988: 252–3), as shown in (17) for the representative verb *graben* 'dig'.

(17)   sg   pl
     1st   *grabe*   *graben*
     2nd   *grebest*   *grabet*
     3rd   *grebet*   *graben*

This (apparent) change is (or would be) unusual in a couple of respects. Most obviously, the pattern of alternation that gets extended seems more complex, in some sense, than the original pattern in (15). It is easier to describe the pattern in (15) (no need to refer to the category of PERSON), and intuitively, it seems like it should be easier to learn as well. Secondly, there were more MHG verbs that followed the pattern in (15) than that in (17), 93 vs. 49, according to Hempen (1988: 191–4). (These numbers are based on counting prefixed verbs separately; if we count only basic verbs, the discrepancy would be greater.) So this development would seem to contradict the most widely accepted of all generalizations about tendencies in analogical change: that numerically dominant patterns strongly tend to be the ones that win out (§7.3.5). Because it is so remarkable, this example has been frequently discussed and cited in support of one theoretical position or another (e.g. Besch 1967: 305; Hock 1986: 212; Albright 2008).

As you might have guessed, this change probably never happened. The MHG forms in (15) reflect the southern dialects that were the basis of most MHG literature. The dialects of this region generally still have the pattern in (15) today (Schirmunski 1962). Central German dialects have played a much greater role in the formation of the modern standard language, and as Grosse (1988) has shown, all of the available evidence suggests that the Central German dialects had always had the pattern in (16), as did Old English. Prokosch (1939: 214) notes that some scholars believe the pattern in (16) reflects the original West Germanic situation, in which case there would have to have been an analogical change (of a much less remarkable kind) in the Southern German dialects to get the pattern in (15). Alternatively, it could just be that the sound changes that produced these patterns in the first place played out differently in the different regions.

This is a good example of a general problem discussed by Janda and Joseph:

> In order to make a meaningful assessment of some possible change, one has to establish beyond a reasonable doubt that . . . there really is some continuity between the 'before' and the 'after' that are being compared. In order to be maximally useful or even meaningful, a comparison of Old English with Modern English would have to control for dialect . . . in order to ensure there is what we might term 'direct lineal descent' between some element in stage 1 and its altered form in stage 2. (2003: 83)

Literary MHG is not the direct ancestor of Modern Standard German; Classical Latin is not the direct ancestor of any of the Romance languages; the dominant West Saxon variety of Old English is not the direct ancestor of Modern English, and the relationship of both Old and Modern English to the various major dialects of Middle English is complicated. Anytime we forget about the dialectal complexity of a language's history, we run the risk that our efforts to understand analogical change will get sidetracked by phantoms.

5.3.1 'Regularization is much more common than irregularization': a case study in circular reasoning

As mentioned in §3.6.4, one of the most often repeated and rarely questioned generalizations about analogical change is that inflectional regularization is much more common than change in the opposite direction. Dozens of originally strong verbs have become weak in English (e.g. *holp* > *helped*), but only a handful of originally regular verbs have assimilated to a strong pattern (e.g. *weared* > *wore*).

There is some truth in this generalization, but the discrepancy between change in the two directions is not always as large as it is claimed to be. Our impressions are greatly skewed by the widespread practice of citing examples of 'regularization' for which one has no actual historical evidence. The reasoning behind this practice seems to go something like this: 'Regularization is much more common than irregularization, so where I know that both a regular and an irregular form of the same item exist or have existed in a language, I can safely assume that the latter is the original form and the former is the result of analogical regularization.' Even if this assumption is correct more often than not, it is problematic to turn around and cite such examples as empirical support for any claim about regularization.[2] Instances of this are astoundingly common in the literature. The following is just one recent example:

In the context of an important argument concerning the ways in which languages sometimes tolerate 'bad' (highly marked) phonological structures for the sake of greater morphological regularity, Carstairs-McCarthy (2010: 52–5) offers four examples of verbs in which he claims analogical regularization has 'undone' the effects of sound changes that had produced past tense/participle forms with fewer phonological 'defects'. The four verbs are *heave, cleave, dream* and *kneel*, and the claim is that the forms *heft, cleft, dreamt* and *knelt* first arose historically by regular sound change and were subsequently replaced, or are still in the process of being replaced, by the regular analogical formations *heaved, cleaved, dreamed* and *kneeled*. In fact, Carstairs-McCarthy has the analogical developments largely backwards in all four cases.

A little background on the history of English/Germanic verbal inflection is necessary here. We have already encountered the distinction between 'strong' verbs, which distinguish their tense forms by means of ablaut (*drive–drove–driven*; *sing–sang–sung*, etc.) and 'weak' verbs, which take a 'dental' suffix, usually *-ed* (*walk–walked*, etc.). More important for our present purposes is the distinction in Modern English between regular (*walk–walked*) and irregular (e.g. *keep–kept, tell–told*) weak verbs and the closely related fact that Old English (and the other older Germanic languages) had a number of distinct classes of weak verbs. What really matters for us is that some classes and sub-classes of weak verbs had a connecting vowel between the stem-final consonant and the *-d* suffix of the past tense, while others did not. This is still true in Modern English, but today the connecting vowel (ə or i) always and only occurs when the stem-final consonant is itself a *t* or a *d*, e.g. *punted* with /-ɨd/ vs. *begged* with /-d/ and *kissed* with /-t/. In Old and early Middle English, the presence or absence of the connecting vowel was not predictable from the final consonant of the stem; it depended instead on which weak-verb (sub)class the verb belonged to. Since we are only concerned with relevance for later developments, we can oversimplify somewhat and identify the absence of the connecting vowel with Old English class 1 and its presence with Old English class 2. The irregular weak patterns of Modern English can be traced back to Old English class 1.

The absence of the connecting vowel in most class-1 verbs meant that the stem-final consonant and the *-t* or *-d* of the past-tense suffix were immediately adjacent to each other, which triggered a number of sound changes that are behind the various irregularities that survive today. The sound change of interest here is the more or less regular shortening in early Middle English (thirteenth c.) of originally long vowels before certain consonant clusters (Mossé 1968: 18). Long stem-vowels of class-1 verbs were followed by a consonant cluster in the past tense (*Ct* or *Cd*) but not in the present tense, so this sound change resulted in the modern alternation between long vowels in the present and short vowels in the past of verbs such as *keep–kept, feel–felt, deal–dealt* and *leave–left*. Unlike these items, none of Carstairs-McCarthy's four verbs – *heave, cleave, dream*, or *kneel* – belonged to weak class 1 in Old English. Thus, contrary to what he indicates, none of the irregular forms, *heft, cleft, dreamt*, or *knelt*, arose as a result of regular sound change.

The most straightforward case is *kneel*, which was a class-2 weak verb in Old English (infinitive *cnéowlian*) and thus generally had a connecting vowel between the stem-final *-l* and the past-tense suffix through early Middle English times (*knelede*) so that it was not subject to the vowel shortening before consonant clusters that we see in class-1 forms like *dealt* and *left*. According to the

OED, 'the past tense and participle *knelt* appear to be late (nineteenth cent.)'. This is one of the clearest cases of irregularization in English verbal inflection: *kneeled* > *knelt*.

The history of *dream* is a little more complicated because this verb is not attested in Old English at all. (It is believed to be a different word from Old English *drȳman/drēman* 'to make music, to rejoice'.) The OED speculates that the modern verb *dream* may well have originated as an early Middle English denominal coinage. As a new coinage, it is possible that there was variation from the beginning in its inflectional properties, but it seems likely that such verbs in early Middle English would have tended to take the connecting vowel in the past tense and participle, since this shows signs of having been the default pattern (Mossé 1968: 73–81). In any case, it is clear that *dreamed*, not *dreamt*, was the dominant past tense and participle form from the very beginning. The MED has 22 attestations with *-ed* or *-yd* versus just three (all from the same text) with *-t* (*drempte*).

The case of *cleave* 'split' is even more complicated, but not in any way that directly concerns the issue at hand. There are actually three originally distinct verbs that probably played a role in the development of the inflection of this verb, but none of the three was a class-1 weak verb in Old English. The direct ancestor of *cleave* 'split' is the OE strong verb *clēofan*. The strong past tense and participle forms *clove* and *cloven* are still sometimes used to this day. The other two OE verbs, strong *clīfan* and weak (class-2) *clifian/cleofian* meant 'stick, adhere' and are thus more directly relevant to the modern verb that has that sense, but *clifian/cleofian*, in particular, seems to have influenced the inflection of *cleave* 'split'. Notice that *clifian/cleofian* was a class-2 weak verb in Old English. There was no class-1 weak verb in the picture here, and thus no historical phonological justification for a form *cleft*. As the OED explains, *cleft* arose as an analogical innovation after the regular weak form *cleaved*, originally the past-tense form of *clifian/cleofian* 'stick, adhere', started being used for the newly homophonous verb meaning 'split' as well.

Finally, *heave* was also originally a strong verb, and the old past-tense form *hove* is still listed in modern dictionaries. Weak past-tense forms already start appearing in late OE times and become somewhat more common in the course of the ME period, although the original strong forms continue to dominate. We do find occasional weak forms both with and without a connecting vowel (*hefde*, *hevede*) from very early on, but the former are extremely rare. For Middle English, the MED has only two attestations in the early thirteenth century and then no trace until the form *heft(e)*, which Carstairs-McCarthy cites, occurs twice in Spenser's *Faerie Queene* and once in another sixteenth-century text, only to promptly vanish once again. Carstairs-McCarthy claims that: 'What has happened since Spenser's time is that, for the verb *heave*, the effect of the sound-changes that yielded *heft* as a past-tense form has been undone, so as to regularize the morphology of this verb' (2010: 53). The evidence from the MED and the OED points to a very different scenario: the close analogical model of *leave–left*, with the support of other verbs that have similar alternations, has given rise to *heft* as an occasional morphological innovation more than once in the history of English. Not only *cleft* (see above) but also *(be)reft*, from the Old English class-2 weak verb *(be)réafian*, provide additional evidence for the irregularizing effects of this analogical model.

There are, however, legitimate examples to illustrate Carstairs-McCarthy's point. At least nine Modern English verbs descend from Old English class-1 weak verbs with long vowels followed by stem-final fricatives, liquids, nasals or non-alveolar stops, such that regularization did/would result in past-tense forms ending in a long vowel followed by a consonant cluster: *believe, deem, deal, heal, hear, keep, leave, rear* ('raise'), *steer* (Wright and Wright 1908: 263–4), and five of these (*believe, deem, heal, rear, steer*) appear to have undergone the kind of phonologically undesirable regularization that Carstairs-McCarthy is talking about. In the case of *deem*, forms like *dempt* continue to occur through the sixteenth century before regularized *deemed* finally wins out completely.

The general lesson here is that present-day morphological variation, by itself, reveals nothing about the direction of analogical change. Regularization may be more common historically than irregularization, but irregularizations occur much more often than many linguists seem to realize, and it may be that – at least at some points in a language's history – attested variation is just as likely to reflect irregularization as regularization.

5.4 Summary of types of analogical change (Chapters 3–5)

These three chapters have presented a critical overview of traditional classification schemes for analogical change and explained and illustrated the various types. I argue that 'proportional vs. non-proportional' is a useful fundamental distinction, as long as we understand that the distinction is not really about proportions. Traditional classification schemes for different types of proportional analogy that use labels such as 'four-part analogy' and 'extension' turn out to be fairly arbitrary; the term 'extension', in particular, is used in a variety of subtly different ways. I propose a number of criteria to help clarify the distinction between the main two types of non-proportional analogical change – folk etymology and contamination – as well as to identify distinct subtypes of each, especially of folk etymology. Several types of change, including folk etymology and backformation, are widely characterized as 'minor', but there are grounds for reevaluating that assessment. The proper classification and characterization of paradigm leveling are controversial. Since Neogrammarian times, linguists have noted that a purely proportional account will work for at least most cases of leveling, but many argue that that cannot be the whole story. The evidence suggests that there is indeed something non-proportional going on in many cases of (non-regularizing) leveling, but I explain that this does not – as many have claimed – force us to posit a universal preference for non-alternating paradigms.

Notes

1. Parallel to their *cleave–cleaved* example of leveling, Blevins and Blevins (2009: 6) offer the irregularization *dive–dived* > *dive–dove* as an example of 'extension', which they define as 'the case where an alternating pattern is introduced to a historically nonalternating paradigm'. Again, most scholars

would distinguish between changes that involve only the extension of a morphophonemic alternation, and those that include but are not limited to such an extension.
2. A parallel issue arises in work on grammaticalization (Croft 2003: 272–5).

6

Analogical Change beyond Morphology

6.1 Introduction

As explained in Chapter 1, whenever we talk about analogical change, but especially when we look beyond morpho(phono)logy and syntax, we must keep in mind the distinction between analogy$_1$ ('all change is analogical') and analogy$_2$. The latter is the basis for the traditional distinction between 'analogical change' and other types of change (sound change, semantic change, grammaticalization, etc.). In this chapter, I will focus mainly on changes outside of morphology that – at least arguably – qualify as analogical in the narrow sense of analogy$_2$.

6.2 Syntactic change

The one place other than morpho(phono)logy where we clearly find innovations based on analogy$_2$ is in syntax. In the 'Analogy' chapter of the *Prinzipien*, Paul talks almost as much about syntax as he does about morphology. The most obvious examples of syntactic analogical innovations involve the inherent syntactic properties of lexical items, such as the argument structure of verbs or the gender of nouns (Middleton 1892; Hock 1986: 357–61). One of Paul's own examples involves the change, in German and other Indo-European languages, of verbs that originally took two accusative objects to the much more common pattern of one dative and one accusative object.

In Modern Standard German, the frequent verb *kosten* 'to cost' can still be constructed with two accusative objects:

(18) Die Behandlung wird ihn ein Vermögen kosten.
'The treatment will cost him$_{acc}$ a fortune$_{acc}$'.

In colloquial German, it is now more common to use one dative and one accusative object with *kosten*:

(19) Die Behandlung wird **ihm** ein Vermögen kosten.
'The treatment will cost him$_{dat}$ a fortune$_{acc}$'.

In the past, several other verbs took two accusative objects but have long since gone over to the dative + accusative pattern.

In both English and German, modal auxiliaries and certain other verbs are used in combination with infinitives without *to/zu*, whereas most verbs require *to/zu* with an infinitival complement:

(20) He can go. / Er kann gehen.
(21) He is trying **to** go. / Er versucht **zu** gehen.

Both of these patterns serve as analogical models such that historically, we see a fair amount of change in both directions, and at least some cases of variation in the present-day languages may reflect changes in progress. A well-known case in German involves the verb *brauchen* 'to need'. Like its English equivalent, the semantics of this verb are conducive to its being used in a modal-like way. It originally did not belong to the class of modal auxiliaries, and could only be used with an infinitive with *zu*. In many varieties of German today, however, it is common to use it (at least in the negative) without *zu*:

(22) Er braucht nicht (zu) kommen.
'He doesn't need (to) come.'

English *need* has undergone a similar development (OED, s.v. *need*, v.2), although for many speakers today it may be the younger construction without *to* that has a more archaic feel:

(23) He doesn't need to come. / He need not/needn't come.

These changes are clearly analogical in the sense that we are dealing with two different existing patterns. The change does not involve the creation of any new patterns or any changes in the patterns themselves. All that changes is that one or the other of the existing patterns comes to apply to an item to which it previously did not apply.

This last example also illustrates that analogical changes in syntactic and morphological properties are sometimes intimately connected. Modals are a class of words defined by both morphological and syntactic properties that set them apart from (other) verbs. In English, for example, modals do not have the *-s* ending that all (other) verbs have in the third sg., as reflected in *He need/*(**not** **needs**) *not come*.

Just as analogical change in morphology and morphophonology can sometimes involve not just individual lexical items but entire classes of forms, so too can a syntactic pattern be extended analogically over an entire grammatically defined domain. In syntax, some possibilities exist that have no direct counterpart in morphology. For example, properties of main clauses may be extended to subordinate clauses, as when the inversion of subject and (auxiliary) verb that is restricted to direct questions in standard English is extended to indirect questions in many non-standard varieties (*I don't know when is he coming*).

The most general kind of purported analogical change in syntax involves patterns of 'harmony' in word order (Greenberg 1966; Croft 2003: 53–80). The basic typological observation here is that certain word-order patterns tend to correlate. In languages where verbs generally precede their objects (VO), for example, we also tend to find that auxiliaries precede verb phrases (AuxV), nouns precede dependent relative clauses (NRel) and genitives (NG), and such languages tend to have prepositions rather than postpositions (Dryer 2009). There are many attested cases where the order of such elements has changed historically, and several scholars have argued that an essentially analogical process plays a crucial role in such developments. An initial change in the order of verbs and their objects, either OV > VO or VO > OV, may get the ball rolling. This initial change would presumably not be analogical, and there have been various proposals as to what might trigger it (McMahon 139–60), but analogy is often invoked (though not always by that name) to account for the restoration of word-order harmony after the initial disruption. Thus, an OV > VO change might be followed by analogical VAux > AuxV, RelN > NRel, GN > NG, etc. (Lehmann 1973; Vennemann 1974; Harris and Campbell 1995: 228–32). Many linguists believe that all of these orderings are linked by a common, more general syntactic relationship, e.g. that between head and dependent.

Linguists sometimes present proportional equations for analogical innovations in syntax. Hock and Joseph (1996: 196), for example, offer the following equation to account for the use of *hopefully* as a sentence adverb meaning roughly 'I hope that . . .':

(24) *'Tomorrow it will rain,' John said* **happily** : **Happily**, *it will rain tomorrow.*
'Tomorrow it will rain,' Mary said **hopefully** : X

Paul's syntactic proportions look nothing like this; instead, they reflect syntagmatic relations: *pater* 'father' : *mortuus* 'dead' 'the dead father (masc. sg. nom.)' = *filia* 'daughter' : *pulchra* 'lovely' 'the lovely daughter (fem. sg. nom.)' = *caput* 'head' : *magnum* 'large' 'the large head (neut. sg. nom.)'. This reminds us that Paul conceived of proportional equations as a model of the real grammatical relations in the mental system. His morphological proportions are paradigmatic (e.g. *walking* : *walks*) rather than syntagmatic (*walk-* : *-ing*) because he believed that the mental grammar represents morphological relations paradigmatically. Similarly, his syntagmatic syntactic proportions reflect his beliefs about the syntactic component of the mental grammar. Note that Paul's morphological proportions all involve inflection or derivation. Syntagmatic proportions would be an appropriate way to model compounding, although Paul does not mention this.

To understand why traditional accounts of analogical change focus so much more on morpho(phono)logy than on syntax, we must remember that mainstream historical linguists are often interested in analogy only to the extent that it helps them account for apparent exceptions to regular sound change. The English plural form *days* looks like a problem for the historical linguist because the Old English form *dagas* should have developed regularly into something like *daws (rhyming with *paws*). The problem is resolved as soon as we recognize that *days* is not a direct continuation of Old English *dagas*, but rather a new analogical formation, based on the singular *day* and the regular English plural pattern. Syntactic analogy is not needed to explain problematic forms in this way and is thus of interest only to those linguists who are genuinely interested in grammatically motivated change for its own sake.

6.3 Lexical (semantic) change

Quite a few linguists have argued that certain types of semantic change should be regarded as analogical (Kroesch 1926; Hermann 1931). Most obviously, analogical reasoning undoubtedly plays a role in our semantic interpretation of morphologically complex words that is essentially the mirror image of the role that it plays in the production of such words, and innovative, analogical interpretations clearly can and do give rise to semantic change. If we take the usual semasiological perspective, however, semantic change is defined as a type of change where the form stays the same while the meaning changes, so it would not count as analogical change in the technical sense (Hock 2003: 444); rather, it would be akin to covert reanalysis (see Chapter 2), and indeed many regard semantic change as a type of reanalysis (Fortson 2003; Traugott and Trousdale 2010).

When we look a little closer, however, it becomes apparent that the distinction between analogical change and semantic change in morphologically complex words is largely a matter of perspective. Consider a hypothetical semantic innovation whereby a learner interprets the noun *cooker* to mean 'a person who cooks', based on the analogy of other *-er* agent nouns, and starts using it to express this meaning, even though everyone around her only uses it to refer to a device used in cooking. From the traditional semasiological perspective, the innovation involves only the meaning of *cooker* while the form is unaffected. If we look at the same development from an onomasiological perspective, however, we note that *cooker* is now in competition with the traditional 'irregular' agent noun *cook*, which it may well have completely replaced in the innovator's mental grammar. Of course *cooker* is not a new form but rather a new use of an existing form, but this is true of many textbook examples of analogical change as well, as when English participle forms come to be used for the past tense, or vice versa (*I seen him; you shoulda took it*) on the analogy of the many verbs where past tense and participle have long been identical (see §8.8 below).

Bloomfield (1933: 407–8, 440–2) pushed this flipping of perspectives to its limits and subsumed all semantic change under analogical change, arguing that 'doubtless we have to do, in both grammatical and lexical displacements, with one general type of innovation; we may call it *analogic-semantic change*' (408, italics in original; Samuels 1972: 52–8). From Bloomfield's staunch empiricist perspective, thinking of any change in semasiological terms is a 'methodological error' (440); change in meaning is in fact merely 'the practical result of a linguistic process'. His main example is the word *meat*, which changed its meaning from 'food (in general)' to 'food from the flesh of animals'. He argues that the correct way to think about such a change is in terms of *meat* extending its use analogically to more and more contexts where *flesh* would formerly have been used. He offers the following proportional equation as an example of how this would work (441):

(25) *leave the bones and bring the flesh* : *leave the bones and bring the meat*
= *give us bread and flesh*   : x, x = *give us bread and meat*

His point is that there had always been contexts in which *flesh* and *meat* could be used more or less interchangeably. These can serve as an analogical model for the extension of *meat* into contexts where formerly only *flesh* would have been possible. Although few if any linguists today would agree with Bloomfield's 'methodological error' assessment, it is certainly true that (semasiological) change in the meaning associated with one word typically goes hand in hand with the (onomasiological) replacement of one word by another, and the latter does indeed constitute a kind of analogical change, in the technical sense.

There are a number of other cases of arguably analogical lexical change, always involving the extension of an identity relation, that fall into a gray area on the margins of morphology. English, for example, has many sets of words for animal species, one word each for male, female, young and non-specific: *duck, drake, duckling, duck; gander, goose, gosling, goose; rooster/cock, hen, chick, chicken; buck, doe, fawn, deer*; and so on.

In many cases, there is no morphological relationship among the members of a set at all: *ram, ewe, lamb* and *sheep*. As Carstairs-McCarthy (1992: 47–51) points out, however, there is one important way in which the relationships here are like morphology: the semantic relationships across each set are highly consistent. The organization of these forms in the mental grammar can be reasonably modeled with a spreadsheet-like table, as with inflectional paradigms (see §8.8.2). Speakers/learners cannot necessarily infer any formulas that would allow them to fill in a form in an empty cell. In other words, the proportional equations here may not be solvable, but the matrix could still play an important cognitive role by leading speakers/learners to expect that every cell will be filled, and keeping them on the lookout for that not-yet-encountered word meaning 'male pig', for example.

Where there are no formal morphological relationships, analogy$_2$ cannot be relevant to any overt innovations, but there is one kind of formal relationship that recurs quite often: identity. In some cases, the name for the male is identical to the non-specific term (*dog*); in other cases it is the female and the non-specific term that are the same (*duck, goose*). As explained in §8.8, an identity relation can always be extended analogically:

(26) *goose* (female) : *goose* (non-specific) = *cow* (female) : X, X = *cow* (non-specific)

Many of the lexical items in this particular domain are becoming obsolete. One could characterize these developments as a kind of (proportional) paradigm leveling: The formal identity relation is being extended analogically to more and more sets.

A similar example involves pairs of words such as: *take–give; buy–sell; borrow–lend; learn–teach*. Again, the parallel semantic relationship between the words in each pair is clear, but there is generally no morphological relationship at all. In a proportional equation such as: *buy* : *sell* = *borrow* : X, I know what the meaning of the solution would be, but I have no basis for guessing at its form. As Whitney (1867: 86) points out, however, there are cases here too where the two opposing meanings are expressed by the same word, e.g. *rent*. Whitney sees these as the basis for an analogical extension of the identity relation in innovations such as non-standard *learn* for *teach*, as in *I learnt him to swim*.

More generally, any elimination of a lexical distinction could be regarded as leveling, and wherever there is a parallel semantic distinction elsewhere that is not lexically marked, this leveling could be considered analogical. German normally uses different words for a human mouth – *Mund* – and an animal's mouth – *Maul*. When a speaker uses *Mund* for an animal's mouth, one could treat this as a proportional analogical innovation based on words for other body parts where German does not distinguish between humans and animals, e.g.

(27) *Auge* 'eye' (human) : *Auge* (animal) = *Mund* 'mouth' (human) : X, X = *Mund* (animal)

Is this the right way to account for such changes? The question is really whether the formal analogical model of lexical identity (*Auge* : *Auge*) is crucial here. The case above looks like a straightforward metaphorical extension. Metaphor itself is a kind of analogy$_1$ (Anttila 2003: 431–2), but the equation in (27) suggests that analogy$_2$ is at work. Such proportional models of lexical sameness across domains are surely not essential for metaphorical extension, however. Even if a language systematically used different words for humans and animals for every single body part, a speaker could still discern the functional parallels between the two and make metaphorical extensions on that basis. Still, it does seem likely that speakers of a language that generally uses the same word for parallel elements in two domains, and distinguishes in just a few cases, would show a much stronger tendency to level the few distinctions than would speakers of a language where lexical distinctions between the two domains are the norm. In this sense one could argue that analogy$_2$ might play an important supporting role in metaphorical extension.

6.4 Morphophonological change

There is no consensus on exactly where to draw the lines (or even whether to draw lines) between morphophonology and phonology on the one hand, and morphophonology and morphology on the other. Examples of alternations that many linguists would classify as morphophonological (or morphophonemic) include final devoicing in German: /taːge/ 'days' vs. /tak/ 'day' and 'velar softening' in English: *electric* (with final /k/) vs. *electricity* (with /s/) and *electrician* (with /ʃ/). Such alternations are common in the world's languages. Their conditioning may be entirely phonological (as with German final devoicing), entirely morphological (e.g. ablaut in Germanic verbs such as *sing–sang* or *drive–drove*) or somewhere in between, as in the English alternation between /ŋ/ and /ŋg/, where only the former is possible word-finally (*long* = /loŋ/), only the latter occurs medially within a morpheme (*finger* = /fɪŋɡɚ/), but medially at a morpheme boundary it depends on the grammatical properties of the following morpheme: (*singer* with /ŋ/ but *longer* with /ŋg/). Again, linguists differ on which of these kinds of alternations they call 'morphophonological'.

Morphophonology in the broadest sense figures almost as prominently as morphology in traditional discussions of analogical change. The Neogrammarians generally draw no fundamental distinction between morphology and morphologically conditioned alternations in their accounts of analogy, and the latter have therefore already been discussed in the appropriate sections of Chapters 3 and 5. The remainder of this section will thus be devoted to purely phonologically conditioned alternations. Paul models such alternations (*Lautwechsel*) as 'material-phonetic' (or 'etymological-phonetic') proportional equations, which he distinguishes from the more familiar 'material-formal' equations of morphology (1886: 61, 87, 95–8).

A phonologically conditioned alternation could, logically, be extended or leveled in the same way as any other morphophonological pattern. As long as the conditioning of the alternation remains purely phonological, however, leveling in one direction is impossible. For example, German /taːk/–/taːge/ cannot be leveled to /taːg/–/taːge/ because /taːg/ is not a possible phonemic form in current standard German. For the same reason, there is no potential for extension of the alternation to existing items with non-alternating /g/, since there can be no such items. In the other direction, both leveling (hypothetical /taːk/–/taːke/) and extension (hypothetical /sak/–/saːge/ 'sack(s)') can and sometimes do occur on a word-by-word basis, but such developments appear to be rather rare under normal circumstances. Albright (2009: 208–11) suggests one reason why this might be true: Native learners of German figure out early on that if a word's lexical stem ends in an obstruent, they have to listen for a form with a vowel-initial ending in order to know whether the stem-final obstruent is voiced or voiceless and then base their paradigm on that form. They do this systematically and avoid guessing until they have encountered the disambiguating forms.

Proportional change involving purely phonologically conditioned alternations is thus rarely a simple matter of extension or leveling in individual lexical items. Typically, it involves one of the following:

1. New candidates for the alternation arise as a result of an unrelated sound change, as when apocope (for example dative sg. *tage* > *tag*) produced large numbers of newly obstruent-final wordforms in many varieties of German (Hock 1986: 242–3).
2. Moulton (1967, 1961) coined the term 'morphophonemic analogy' to refer to the creation by proportional analogy of new phonemes consisting of new combinations of existing distinctive features. The example that he discovered involved the creation in eastern Swiss German dialects of a new front rounded vowel phoneme that corresponds to an existing back vowel in a way that parallels the other umlaut alternations in these dialects.
3. So-called 'rule inversion' (Vennemann 1972a) involves what Paul called 'a reversal of the proportions that is, strictly speaking, unjustified' (1886: 97, my translation). The best-known example is the *r*–Ø alternation in some varieties of English (Hock and Joseph 2009: 179–81). In non-rhotic varieties of English, words that historically (and orthographically) have a final *r* show an alternation between presence of this *r* when there is a following vowel-initial word or morpheme (e.g *clear issue*, with *r*) vs. no *r* when a consonant follows or when the word is utterance-final (e.g. *clear thinking*, with no *r*). In many of these dialects, this alternation is no longer limited to words with historical/orthographic final *r* but rather has been extended to all words ending in certain vowels, resulting in an 'intrusive' *r* in contexts such as: *the idea-r is*. Rule inversion thus results in predictability of an

alternation in the originally unpredictable direction. Without this inversion, speakers of non-rhotic dialects of English simply have to learn which words have a final *r*, based on hearing tokens where there is a following vowel-initial word or morpheme. After rule inversion, this rote learning is no longer necessary. The *r* is predictably present between certain vowels at word boundaries and – at least in some dialects – morpheme boundaries (*thaw–thawring*). In classical generative terms, one could say that before the change the final *r*'s were present in the abstract underlying representations of the lexical items in question, with a phonological rule deleting them before consonants and phrase-finally. After the rule inversion, there are no longer final *r*'s in any underlying representations, and the inverted rule now inserts them before vowels.

6.5 Phonological change

The changes discussed in the last section are phonological in the sense that they involve purely phonologically conditioned alternations, but they are also uncontroversially analogical in that they crucially involve patterns across grammatically or semantically related wordforms. Linguists have suggested several ways of extending the notion of analogy to include at least some types of phonological change in which patterns across morphologically or semantically related forms play no role at all. The best known of these is perhaps the idea that we should regard as analogical the extension of a sound change either to: (1) a larger class of sounds; or (2) a more general phonological environment. An example of the former would be a rule of final devoicing that initially applies only to fricatives and is then extended to apply to all obstruents (fricatives and stops). An example of the latter is the extension in Modern Standard German of the *s* > ʃ change to apply at the beginning of a syllable before any consonant. At an earlier time, still reflected in colloquial Northern German, this change had only applied before sonorants (liquids, glides and nasals), not before stops (King 1969: 58–62; Vennemann 1972b; Benware 1996).

The Neogrammarians regarded such extensions as perfectly normal sound change rather than analogy. At each stage, the conditioning for the change can be stated in purely phonetic terms. The analogical view of such changes goes back to Schuchardt (1885) and was endorsed by a number of phonologists in the 1960s and 70s. Note that this kind of change is clearly not proportional. The first innovator who used ʃ before stops in words like *Stein* (/ʃtayn/) 'stone' or *Spiel* (/ʃpil/) 'game' was necessarily reproducing rather than producing these words, to use Paul's terms, because she had to have learned the existence and the meaning of the words by hearing other speakers produce the older forms with /s/. A non-proportional account could appeal to something similar to the interference mechanisms that give rise to folk etymology and contamination: Learners might pick up on the distributional generalization that their language has ʃ rather than *s* at the beginning of a syllable before many consonants, and might be biased by this perceived tendency to mishear or mispronounce *s* as ʃ before stops as well. Note that this does not constitute associative interference as defined in Chapter 2, because in this case the generalization that is biasing speakers in their perception or production has nothing to do with any connections to grammatically or semantically related items.

Some linguists have argued that there are other situations as well where a purely distributional phonological pattern leads to a kind of analogical 'regularization' of the items that do not conform to the dominant pattern. Best known are cases where the distributional pattern arises largely by chance. Kiparsky (1992: 58) mentions the example of voiceless aspirated palatals in Sanskrit, which happened to almost always occur as geminates when medial. The few non-geminate exceptions appear to have simply been assimilated to this dominant pattern.

Perhaps a kind of bridge between non-proportional analogy in the usual sense and these developments based on purely phonotactic generalizations can be seen in cases where the morphemic status of the chunks of words exerting an influence on speakers' perception or production of other words becomes increasingly questionable and there is little or no apparent semantic connection between the affecting and affected items. Nunberg (2002) attributes the highly stigmatized recent change *nuclear* > *nucular* to the influence of words like *molecular* and *particular*. He calls this an example of folk etymology, which suggests that he regards -*ular* as a suffix here, but it is hardly a prototypical suffix. Similarly, the OED attributes the changes in the second syllables of English *pleasure* < Anglo-Norman *plaisir*, *treasure* < Old French *tresor* and *leisure* < Old French *leisir* to the influence of the French-origin suffix -*ure* (from Latin -*ura*, compare *closure*, *scripture*, *fissure*, etc.), but it is not at all clear (to me at least) that -*ure* is really a suffix in all of these words.

According to Wheeler (1887: 29), the final *l* in Anglo-Norman *sillable* (whence English *syllable*) < Old French *sillabe* is due to the general influence of other words ending in -*ble*. The OED explains *rambunctious* (1830) as an alteration of earlier *rambustious* 'apparently influenced in form by nouns and adjectives with -*unct*-' and speculates that *crouch* (1394) may owe certain aspects of its phonetic make-up to 'the analogy of *pouch*, *avouch*, etc.'

One of the most theoretically significant proposals along these lines is Kiparsky's (1995) account of so-called sound change by lexical diffusion as a kind of 'non-proportional analogy'. One of his primary examples is the set of English words that had long /u:/ following the great vowel shift: e.g. *food*, *roof*, *hood*, *book*. The vowel in a subset of these words has since undergone shortening, which has been spreading through the set. Kiparsky accounts for the lexical diffusion of this shortening as follows: The phonological rule assigning a single mora to stressed /u/ is first generalized beyond its original environment to become the default wherever the vowel is followed by a velar. This extension has no immediate overt consequences, however, because all of the words with initial coronals are specified in the lexicon as having long vowels, i.e. as exceptions to the default rule. These exceptions are then subject to being 'regularized' through 'item-by-item simplification of the lexicon' (648). Kiparsky recognizes that this process is 'non-propotional' but he nevertheless claims, confusingly, that it 'is analogical in just the sense in which, for example, the regularization of *kine* to *cows* is analogical' (641). Lexical diffusion is clearly not analogical in this narrow (proportional) sense. To the extent that it involves bringing exceptional items into line with a dominant tendency in the language (in this case simply the tendency for stressed /u/ to be short), it is easy to see that there is a non-proportional sense in which it is analogical, but as with the examples discussed earlier in this section, extending the analogy umbrella to cover such changes entails abandoning what has traditionally been the defining criterion of analogical change – that it is based on (perceived) semantic or grammatical relationships among forms, and abandoning this criterion would raise questions about whether the Neogrammarian distinction between sound change and analogical change can be maintained at all.

6.6 Regular sound change as analogy

For the Neogrammarians, a speaker's mental grammar was a system of morphological, morphophonological and syntactic relationships among distinct wordforms. These are the relationships that Paul modeled with his proportions and his formal and material groups. A complete linguistic theory must also model another kind of relationship: that among different phonetic realizations of the same wordform. Take the word *potato*, for example. My pronunciation of this word varies a great deal from one occurrence to the next, depending on how fast and how carefully I am speaking, as well as a variety of other details about the situation. Sometimes I produce the first syllable without any vowel at all, releasing the *p* directly into the *t*; the aspiration on the *p* can also disappear, making it indistinguishable from a *b*. In very fast, casual speech, the initial unstressed syllable might not be audible at all – as reflected in the familiar dialectal form *tater*. Similarly, I sometimes reduce the final vowel essentially to a schwa. If I hyperarticulate somewhat, on the other hand, the vowels of both the first and last syllables come out as full [ow], and I might even pronounce the last consonant as a fully aspirated *t* rather than a tap. Somehow, English speakers have very little trouble connecting all of these diverse pronunciations with the word *potato*.

At least initially, the Neogrammarians regarded this aspect of language as a purely mechanical, physiological matter. The different pronunciations of a word were attributable to properties of the articulatory organs, and the relationships among these pronunciations thus did not constitute a cognitive system in the way that the relationships among morphologically related wordforms do. It has long been clear, however, that the ways in which sounds differ across different realizations of the same word – the exact ways in which they are reduced in fast, casual speech, for example – are part of a complex cognitive system that learners must acquire, just as they acquire the patterns for forming the plural forms of nouns or for combining words into phrases and sentences.

This means that analogy, in some sense, is crucial for every token we utter. Even if speakers restrict themselves to using wordforms that they have heard from others and memorized, they cannot have heard every possible pronunciation of every form they use. There must be many occasions where they have to come up with a carefully articulated version of a word having only heard more casual variants, or vice versa, and this would require some kind of abstract rules, or proportional equations, or a network of mental representations of different pronunciations of words that would allow speakers to figure out what pronunciation of a known word would be appropriate for a specific speech situation. When we look at things this way, Paul's fundamental distinction between production and reproduction breaks down. So-called 'reproduction' of forms heard from others involves analogical reasoning just as much as do our own grammatical formations.

The theory of sound change as 'phonetic analogy' goes back at least to Schuchardt 1885. It was further developed and propagated as an alternative to Neogrammarian theory by scholars such as Vossler (1905), Sturtevant (1917), Schürr (1925), Hermann (1931) and Vennemann and Wilbur (1972). Two questions about phonetic change are sometimes confused in this context: (1) Is it analogical? (2) Is it 'regular', i.e. does it apply across the board to all candidate items simultaneously? A positive answer to the first question does not by any means entail a negative answer to the second. Schuchardt and his followers argue that all phonetic change is analogical, but some changes proceed word by word while others are sweeping and exceptionless. In this regard, sound change is no different from analogical change in morphophonology, morphology, or syntax (§3.6.5). It is also not hard to understand why phonetic change would tend to apply across the board more often than analogical change at other levels. It has nothing to do with whether or not the changes are analogical but rather with how close the (sub)system in question comes to the ideal of a 'complete harmony of the form system' (Paul 1886: 92).

The restriction of the term 'analogical' to processes based on morpho(phono)-logical and syntactic patterns has long since outlived its original rationale, but the distinction between changes motivated by grammatical relations among different wordforms and those motivated by phonetic relations among different realizations of the same wordform remains a valid and important one. The essence of the Neogrammarian 'regularity' hypothesis is that these two systems are separate and that they interface only through the mental representation of a single, citation pronunciation of each wordform. The representations of non-citation realizations are invisible to the morphological and morphophonological systems, and relations among different wordforms are invisible to the phonetic system. If we keep in mind that this is really what we are talking about when we distinguish analogical change from sound change, these traditional terms can continue to serve us well.

6.7   *The interaction of analogy$_2$ and sound change*

Since Neogrammarian times, historical linguists have loved to characterize language development as a perpetual battle between sound change and analogy. Sound change is 'blind' (Osthoff 1878a: 326) to the regular grammatical patterns of the language and is thus constantly disrupting them. Analogy$_2$ is based on these very patterns and thus tends to restore them where they have been disrupted. This epic struggle is a major leitmotif of Paul's *Prinzipien*. The following well-known passage is worth citing in full:

> In sound change, the symmetry of the form-system is confronted with an enemy working tirelessly to destroy it. It is hard to imagine the degree of disconnectedness, confusion, and incomprehensibility that language would

gradually reach if it were obliged to patiently endure the devastations of sound change, if no *reaction* against this were possible. But a means for such a reaction is available in *analogical formation*. With its help, language gradually works its way back, again and again, to a more tolerable situation, to firmer connectedness and more functional groupings in inflection and word formation. Thus we see in language history a perpetual ebb and flow of two opposing currents. Every *disorganization* is followed by a *reorganization*. The more forcefully the groups are attacked by sound change, the more the innovative activity comes to life. (1886: 161, my translation, emphasis in original)

Many textbooks focus especially on paradigm leveling to exemplify this restorative function of analogical change. Morphophonological alternations can almost always be traced back to regular (conditioned) sound changes. Here are a couple of examples: The English alternation between voiceless and voiced fricatives in pairs like *knife–knives*; *house* (/s/)–*houses* (/z/); and (at least for many Americans) *moth* (/θ/)–*moths* (/ðz/) originated in a regular allophonic alternation whereby voiced fricatives occurred medially between voiced segments and voiceless fricatives occurred word-finally; the vowel mutation in singular–plural pairs like *mouse–mice*; *tooth–teeth*; *man–men* and in comparatives and superlatives like *old–elder–eldest* and in denominal verbs like *bleed* < *blood* and *fill* < *full* goes back to a regular assimilative vowel fronting before front vowels or palatal glides that were formerly present in the following syllable of these words.

From the beginning, such alternations almost always affect only a part of any lexical class because their conditions are not met in every item (§7.3.8). The *knife–knives* alternation, for example, could only apply to nouns ending in fricatives. This means that if such an alternation survives after it can no longer be associated with any straightforward phonological conditioning factors, speakers have to learn and remember, typically item by item, whether a word has the alternation or not. This complicates the task of the learner, and perhaps that of the language user as well. Analogical change frequently comes to the rescue in such cases, usually by eliminating the alternation. Many alternations have been leveled without a trace in English, such as the expected *ay–aw* alternation between the singular and plural of *day* mentioned above, and many surviving alternations have been leveled in most of the items that originally had them. Regularization has eliminated plural umlaut in eleven English nouns, including *book*, *oak*, *cow* and *goat* (§7.3.4). We have also seen (§3.6.2) that alternations are sometimes generalized rather than being eliminated (*dwarfs* > *dwarves*, on the model of *elf–elves*, etc.), which can also restore a higher degree of regularity/predictability.

Hock claims that the idea of analogy restoring order where it has been disrupted 'is limited to leveling and sound change; other analogical processes have the relation only incidentally, if at all' (2003: 450; 1986: 171). This statement is puzzling since the Neogrammarian accounts of the struggle between sound change and analogy are not primarily concerned with leveling and paradigm alternations, but rather with sound changes that obscure the features of words that formerly made their inflectional behavior predictable (Brugmann 1876: 319 n. 33; Kuryłowicz 1964 [1945–9]: 161). The merger of the nominative singular endings *-us* and *-os* in Latin is a classic example. These originally distinct endings made it possible to know whether a noun belonged to the second or the fourth declension. The merger left the nom. sg. form indeterminate. The analogical response to this situation was the gradual elimination of the smaller fourth declension as its members adopted the inflectional pattern of the second.

As mentioned in Chapter 1, Paul pointed out that inconsistencies or indeterminacies in the grammatical system are a prerequisite for the occurrence of (proportional) analogical innovation/change. If the whole system were completely regular and learning one form of a word always allowed you to predict all the other forms, then speakers would invariably produce exactly the same forms as others before them. Left to itself, morphologically motivated change would always be moving the system closer to 'complete harmony' and thus perfect stability. Given enough time, it would eventually reach this goal, and there would be no further need for analogical change. That this does not happen is due to the incessant disruptive effects of sound change, and to a lesser extent semantic change. In this sense, morphologically motivated change is always a reaction to changes with other motivations (Wurzel 1989). If these other changes were to cease, morphologically motivated change might have a chance of finishing its job and retiring, but since sound change will clearly never shut down, we can be sure that analogy$_2$ and morphological reanalysis will be at their Sisyphean task until the end of time (Paul 1886: 188).

Schuchardt is one lonely voice who questions the idea that analogy and sound change are generally opposing forces in language development: 'If we admit the gradual spread of sound change, could not the thought arise that conceptual analogy only works against the sound laws in individual cases but in general works much more often in concert with them' (1972: 30 [1885: 29], my translation).

6.7.1 Sturtevant's so-called paradox

Long before there was a Philosoraptor, historical linguists had 'Sturtevant's Paradox': 'Phonetic laws are regular but produce irregularities. Analogic creation is irregular but produces regularity' (Sturtevant 1947: 109). It is catchy and memorable. It has undoubtedly helped generations of linguistics students remember the battle between sound change and analogy, and, on the tiny scale of our subdiscipline, it is no exaggeration to say that it has 'gone viral', making appearances in numerous textbooks (e.g. Anttila 1989: 94; McMahon 1994; Trask 1996: 108; Campbell 2004: 109) and other works (e.g. Lass 1997: 342; Hock 2003: 450).

Like a lot of memorable sayings, Sturtevant's Paradox is really more of a clever play on words than a paradox, kind of like 'Isn't it funny how you drive on a parkway and park on a driveway.' There is nothing paradoxical about the fact that phonetically regular change gives rise to morphological irregularities. Similarly, it is no surprise that morphologically motivated change tends to result in increased morphological regularity. 'Analogic creation' would be even more effective in this regard if it were regular, i.e. if it always applied across the board to all candidate forms, but even the most sporadic morphologically motivated change is bound to eliminate a few morphological idiosyncrasies from the system.

If we consider analogical change from the perspective of its effects on phonotactic patterns, it is sometimes disruptive in just the way that one would expect (Vennemann 1993: 323). At one point in the history of Latin, for example, it was completely predictable that *s* would not occur between vowels. Analogical change destroyed this phonological regularity, as it has countless others. Carstairs-McCarthy (2010: 52–5) points out that analogical change in English has been known to restore 'bad' prosodic structures, such as syllable codas consisting of a long vowel followed by two voiced obstruents. Although Carstairs-McCarthy's examples are all flawed, there are real instances, such as *believed* < *beleft*, of the kind of development he is talking about (§5.3.1).

What the continuing popularity of Sturtevant's formulation really reveals is that one old Neogrammarian bias is still very much with us: When Sturtevant talks about changes resulting in 'regularity' and 'irregularities', present-day historical linguists still share his tacit assumption that these terms can only refer to morphology. If we were to revise the 'paradox' to accurately reflect the interaction between sound change and analogy, we would wind up with something not very paradoxical at all:

> Sound change, being phonetically/phonologically motivated, tends to maintain phonological regularity and produce morphological irregularity. Analogic creation, being morphologically motivated, tends to produce phonological irregularity and morphological regularity. Incidentally, the former tends to proceed 'regularly' (i.e. across the board with no lexical exceptions) while the latter is more likely to proceed 'irregularly' (word-by-word).

I realize that this version is not likely to go viral.

6.7.2 'Therapy, not Prophylaxis'

The slogan 'languages practice therapy, not prophylaxis' is widely attributed to Lightfoot (1979: 123) but as Harris and Campbell (1995: 28) point out, the wording is actually several years older and the idea goes back much further than that. Lightfoot is talking about syntax, specifically about the alleged tendency for small changes with various motivations to result in a gradual increase in the opacity of syntactic patterns. His claim is that speakers do not take any action to prevent this from happening. According to his Transparency Principle, it is only when the degree of opacity/exceptionality reaches an intolerable level that we get a 'therapeutic' reaction restoring greater transparency. Paul proposed a kind of Transparency Principle for analogical change:

> So-called false analogy is not only a necessary consequence of this disruption of the harmony [*DF: caused by sound change*] but also, at the same time, a reaction against it, by means of which the memory is freed from the crushing burden of the mass of peculiarities that have imposed themselves on it. Due to the seemingly arbitrary randomness of this burden, the memory is no longer capable of dealing with it. (Paul 1877: 328, my translation)

Paul applies the therapy-not-prophylaxis principle in a number of places (e.g. 1886: 208), and the idea that analogy can never prevent the operation of sound change is often mentioned in this context. Paul himself only came to this view after being scolded by Osthoff (1878a: 325–7, 1879a: 5–6) for suggesting the opposite. Previously, both Paul (e.g. 1877: 395–6) and Brugmann (e.g. 1876: 319 n. 33) had argued that preventive analogy could in some cases block an otherwise regular sound change from affecting certain words or classes of words (Esper 1973: 42). Hermann (1931: 56) cites evidence that Brugmann later returned to this view. Jespersen (1928: 18) was always a firm believer in 'preventive analogy'.

The idea that analogy cannot block sound change is often taken to be a central pillar of the Neogrammarian 'regularity hypothesis', a correlate of the tenet that sound change is subject only to phonetic – never to morphological or lexical – conditioning. It seems that most of the Neogrammarians themselves came to see it this way, but there are a couple of important points that are often misunderstood in this context. It is certainly not true that analogy can never restore a morphological regularity disrupted by a sound change while the sound change is still active. The Neogrammarian claim is merely that analogy cannot do this by protecting some words from the active sound change, but as explained above in §5.1, analogy can, first of all, often tidy things up by bringing about the overapplication of a sound change to forms where its conditions are not met. Kuryłowicz argues, for example, that the leveling of the s–r alternation that had arisen in Latin as a result of rhotacism (*honōs–honōris* > *honor–honōris* 'honor') occurred while rhoticism was still an active sound change. Leveling in the other direction (*honōris* > **honōsis*) would have been phonologically impossible at that point because s could not occur intervocalically, but there was no phonological problem with r occuring word-finally or next to a consonant.

Secondly, the Neogrammarian position does not – in all cases – rule out the possibility of analogy essentially canceling out the effects of an active sound change. The example that Osthoff initially uses to make his point is the well-known deletion of intervocalic s in Greek (see also Brugmann 1885: 52–3). In this particular case, intervocalic s was completely impossible in Greek as long as this sound change was active (as it was in Latin while rhotacism was still active), and therefore analogy could not restore s until this situation changed, i.e. until – in Neogrammarian terms – the sound change was no longer 'alive' (*lebendig*). In more modern terminology, we might say that analogy has to wait until the phonological rule $s \rightarrow \emptyset / V\_V$ has been 'lexicalized' (Kiparsky 1995), or until the constraint against intervocalic s is no longer 'undominated' (Kager 1999).

Consider, however, the following hypothetical scenario (cf. Raffelsiefen 2000): A language is undergoing regular phonetic reduction of word-final vowels such that short vowels are regularly dropped (apocope) and long vowels are regularly shortened. Imagine further that this language has two noun classes which differ only in that one of them originally formed its plurals with the suffix -*a* while the other used -*ā*. Membership in these classes is completely unpredictable from the singular form or the meaning of the noun, but the *ā*-class is considerably larger and there has been a tendency for items to shift from the smaller *a*-class into the dominant class throughout the history of the language. Finally, imagine that at some point after the $a > \emptyset$ and $\bar{a} > a$ sound changes, we observe that all of the nouns in the language now have an -*a* plural ending. For nouns that originally belonged to the $\bar{a}$-class, this would be the expected reflex of $\bar{a}$ by regular sound change. For nouns that originally had -*a*, the new -*a* would have to be explained as an analogical development that has the effect of maintaining or restoring the same plural ending these nouns had before the sound change.

Two questions arise here: (1) Would the analogical 'restoration' of -*a* in nouns of the *a*-class have to wait until the $a > \emptyset$ change was no longer active? The answer (Neogrammarian or otherwise) is clearly no. The speakers who are producing these analogical innovations do not necessarily know that the nouns in question ever belonged to the *a*-class; they may have never encountered any plural forms for these nouns at all, or not recognized them as plural forms if they did. They are essentially treating these nouns as if they belonged to the other class, and this could clearly happen at any time, before, during, or after the $a > \emptyset$ sound change. (2) If it turned out that there was never a time when the *a*-class nouns actually lost their endings to apocope – in other words, if at the very moment when the $a > \emptyset$ sound change would have left these nouns endingless they all shifted over to the other class and thus 'kept' their endings – would it then be accurate to say that analogy 'prevented' the $a > \emptyset$ sound change in these words? Again, the answer is no. To the extent that the 'retention' of -*a* is attributable to proportional analogy, it is not really a retention at all, regardless of when it happened. The new forms with -*a* are speakers' analogical creations, based on their knowledge of other wordforms. If the new -*a* happens to appear just when the old -*a* is being lost, this might create the illusion of continuity, but the new -*a* is in fact a different -*a*. The sound change eliminating the old -*a* has not been blocked; some of the forms that would have reflected that sound change have simply been replaced by different forms. There are reasons why we might expect this analogical change to be especially likely precisely at the moment when the old -*a* is being lost: Unmarked plurals would obviously violate 'constructional iconicity' (§7.3.4) as well as being at odds with 'system congruity' (§7.3.5) in a language where most nouns do have a plural suffix.

The Neogrammarian argument that it does not make sense to talk about (proportional) analogy blocking a sound change is sometimes confused with the empirical observation that some sound changes result in exceptionless phonotactic constraints, in which case there is a period when a 'restorative' analogical change is phonologically impossible. The point about (proportional) analogy not being able to prevent regular sound change has nothing to do with the relative chronology of the two. The effects of a sound change (e.g. a chain shift) that does not result in a relevant phonotactic constraint can be preempted by analogy in some wordforms at any time, including just at the moment when those effects would otherwise have been manisfested. This only constitutes preventing the sound change from applying to those forms in the sense that sound change can obviously not apply to forms that no longer exist. A more accurate characterization would be to say that preemptive analogy can bleed a sound change by replacing candidate forms with different forms.

6.8 Chapter summary

While this book is primarily about morphological change, this chapter looks beyond morphology and considers various ways in which aspects of syntactic, semantic and phonological/phonetic change could be (and have been) considered analogical. Syntactic change is reasonably straightforward, since the role of something quite analogous to morphological analogy has long been recognized here. Semantic change is often highly analogical in a general sense, and I elaborate on Bloomfield's point that a great deal of semantic change can start looking much more like analogical change in morphology if we flip our perspective and look at it onomasiologically rather than semasiologically.

Consideration of the role of analogy in phonological/phonetic change, including 'regular' sound change, introduces us to the important theoretical work of Schuchardt and his followers, who have questioned the fundamental Neogrammarian dichotomy between sound change and analogy all along. The chapter concludes with a look at several controversial issues related to the historical interaction between sound change and morpho(phono)logical analogy.

7

Constraints on Analogical Innovation and Change

7.1 Introduction

One of the major focuses of work on analogical innovation and change has long been the question of how these processes are constrained. Restricting our attention to proportional analogy, a null hypothesis might be that any innovation or change that can be modeled as the extension of an existing pattern is equally likely to occur: *think : thought = blink : **blought**; child : children = kite : **kittren**; knee : kneel = elbow : **elbowl*** would all be just as likely as *oxen > oxes* or *clung > clinged*. No one has ever really believed that this is the way it works. Intuitively, it is obvious that some analogical innovations/changes are much more likely than others. This chapter will explore some of the attempts to identify the factors responsible for these differences and to develop comprehensive models to account for how these factors interact and make predictions about the possibility or probability of various conceivable changes.

Constraints on analogy are sometimes claimed to be a relatively recent concern, but in fact this was a major preoccupation of nineteenth-century scholars. The importance of the issue was already stressed in the 1860s by the Neogrammarians' great role model, Scherer:

> It would be a great service if someone were to discuss this imposition, this form transfer or operation of 'false analogy' in the most general terms and above all try to determine the constraints (*Einschränkungen*) by which this process is bound. (1866: 177, my translation)

Wheeler is also emphatic on this point:

> The explanation by analogy is never complete when the possibility of influence from a given source is indicated; it must also be shown how, out of many possible associations, the language was naturally impelled to choose the one in question; also why the retention of the old form was impracticable. (1887: 38)

The critique implicit in this passage is as relevant today as in was in 1887. Then as now, analogy typically reared its ugly head in historical accounts as a post hoc device to account for an attested change. Linguists start from the fact that a change has occurred and are satisfied as soon as they have identified a plausible proportional model to account for it. The Neogrammarians themselves were very sensitive to this issue because the arbitrariness and unpredictability of analogy was one of the main themes at which their critics kept hammering away (e.g. Curtius 1885). In addition to proposing a variety of factors that do impose soft constraints on analogical change, the Neogrammarians offered reasons why it was impossible in principle to go beyond identifying very general tendencies. The following quote from Delbrück is typical:

> Why and under what circumstances such [analogical] transformations occurred at a particular time and why only in some dialects but not in others is something we can determine with certainty only in the rarest of cases. Most of the time, we must instead be content with the observation that of the two competing drives, namely the drive to maintain individual forms in their transmitted shape and the drive to assimilate them to related forms, the latter won out. (1893: 122, my translation)

Paul gave considerable thought to the reasons why analogical change is often unpredictable:

> Moreover, the path of development is influenced by a large number of chance processes in the cognitive activity of each individual and in the effect of individuals on each other, processes that are inaccessible to our analysis as well as to our observation ... We would have to be omniscient in order to be able to determine in every instance the reason why the decision went one way in this case and the other way in that one. (Paul 1886: 170, my translation)

Osthoff relates this unpredictability to free will:

> Indeed, compared to the inescapable force with which the physiological laws of language are implemented, there is some freedom of movement in the associative transformations of speech and language. To the extent that one can talk of free will at all, it is here, in mental actions, that it comes into play. (1879a: 22, my translation)

Later scholars have echoed many of these views. Saussure – in keeping with his atomistic conception of diachrony, according to which synchronic grammatical structure could have no relevance for the direction of change – emphasized the role of 'caprice' (1995 [1916]: 222) in analogical developments. Much more recently, Spina and Dressler come to a conclusion that is at least as pessimistic as those of Delbrück and Paul:

> Predictions of a finite range of outcomes in morphological change and of the probability of which competing variant wins appear possible and testable only in very small, self-contained domains and when domain-external influences can be excluded. In other words, predictions about diachronic change only have a chance of success in exceptional cases. (2011: 535)

7.2 Predictability and directionality

Identifying constraints on analogical change allows us to make certain kinds of predictions. We find two types of constraints in the literature corresponding to two types of predictions: (1) categorical (inviolable) constraints entail absolute predictions; (2) soft constraints entail probabalistic predictions. Absolute predictions about analogical change are always negative in the sense that they say that certain kinds of change will not happen, but never that a particular change will happen.

Scholars who believe that certain kinds of analogical change can be categorically ruled out frequently cite a passage from Kuryłowicz (1966 [1945–9]: 174; Vincent 1974: 437; Lightfoot 1979: 361; Joseph 1998: 366), who argued that we can never predict whether analogical change will happen in a given context; we can only predict what course it will take if it does happen. He famously compares this to the contrast between our inability to predict with certainty when it will rain versus the high degree of predictability of the course that the run-off will follow when it does rain.

This issue does not really arise in the same way with soft constraints and probabalistic predictions. Here, the claims always concern the relative likelihood of different kinds of change. Such predictions can be positive in the sense that they identify certain changes that are very likely to occur, but of course a probabalistic prediction would never say that a particular change is bound to occur.

There are two dimensions of directionality in analogical change. On the interparadigmatic axis, proportional change typically involves the spread of a pattern found in one set of items (e.g. in one inflectional class) to items that previously followed a different pattern. Logically, the change could always go in either direction, and sometimes we do see change in both directions: e.g. earlier *glide–glode* has become *glide–glided* whereas – at least for most Americans – *dive–dived* has become *dive–dove*. One direction usually seems to be much more common than the other, however.

On the intraparadigmatic axis, directionality is a question of which forms within a paradigm serve as the unchanging 'pivots' (Hock 1986: 215) around which other forms are replaced. Changes in the inflectional properties of Modern English verbs almost always affect the past tense and participle, while the present tense remains unchanged. If *sell–sold* were to regularize, both *sell–selled* and *soll–sol(le)d* are, in principle, possible outcomes, but I think most people would agree that the former seems much more likely than the latter.

7.3 Constraints on the interparadigmatic direction of change

7.3.1 Analogical change as 'optimization'

A theoretically diverse set of approaches over the past several decades have regarded analogical change as, in one sense or another, 'optimization' of the morphological system. An optimization approach entails constraints on change in that it rules out or disfavors logically possible changes that would result in a less

7.3.2 Formal simplification/optimization of the grammar

Some generativists have presented the notion of formal simplification or optimization of the grammar as an absolute constraint on analogical change (Kiparsky 1968, 2000, 2012; King 1969). To understand how this constraint would operate, it is helpful to consider a logically possible proportional development that would complicate the grammar. We can, for example, imagine changes that would replace exceptionless generalizations with lists of lexical exceptions. Take word-final devoicing in German. The paradigmatic alternation of voiced obstruents with their voiceless counterparts in word-final position is completely regular and exceptionless (e.g. /taːgə/ 'days' vs. /taːk/ 'day'; /leːbən/ 'to live', inf. vs. /leːp/ imp. sg.). We can easily construct proportional equations based on words with stem-final sonorants that look like good models for leveling of the final-devoicing alternation: e.g.

(28) *fallen* (/falən/) : *fall* (/fal/) = *leben* /leːbən/ : X, X = /leːb/

So we might expect to see analogical leveling of this voicing alternation in some (perhaps low-frequency) words while it is retained in others. But there is an obvious sense in which such a change would result in a more complicated system. If leveling occurred in some items but not others, there would be a need to indicate which words have the alternation and which do not, either by marking items or simply by storing whole wordforms in the mental lexicon.

It is conceivable that a learner confronted with the current pattern might fail to notice the final devoicing alternation altogether and thus innovate by leveling across the board, but if learners notice the alternation at all, they will never encounter any evidence from other speakers to suggest that there are lexical exceptions to it, so why would they ever entertain this more complicated possibility rather than the simpler exceptionless rule that is consistent with all of the evidence they are hearing?

Informally, we can say that learners do not spontaneously posit complexity for no reason. They must encounter evidence of complexity in the forms that they hear from others. The grammars that learners construct may well be more complex than those of the speakers who are providing input to them, but this would always result from factors such as sound changes that render formerly transparent patterns opaque. To the extent that a change is morphologically motivated, it should never result in greater complexity within the morphological system.

Kiparsky recognized that analogical changes sometimes do complicate the grammar but argued that these exceptions 'yield to the interpretation of analogical change as simplification under a more realistic interpretation of change ...' (1978: 92). What he means is that the simplification constraint is categorical in an idealized model where analogical change is driven exclusively by the transmission of grammar to new learners, but in the real world where various extragrammatical factors also play a role, we inevitably find (apparent) exceptions. One is reminded again of some of the quotes in §7.1 above.

7.3.3 Preference theories

The prevailing interparadigmatic directions of analogical change cannot be accounted for entirely by formal simplification of the grammar. Generativists commonly supplement their formal theories with substantive preferences that appeal to notions of inherent 'markedness' or 'naturalness' of certain structures and patterns.

Proponents of Natural Morphology and related approaches strive to account for all directional tendencies in analogical change in terms of semiotically, cognitively, or functionally motivated preferences, making no reference at all to the notion of formal simplicity of the grammar. They generally downplay the role of the learner and may instead invoke ease of processing – for the speaker or the hearer or both – as an important factor driving change.

'Natural(ness)' is merely a convenient term for the inverse of the more familar notion of 'marked(ness)'. This latter term has come to be used in linguistics in a wide variety of different ways that are 'related only by family resemblances' (Haspelmath 2006: 25). For our purposes, the most important sense involves relative cognitive difficulty. Saying that one morphological structure or pattern is less marked/more natural than another essentially amounts to saying that it is, in some (often only vaguely defined) way, easier for the brain to deal with (Mayerthaler 1987: 27). Purported empirical correlates of this notion of markedness/naturalness are discussed in §7.3.8 below.

7.3.4 System-independent constraints

'One-function-one-form'

The purported preference for a one-to-one correspondence between form and meaning/function in grammar, often referred to as 'isomorphism' (Haiman 1985; Croft 2003: 102–10), has both a paradigmatic and a syntagmatic dimension. Proponents of Natural Morphology refer to the paradigmatic aspect of this principle as 'uniform encoding' (Mayerthaler 1981, 1987) or 'biuniqueness' (Dressler 1987), and the syntagmatic aspect is related to the notion of 'morphotactic transparency'. On each of these dimensions the preference can be violated in one of two ways: by one form mapping to multiple functions, or by multiple forms corresponding to a single function. The four dispreferred pattern types are thus: (1) allomorphy/synonymy (paradigmatic, multiple forms with the same function/meaning, e.g. -s and -en mean 'plural' in *bulls* and *oxen*, respectively); (2) syncretism/homonymy/polysemy (paradigmatic, one form with multiple functions/meanings, e.g. -t on German verbs can mean either 'second person pl.' or 'third sg. pres. indic.'; (3) multiple exponence (syntagmatic, more than one formative expressing a single function, e.g. in English *sold*, the meaning 'past tense' is expressed by both the *e–o* vowel alternation and the -*d* ending); (4) cumulative exponence (syntagmatic, one formative expressing multiple functions, e.g. -*ōrum* on Latin nouns means both 'genitive' and 'plural').

In morphology, paradigmatic and syntagmatic violations of one-form-one-function often amount to two sides of the same coin: The umlaut alternation in German *Buch–Bücher* 'book(s)', for example, is both allomorphy (the lexical stem has two forms: *Buch(-)* and *Büch-*) and multiple exponence (the meaning 'plural' is expressed by both umlaut and the *-er* ending).

The prediction for grammatical change is that morphologically motivated developments should tend to eliminate all of these types of violations and restore the preferred one-to-one mapping between form and function. It is not difficult to find examples of changes that do just that: Allomorphy in English plural markers has been nearly eliminated by the extension of the *-s* plural, and this same extension has eliminated homonymy/syncretism in a number of once unmarked plurals such as *word*. Similarly, the examples of paradigm leveling that we have seen typically eliminate both (stem) allomorphy and multiple exponence. The extension of the German *-st* second sg. ending to all tenses and all verb classes eliminated an instance of cumulative exponence, as this ending now means only 'second sg.' and provides no information about tense, mood, and so on. There are also many counterexamples, however, where analogical change results in new violations of one-form-one-function. We saw instances of analogical extension of stem alternations in §3.6.2. Homonymy/syncretism has increased with the spread of unmarked plurals to more animal names in English (e.g. *swine, elk*; *fish*).

Many, though by no means all, anti-isomorphic historical developments can be accounted for in terms of a competing principle of 'economy' (Croft 2003: 105–10), which essentially says that, all else being equal, speakers try to get their messages across as efficiently as possible. Cumulative exponence is highly economical, whereas multiple exponence and synonymy arguably violate both isomorphism and economy. Many have argued that economy tends to trump isomorphism in high-frequency items, whereas isomorphism matters more as token frequency declines (e.g. Wurzel 1990a; Nübling 2000).

The idea that the course of change can be influenced by speakers' avoidance or repair of 'dysfunctional' (near) homonymy is an old one (e.g. Paul 1877: 329–30; Brugmann 1885: 84–5; Samuels 1972: 67–75). Many of the developments discussed in this context are analogical. (Compare Andersen's discussion of 'remedial innovations' (1974: 21, 1980: 10–11). One example involves the spread of the masculine/neuter genitive singular *-(e)s* ending in Old High German and Old English. This ending was originally restricted to *a*-stem nouns. In certain other declensions, normal sound change would have led to genitives that were nondistinct from other singular forms, but the distinctive *-(e)s* ending was extended to many strong masculine and neuter nouns, such as OE *wine* 'friend' (*i*-stem), *fot* 'foot' (consonant stem), *fæder* 'father' (relationship noun in *-r*) (Osthoff 1879a: 33–4; Wright and Wright 1908).

There are also instances where avoidance of homonymy has been invoked to account for the (intraparadigmatic) direction of paradigm leveling (see §7.4 below). In some classes, the vocalic ablaut alternations in the Germanic strong verbs originally included a vowel difference between the preterite indicative singular (excluding the second person in West Gmc.) and the other finite preterite forms. This difference has been leveled in all of the modern standard languages, with the exception of a few relics such as English *was–were*. In both English and German, the modern preterite sometimes preserves the vowel of the indic. sg. (e.g. *ride–rode–ridden*) and sometimes that of the other forms (*bite–bit–bitten*). In German, verbs of strong Class I (the *ride/bite* class) systematically kept the plural/subjunctive vowel, e.g. MHG *rîten–reit–riten–geriten* > *reiten–ritt–ritten–geritten*. This is surprising, since other classes generally keep the indic. sg. vowel. A common explanation is that the regular merger (in Modern Standard German) of the reflexes of MHG *î* and *ei* would have resulted in homophony of present and preterite forms if the indic. sg. vowel had been retained (Osthoff 1879a: 23; Brugmann 1885: 84; Wheeler 1887: 38).

Avoidance of homonymy/syncretism is sometimes also invoked to account for the direction of movement of lexical items from one inflectional class to another. As we will see below, relative class size (in terms of type frequency) is widely recognized as the primary factor responsible for the direction of such movement, but distinctness of category markers is sometimes cited as an additional factor, the claim being that classes that (clearly) mark (important) distinctions tend to attract items from classes where these distinctions are not (so clearly) marked (Paul 1877: 329–30; Osthoff 1879a: 33).

As we move beyond cases involving actual homonymy/syncretism and start talking about differences in how clearly a distinction is marked, we enter the realm of what Hock (1986: 211–12) regards as the spirit of Kuryłowicz's first law of analogy. The letter of that law says that 'bipartite' markers tend to replace simple markers. Kuryłowicz's own example, which seems to be just about the only good example that anyone can come up with, is the extension of umlaut as an additional plural marker to many German nouns which had previously marked the plural only with the ending *-e* (Osthoff 1879a: 34, 41–2; see §3.6.2). This 'law' has been widely criticized because this kind of development is much less common than its opposite: the simplification of a bipartite marker through leveling. Hock (212) acknowledges this, but argues that the spirit of Kuryłowicz's law is simply that 'forms which are more "clearly" or "overtly" marked tend to be preferred in analogical change.' Avoidance/repair of complete homophony could be regarded as a special (limiting) case of this more general principle.

Hock and Joseph (2009: 153) suggest that the contrast between the analogical spread of plural umlaut in German and the tendency to level the alternation in English may show that 'different speakers evidently had different ideas' on the question of 'whether a given alternation is significant or not' and that 'the effects of umlaut were considered significant in German, in contradistinction to English where they were considered insignificant.' The historical detail points to a much more prosaic explanation. Before analogical leveling or extension came into the picture at all, there was already a very large difference between English and German in the extent of phonological umlaut. This was primarily due to a difference in the relative timing of the umlaut sound change and the loss of final unstressed vowels after heavy syllables in a major class of nouns known as *i*-stems. In English, the final *-i* of these nouns was retained in all forms long enough to cause umlaut throughout the paradigm, so no alternation resulted. In German, by contrast, the *-i* was lost in the singular before it had a chance to cause umlaut, but remained long enough in the plural to do so. Thus – where they exist – the English cognates of German umlaut-plural nouns often have a front vowel (or what was a front vowel before the great vowel shift) in both singular and plural, e.g. English *guest* = German *Gast–Gäste*, and similarly *stench, bench, bride, fist, hide*, etc.

Hock and Joseph claim that 'the effects of umlaut have in English largely been eliminated. Only a small set of "irregular" forms preserves them . . .', but English never had umlaut alternations in more than a relatively small set of nouns in the first place. The alternation arose primarily in a couple of minor 'consonant-stem' noun classes. Wright and Wright (1908: 192–9) list about two dozen such nouns that had umlaut alternations in Old English, of which 18 still exist today. The alternation has been eliminated (through regularization) in eleven of these (*book, nut, oak, borough, cow, goat, grout, turf, furrow, friend* and *fiend*), and retained in the other seven (*foot–feet, tooth–teeth, goose–geese, mouse–mice, louse–lice, man–men, woman–women*). An interesting special case is *breeches* 'trousers'. If the Old English singular and plural of this noun had survived, the modern forms would be *brook* and *breech*. As it happens, this noun has only survived in the plural (similar to *pants* and *trousers* for many English speakers), with a form consisting of the regular *-es* ending tacked on to the old umlauted plural.

Lass (1997) emphatically rejects avoidance-of-homonymy arguments. His most general and obvious point is that changes often do lead to homonymy/syncretism, and in countless instances speakers tolerate this 'dysfunctional' aspect of their language for centuries without showing the least inclination to repair it (Osthoff 1879a: 13). English speakers, for example, show no signs of doing anything to resolve the present-past homonymy in some of our most common verbs, e.g. *let, put, cut, set, hit*, and in fact there has even been some partial attraction of formerly regular verbs, such as *fit* and *wet*, into this class (American English: *the suit fit me well*; *the baby wet its diapers*). Furthermore, the same kinds of analogical changes that have the effect of undoing homonymy/syncretism also occur frequently where there is no homonymy to undo. By pure chance, we would expect such changes to result sometimes in disambiguation of homonymous forms, so pointing to instances of such disambiguation does not prove that a distaste for homonymy has anything to do with the motivation for these changes.

Constructional iconicity

Readers familiar with semiotic theory may know the **icon** as one of the three basic types of signs identified by the philosopher Charles Sanders Pierce. Unlike symbols and indices, an iconic signifier bears some kind of crucial resemblance to the meaning associated with it. The type of icon that has been of greatest interest to morphologists is not the **image icon** exemplified by onomatopoeia, but rather the **diagram**, where the signifier and the signified resemble each other only in the relationship among their parts. Grammatical diagrams can be either paradigmatic or syntagmatic or both. Syntactic diagrams are typically syntagmatic, as when linear word order reflects the chronological order of events (*Veni, vidi, vici*). Most morphological diagrams are primarily paradigmatic, although some also have a syntagmatic dimension. The 'one-form-one-function' principle is a very basic kind of morphological diagram: sameness vs. difference of form corresponds diagrammatically to sameness vs. difference of meaning/function.

Another widely recognized kind of morphological diagram is seen in the tendency for the morphosyntactically marked members of grammatical categories to have more phonological substance than the unmarked members, so that, for example, plural forms tend to have an affix that the corresponding singulars lack, rather than vice versa. Mayerthaler (1981, 1987) refers to this tendency as 'constructional iconicity'. This preference is violated to different degrees by structures that are 'minimally iconic' (e.g. marking the plural only by a stem alternation, as in *teeth*), 'non-iconic' (unmarked plurals such as *deer*) and 'counter-iconic' (the plural is shorter than the singular, as in some German dialects where *hun* 'dogs' is the plural of *hund*). The claim is that analogical change will tend to make paradigms more constructionally iconic.

7.3.5 System-dependent constraints

A number of system-dependent factors that play a role in making some analogical changes more likely than others have been well known to linguists since the nineteenth century. Foremost among these is type frequency (e.g. Paul 1877: 329; Osthoff 1879a: 33; Bloomfield 1933: 409).

The most systematic account of system-dependent factors and their role in constraining analogical change is Wurzel's (1984, 1987, 1989; Fertig 2000: 19–22). Wurzel equates naturalness/optimality of an inflectional system with internal consistency, or, to use Paul's expression, 'harmony of the form system' (1886: 92). Historically, a perfectly harmonious system, if such a thing existed, should be perfectly stable, with no possibility for morphologically motivated change. All other systems should show a tendency to eliminate their internal inconsistencies by expanding some patterns at the expense of others.

This prediction raises the question of which patterns will expand and which will be eliminated in evolving toward greater harmony. Wurzel appeals here to the familiar criterion of numerical dominance: What he calls the 'system-defining features' are the pattern types that recur most often and the morphological classes and markers with the highest type frequency (Bybee 1995, 1996; Bybee and Newman 1995). Wurzel extends the use of the terms 'natural' and 'unmarked' to refer to these dominant features of a system.

Wurzel sees the naturalness of internal consistency and of quantitative dominance operating on two levels. He coins the terms *inflectional-class stability* (along with *marker stability*) and *system congruity* to refer to naturalness on the level of (paradigmatic sets of) concrete, specific inflectional markers and on the level of more abstract patterns, respectively.

Inflectional-class stability says that: (1) ideally, inflectional class membership should correlate perfectly with extra-morphological properties, and there should thus be no competition among inflectional classes; and (2) when this ideal is not realized, the largest inflectional class among those competing for the same lexical items will be the dominant one and will thus define the set of forms that counts as 'normal' for words with the extra-morphological features in question.

Parallel to this, the principle of system congruity says that (1) ideally all inflectional classes, subclasses, and certain broader patterns of a given inflectional system or subsystem should exhibit the same structural features on a number of parameters; (2) when this ideal is not realized, the most widespread (within the system or subsystem) of the competing structural features on a given parameter will be the dominant one and thus define the 'system congruous' value of that parameter for the system or subsystem in question. Wurzel coins the term 'system-defining structural properties (SDSPs)' to refer to the whole set of dominant features of a given inflectional system.

The parameters that Wurzel identifies as being relevant to system congruity, with an illustration of each from Modern Standard German verbal inflection, are the following:

1. The grammatical categories and properties that occur for a given word class. Example: The categories of the finite verb in German are: (1) *tense*, with the properties *present* and *preterite*; (2) *mood*, with the properties *indicative*, *subjunctive* and *imperative*; (3) *voice*, with the properties *active* and *passive*; (4) *person*, with the properties *first*, *second* and *third*; and (5) *number*, with the properties *singular* and *plural*.
2. Base-form vs. stem inflection: base-form inflection means that the form that occurs in the maximally unmarked position in the paradigm is used 'as is' as the base for the other forms, whereas stem inflection means that the base form itself includes some kind of inflection that must be removed to arrive at the stem that serves as the base for other forms (Wurzel 1990b). Example: The German verb shows stem inflection (in the present), since – at least according to Wurzel (1984: 54) – the infinitive serves as the base form, and the infinitive itself has an ending which must be dropped before adding the endings for the other forms.
3. Separate vs. combined expression (cumulative exponence) of the various grammatical categories. Example: Person and number always show combined expression in German verbs; one can never identify a part of a verb that just means 'second person' and another part that just means 'singular' for example. The expression of tense, on the other hand, is usually separate from that of person/number, with the dental suffix marking preterite in the weak verbs and stem-vowel alternations marking it in the strong verbs.
4. The number and location of distinctions and identities among the forms of a paradigm. Example: There are four or five distinct forms in the present indicative in Modern Standard German, with the first and third plural always identical to each other, the third singular and the second plural sometimes identical, and all other forms distinct. Wurzel symbolizes such a pattern as follows (for the situation with five distinct forms): $1s \neq 2s \neq 3s \neq 1p = 3p \neq 2p$.
5. The types of formal markers (e.g. suffixes, reduplication, stem alternations) that occur and the categories that each type is associated with. Example: German verbal inflection makes use of suffixes, stem-vowel alternations, compound forms with auxiliaries, one prefix (preterite participle *ge-*) and marginally some stem-final consonant alternations (e.g. *ziehen–zogen*; *schneiden–schnitten*; *sitzen–saßen*) and suppletive alternations. The suffixes are most typically associated with person/number and, in the weak verbs, with tense. A secondary association between a suffix and tense is found in the third singular, where there are distinct person/number endings in the two tenses. Stem-vowel alternations are generally associated with tense in the strong verbs and a small subset of the weak verbs. Some strong

verbs show a secondary association between stem-vowel alternations and person/number in the present (e.g. *gebe, gibst, gibt, geben*).
6. The presence vs. absence of inflectional classes. Example: The German verb does have inflectional classes: weak verbs, the various subclasses of strong verbs, modals, etc.

Change plays a central role in Wurzel's theory. As mentioned above, Wurzel's key historical hypothesis is that morphologically motivated change will always tend to increase the internal consistency (harmony) of the inflectional system by favoring the spread of the most stable inflectional classes and the System Defining Structural Properties at the expense of recessive classes and patterns. Wurzel has little to say about the mechanism responsible for this pattern of development. One can easily imagine how it could be largely due to the transmission of language to new learners, in much the same way as Kiparsky's formal simplification. For the language learner, non-dominant structural features represent local complexities that must be mastered above and beyond the 'overall design' (Andersen 1980: 18) and productive rules of the inflectional system (Wurzel 1984: 87). The learner must presumably either memorize whole forms or acquire an extra mark in the lexicon entry of each item that does not belong to the dominant inflectional class for words of its type (Wurzel 1984: 131–3, 151–2). These non-dominant features will tend to be mastered relatively late in the acquisition process and thus be vulnerable to not being acquired at all. For the adult who has mastered the complete inflectional system with all its quirks and inconsistencies, the system-defining properties and dominant paradigms still have a special status in the grammar (Wurzel 1984: 89). Innovative forms that are in agreement with these dominant features will be more readily accepted and adopted by the adult speaker than forms that are at odds with them (Wurzel 1984: 73, 126; Andersen 1973).

By enumerating specific parameters on which the significant structural features of an inflectional system can be defined, and by suggesting that the 'unmarked' features of a system are simply those that occur most often, Wurzel has given us explicit, testable hypotheses about morphological change.

Wurzel is aware that the correlation between inflectional-class membership and phonological shape is not entirely captured by his strict principle of class stability/motivation. He discusses the phenomenon of words being attracted into an inflectional class by existing members with which they rhyme, and regards this as just one example of 'highly specific phonological properties' serving as the basis for 'very small subclasses' (1989: 132).

As demonstrated convincingly by Bybee and Moder (1983) and Pinker and Prince (1988: 114–23, 1994: 323–4), however, some aspects of the structure of complex systems of small inflectional classes, such as the strong verb systems of German and English, are better captured by a prototype-based approach that looks for 'somewhat disjunctive "family resemblances"' (Pinker and Prince 1988: 116; but see also Yang 2002), rather than by breaking down inflectional classes into discrete subclasses. In their analysis of the English class with [u] as past-tense vowel, for example, Pinker and Prince show that the prototypical shape of the present tense is [CRo] (where R stands for any sonorant). Of the seven members of this class (eight if one counts *withdraw* as distinct from *draw*), three are perfectly prototypical (*blow, grow, throw*). The rest diverge from the prototype in various minimal ways: *know* has only a single initial consonant (in the modern standard), while *draw* (along with *withdraw*), *slay* and *fly* fit the prototype in their onsets but have a different stem vowel. In the participle, the prototypical members again have [o], but this could either be interpreted as meaning that it is prototypical to have [o] in the participle, or that it is prototypical for the participle vowel to be the same as the present vowel. Members with a non-prototypical vowel in the present can have either of these properties, but not both. Thus, *fly* has [o] in the participle, while *draw* and *slay* have the vowel of the present.

With Wurzel's approach, we could do no better than break this class down into discrete subclasses, which would fail to capture the subtle structure revealed by Pinker and Prince's analysis. This kind of analysis also raises questions about Wurzel's position that it is always the base form whose phonological properties are relevant for inflectional-class motivation (see §8.8.1).

7.3.6 Analogical extension of patterns with initially low type frequency

Although almost everyone seems to agree that the patterns with the highest type frequency are generally the ones most likely to be extended analogically, there are a number of cases where a pattern (eventually) spreads significantly in spite of having once been restricted to a very small number of items. Critics of the Neogrammarians regarded such cases as particularly dubious appeals to analogy, but the evidence for many of them is irrefutable (Curtius 1885: 56–8; Brugmann 1877: 50–1, 1878: 82–4). In Modern German, a large number of neuter and several masculine nouns form their plurals with the suffix *-er*, e.g. *Feld* (neut.)– *Felder* 'field(s)'; *Geist* (masc.)–*Geister* 'spirit(s)'. In Old High German, the predecessor of this class was much smaller, and the comparative evidence suggests that in proto-Germanic it contained only a handful of nouns (Krahe/Meid 1969: 43–4). The spread in Czech of the *u*-stem dative singular ending *-ovi* provides another example (Andersen 1980: 29). Old Church Slavonic retained the Indo-European distinction between *o*-stem and *u*-stem noun declensions, but the latter contained only a few masculine nouns. Most theories would predict that this tiny class would be very unlikely to show much productivity. The complete loss of the *u*-stem paradigm in Russian is thus unsurprising. In Modern Czech, however, the *-ovi* ending, originally restricted to *u*-stems, has become associated with animacy and been extended to a large number of nouns.

Especially interesting are cases where a pattern that originally occurred in just a single item comes to be highly productive. A famous example is the suffix *-ess*, as in *actress* and *lioness*. This was originally an ancient Greek suffix that occurred in just a single word: *basílissa* 'queen'. It was eventually used to form a couple of other feminine nouns in Greek and was then borrowed into late Latin where it became somewhat more productive. It really took off in the Romance languages and has also had periods of strong productivity in English, which borrowed it from French. For some further examples, see Brugmann (1885: 95–7).

7.3.7 System-dependent naturalness vs. formal simplicity/optimality

Whereas the system-independent parameters of constructional iconicity and the various aspects of the one-form-one-function principle do not correlate in any obvious way with formal simplicity of the grammar, the same is less true of inflectional-class stability and system-congruity. A key prediction of both formal-simplification and system-dependent-naturalness approaches is that analogical change will tend to elminate exceptional forms and other deviations from dominant patterns. Arguably, Wurzel's theory of 'system-dependent naturalness' is not really a naturalness theory at all, but rather a translation of the notion of grammatical simplicity into the terms of a more surface-oriented model of morphology.

7.3.8 Universal preferences and 'evolutionary' grammatical theory

In §5.1, I raised the question: If there is no system-independent preference for uniform paradigms (paradigms with no stem alternations), how do we account for the prevalence of non-alternating patterns and the relative rarity of stem alternations across the languages of the world? We can generalize this question to apply to any alleged universal preference in morphological patterning.

One answer to this kind of question that has been gaining momentum in recent years is that many universal generalizations that hold true across most or all languages may have more to do with the way languages develop historically than with any universal grammatical, cognitive, or functional constraint or preference. In her work on phonological patterns, Juliette Blevins (2004) labels this kind of approach 'evolutionary', and Bybee et al. 1994, which looks at morphology in a similar spirit, is titled *The Evolution of Grammar*. This is the sense of 'evolutionary' intended here. Any connection with biological evolution is purely metaphorical, although as works such as Carstairs-McCarthy 2010 make clear, investigations into the biological evolution of morphology may have a lot to contribute to our understanding of the issues raised here.

It is not hard to imagine an evolutionary explanation for the cross-linguistic prevalence of non-alternating paradigms. Almost all stem alternations arise from conditioned sound change. Since a sound change only affects certain segments, an alternation will almost always be limited to a subset of the items in a lexical class. The umlaut alternation is limited to words that originally had back vowels; German final devoicing only creates alternations in words ending in voiced obstruents; the Germanic Verner's Law alternation discussed in §5.1 only affected strong verbs with stem-final voiceless fricatives; Latin rhotacism only gave rise to alternations in stems ending in *s*. This means that, for reasons that have nothing to do with any cognitive preference, a given alternation will typically occur in only a relatively small portion of the items of a lexical class. The tendency of analogical change, both proportional and non-proportional, to eliminate stem alternations (Mańczak 1958) would thus follow from its tendency to reinforce dominant patterns at the expense of minor patterns (Wurzel 1984: 169–72). If we could find a language where stem alternation has somehow become the norm rather than the exception, would we still see a tendency toward paradigm leveling? Albright (2005: 39–41) claims that Korean is such a language, and that the tendency there is toward extension of alternations.

Some might object that learners must surely have a bias toward non-alternation simply because an alternation amounts to a rule or pattern that must be learned, whereas non-alternation is the absence of a rule, and would thus presumably be what a learner would assume from the outset (Hale and Reiss 2008: 241). This reasoning would apply equally, however, to all morphology and morphophonology, and does not explain why affixal marking of paradigmatic distinctions would be favored over stem alternations. There may well be a universal constraint against morpho(phono)logy of all types, or as Aronoff puts it, morphology may well be an 'inherently unnatural . . . disease, a pathology of language' (1998: 413).

Affixal inflection contrasts sharply with stem alternations in terms of its typical historical origins, however. Affixes typically develop out of separate words. In §2.5, we saw the example of the Romance future-tense forms that arose from an infinitive followed by an auxiliary. This kind of structure can, and frequently does, develop in exactly the same way for every single item in a lexical category.

Natural Morphologists present several empirical correlates of the claim that affixal inflection is more natural, in some universal sense, than stem alternations. According to Dressler et al. (1987: 13–14), more natural structures: (1) are processed more easily in perception; (2) give rise to fewer speech errors; (3) are less likely to be affected by aphasia; (4) are acquired earlier; (5) occur more in child-directed speech; (6) are cross-linguistically more prevalent; (7) tend to be the dominant structures within individual languages; (8) are more likely to be reinforced and less likely to be eliminated in language change. Inherent ease of cognitive processing is sometimes hypothesized to be at the root of all of these correlates of naturalness. But if we can account in purely evolutionary terms for the fact that certain types of structures and patterns (e.g. affixal inflection) occur with greater frequency than others (e.g. stem alternations) – without invoking anything like inherent ease of processing – then all of the other characteristics mentioned above could simply be consequences of this greater frequency (Bybee and Newman 1995; Haspelmath 2006).

An evolutionary approach that emphasizes the role of frequency may be a better fit for morphology than for any other branch of linguistics. In phonology, the above-listed correlates of naturalness surely have something to do with the physiology of articulation, which has no direct counterpart in morphology. There are arguably no inherent qualities of morphological patterns that play any role in determining speakers' preferences. Speakers simply prefer what they are most familiar with. We might say that morphology is the reality TV of language. It is the domain of dominant patterns that have nothing to recommend them other than their dominance, just as reality shows are the domain of celebrities who are famous for being famous. The only principle governing morphological change would then be the one that Merton (1968; Rigney 2010) dubbed 'the Matthew effect', an allusion to Matthew 13:12: 'For whosoever hath, to him shall be given, and he shall have more abundance: but whosoever hath not, from him shall be taken away even that he hath.'

Recent experimental studies do suggest that some conceivable types of morphological patterns are inherently unlearnable (Gerken 2006; Gerken et al. 2009), and it may well be that among learnable patterns, some would be inherently harder to acquire or to process even if we artificially created a situation where they occurred very frequently in the input to hearers/learners. In historical linguistics, this could be highly relevant to certain types of reanalysis, such as morphologization (§2.5) and exaptation (§2.5.6), where learners are faced with the task of acquiring patterns that have lost their original motivation, and especially to the levelings of stem alternations and losses of other formal distinctions that occur in situations where such a reanalysis could conceivably take place but does not (Dresher 2000). For most analogical change, however, the Matthew effect seems to matter much more than anything else.

7.4 Constraints on the intraparadigmatic direction of change

As we turn our attention to the other dimension of directionality in analogical change, an initial observation is that a single proportional development can never affect every form in a paradigm. At least one form must remain unchanged, serving as the pivot around which other forms are replaced. Can we predict which forms will (tend to) serve as pivots and which will change? This is often posed as a question specifically about the direction of paradigm leveling, but in principle, it is relevant to any kind of proportional change. This is clear from some of the examples of backformation in §3.6.3. Most instances of extension of umlaut alternations in German nouns (§3.6.2), for example, involve existing singulars with back vowels serving as pivots for the creation of innovative plurals with front vowels (*Faden–Faden > Faden–Fäden*), but we also encountered occasional backformations where existing plurals with front vowels serve as pivots for the creation of singulars with back vowels (*Fisch–Fisch > Fusch–Fisch*). The question of intraparadigmatic directionality comes up most often in connection with leveling simply because leveling is always a logical possibility in both directions, since the identity function imposes no constraints on its input: *knife–knives* could be leveled either to *knife–knifes* or (as we saw in §3.6.3 with the real example of *glove*) to *knive–knives*, and these two directional possibilities exist, in principle, for every single case of leveling, although sometimes only one direction is phonologically possible.

The very fact that we characterize some proportional changes as 'backformations' shows that we have strong intuitions about the 'normal' intraparadigmatic direction of analogical change. Backformations are precisely those that go against the expected directionality. But what is the basis for these expectations? Can we formulate an explicit, testable hypothesis that captures our intuitions about the normal direction of change on the intraparadigmatic axis? Many start with the claim that analogical innovations follow a basic → derived direction (Kuryłowicz 1966 [1945–9], 1964, 1977; Andersen 1980), i.e. basic forms function as the unchanging pivots around which derived forms are replaced. This assertion is only meaningful if we can define basicness. In prototypical derivational morphology, the basic form is presumably the shorter one, to which one or more affixes are added to yield the derived form. Even here, there are many cases where things are not so clear-cut: What about conversion, for example?

Debates over the definition of basicness have focused largely on inflectional morphology. There is often no form in an inflectional paradigm that has fewer affixes than any other, so this criterion is usually of no help in identifying the basic form, and even where there is a form that corresponds to the bare lexical stem, this is by no means always the one that most linguists would consider basic (e.g. the imperative singular in German verbal inflection).

Many equate inflectional basicness with morphosyntactic unmarkedness. Of course this is, again, only helpful to the extent that we know what the latter term means. The direction of leveling is sometimes cited as evidence for markedness relations, but the arguments here quickly become circular if we are trying to explain the direction of leveling. There may be widespread agreement that, in general, singular is the basic number, present the basic tense, indicative the basic mood, active the basic voice, etc. For some categories, the consensus is less clear. Many consider third person to be basic, but others argue for first. Nominative is often regarded as the basic case, but some historical developments point to the accusative. What about perfective vs. imperfective aspect? Can such questions sometimes have different answers for different languages? Objective criteria for identifying basic or unmarked categories remain a major desideratum.

Other linguists define basicness in purely formal terms. Some have argued, for example, that the basic form is the one from which the shapes of others in the paradigm are predictable (Vennemann 1972a, 1972b; Albright 2005, 2008; but see also Becker 1990: 52–5). Any account of intraparadigmatic directionality must deal with both the strong tendencies and the undeniable exceptions, the more or less scattered cases like *Fusch–Fisch, glove, lend, sigh*, etc. Such exceptions are often attributed to 'local markedness' or 'markedness reversal' (Mayerthaler 1981; Tiersma 1982; Bybee 1985, 1988).

Many have argued that so-called paradigmatic 'basicness' is simply a matter of token frequency. Wheeler (1887: 21) already stated this position clearly: 'The form most frequently recurring in use, as having the strongest hold upon the memory, is most liable to be the favored form in the process of levelling.' The number of forms in the paradigm that each stem alternant occurs in is also sometimes regarded as relevant. The mechanics of directionality are most straightforward in frequency-based accounts: Learners are most likely to acquire the highest-frequency forms first and best, and guess at others on that basis. Token frequency usually correlates strongly with morphosyntactic basicness, and frequency-based accounts have the advantage of providing a non-ad-hoc explanation for the directional exceptions attributed to local markedness (Bybee 2001: 114–15). But many reject the idea that high token frequency is the reason why a particular form serves as pivot, insisting instead that it is the form's basicness that explains both its high frequency of use and its role in analogical change (e.g. Kuryłowicz 1977: 20–1). Some have presented evidence that learners do not just base their paradigms on whichever forms they happen to learn first or whichever have the greatest 'lexical strength'. Universal principles and/or what learners have already figured out about their inflectional system guide them to base their guesses only on certain forms: those that are morphosyntactically unmarked (Lahiri 2000; Andersen 1980, 2001a) and/or those that they have discovered to be generally most reliable for predicting the rest of the paradigm (Albright 2005, 2008, 2009; James Blevins 2004; Wurzel 1984).

The function of an alternation may also be relevant to the direction of leveling. Alternations that are important markers of grammatical distinctions seem to show much more consistent directional tendencies based on morphosyntactic markedness than do alternations that are largely or entirely phonologically conditioned (Andersen 1980; Fertig 2000). It also seems likely that the leveling of some alternations occurs essentially simultaneously with the demise of their phonological motivation: Learners are unable to make any sense of the alternations and simply interpret them as noise, choosing one alternant or the other, perhaps more or less at random, to use throughout the paradigm (Dresher 2000).

7.5 Token frequency

Token frequency has been claimed to affect the likelihood of analogical changes in a number of different ways (Phillips 2006). Most widely accepted and repeated is the claim that high-frequency forms are relatively resistant to analogical influences. In exemplar-based and dual-mechanism approaches (§8.5; §8.6.1), this resistance is attributed to the 'lexical strength' (Bybee 1988: 131–4, 1991: 76–8) of the mental representation of the form, i.e. to the fact that high-frequency forms are 'strongly impressed upon the memory by constant use' (Wheeler 1887: 39; Paul 1886: 170, 188). In a strictly rule-based approach, where there are no mental representations of inflected wordforms, high-frequency forms would be less vulnerable to imperfect learning since learners would be likely to hear them often enough to assign them to the correct class (Yang 2002). In §8.6.1, I address the question of whether high-frequency forms are truly resistant to all kinds of analogical change or only to regularization.

It is much less clear how token frequency correlates with the likelihood that an item will serve as an analogical model. Many scholars have argued or tacitly assumed that high token frequency would make an item more likely to have an influence on other items, but Bybee and Moder (1983) argue just the opposite, that high-frequency items tend to be 'autonomous', i.e. both resistant to the influence of other items and unlikely to exert an analogical influence themselves. The analogical force of a pattern is thus based primarily on type frequency (the number of items that follow that pattern) rather than token frequency.

7.6 Teleology

Many historical linguists see language change in teleological terms, specifically in terms of a 'teleology of purpose' (Andersen 1973: 789–90; Anttila 1989: 403–4) or of 'final causes'. Such teleological accounts can yield predictions about directional tendencies in analogical change (Vennemann 1993). Advocates of some of the approaches discussed above, such as Natural Morphology, tend to see change in teleological terms, although these approaches may also be amenable to non-teleological interpretations.

Scholars sometimes claim – or at least seem to be claiming – that it is somehow the language – or the 'system' – itself that is striving to reach a goal (e.g. Brugmann 1885: 82; Paul 1886: 188; Shapiro 1991), a position that has been widely and justly criticized (e.g. Lass 1997). Others clearly understand that if language change is in any sense goal-directed, it can only be language users who have a goal or purpose in mind. The idea that language change is fundamentally goal-directed is sometimes held up as a principle of 'humanistic' and speaker-centered approaches to language change.

Anttila (1989: 88) defines analogy as 'a mental striving for simplicity or uniformity' and sums up his views with the slogan: 'the mind shuns purposeless variety' (181; but see also Lass 1997: 340–52). As Anttila notes, this echoes the views expressed more than a century earlier by Wheeler:

> The phenomena of analogy are in the last analysis referable to the unconscious effort of the mind, in its quest for unity, to reduce the apparently incongruous elements of speech to systems and groups; that is, to put simplicity in the place of complexity. The laws of sound tend generally to ... introduce a diversity out of which the mind seeks again to restore simplicity ... (1887: 5)

> The operation of analogy in language is in every case ultimately conditioned and determined by the natural quest of the mind for unity to replace multiplicity, system to replace anomalous diversity, and groups to replace monads ... It aims to eliminate purposeless variety. (1887: 35–6)

Do we need to assume that speakers are striving to tidy up the morphological system in order to account for the fact that analogical change has this effect? The answer is clearly no. Computational models show that the general trend that we see in analogical change toward the elimination of arbitrary complexity and increased system congruity do not even depend on an agent capable of intentional activity (Hare and Elman 1995; Albright and Hayes 2002; Wedel 2009), and Lass (1997) points out that more or less elaborate patterns and orderly structure are characteristic of many self-organizing systems (crystals, molecules, weather systems, solar systems) and that the ways in which dynamic physical systems change over time bears some resemblance to analogical change in language.

There is of course no question that language acquisition and communication involve goal-directed human activities, but the relationship between individual goal-directed activity and the cumulative effects of that activity is often very indirect and surprising. Keller (1994, 2005) argues that historical linguists should think of this relationship in terms of Adam Smith's notion of the 'invisible hand.' A classic example of the invisible hand effect is the footpath that gradually forms when people or animals repeatedly cross a grassy or wooded area. The goal of each individual is simply to get to the other side. The emergence of the path is independent of any intentions (Deutscher 2005: 61).

So rather than being a direct result of purposeful human activity, language change would be an indirect by-product of such activity. Human beings do not intend to change language in the ways that it changes, but language change is a consequence of things that speakers do intentionally.

Note that the emergence of the footpath, while unintended, is a felicitous outcome. It makes it easier for the individuals to achieve their goal. This is often regarded as a defining characteristic of the invisible hand. For historical linguistics, this would mean that in spite of being unintended, language change is functional. Through change, languages become better suited for the things that speakers want to do with them, including learning them and effectively communicating with them.

As a general claim about the relationship between goal-driven individual activity and the cumulative effects of that activity, this notion of felicitous outcomes is patently absurd. As Deutscher points out, it is easy to think of numerous counterexamples for every example like the footpath. Millions of people drive their cars with the goal of getting to work, which results in traffic jams that keep them from reaching their destinations; thousands of people drive their SUVs deep into the woods with the goal of enjoying unspoiled wilderness.

In historical linguistics, there are also obvious examples where speakers' goal-directed communicative activity results in changes that undermine what they are trying to do, rather than facilitating it. In the discussion of intentional overt innovations in Chapter 2, I pointed out that speakers sometimes knowingly produce forms that deviate from current norms of usage for communicative or social purposes (such as calling attention to themselves or trying to be funny), and that this kind of activity can lead to grammatical change when people gradually stop regarding the new forms as deviations and/or new learners fail to recognize them as such, and they become the new normal. Here, grammatical change is constantly undermining what speakers are trying to do with their overt innovations. Speakers deviate from prevailing norms because innovations inherently have a special communicative force, but the most effective innovations inevitably become victims of their own success and lose the force that led speakers to start using them in the first place (driving them to keep coming up with new innovations).

As we have seen, morphologically motivated change generally increases the 'simplicity', 'system-congruity' and 'harmony' of the morphological system. Is this a desirable outcome? Is it, as Vennemann (1993: 330) argues, the most obvious example of his general principle that 'language change is language improvement' (322)? It presumably makes the morphology easier to learn and perhaps makes wordforms easier to process. Are these unambiguously 'good' things? Many linguists argue that they are, but these arguments have never made any more sense to me than the opposite view of the pre-Neogrammarians who associated 'false analogy' with the deterioration of a complex, pristine system. Languages with easy-to-learn morphological systems serve certain societal functions well, and a language that is in widespread use as a lingua franca, for example, will tend to evolve in this direction (if it is not already there). But a language with an enormously complex system, full of arbitrary exceptions, can be well suited for other functions, such as clearly marking ethnic boundaries, and it may even have cognitive benefits for its speakers.

7.7 Chapter summary

The question of how analogical change is constrained has been a major preoccupation of historical linguists since at least Neogrammarian times. Linguists have proposed absolute and probabalistic constraints, formal and substantive constraints, system-independent and system-dependent constraints. Token frequency has long been recognized as an important factor, but its status and theoretical interest is highly dependent on one's model of the mental grammar.

I argue that there is little evidence that system-independent preferences, such as the one-form-one-function principle, play any significant role in determining the likelihood of different analogical developments. The main principle that really seems to matter is that analogical change favors whatever patterns and pattern types happen to be most common in a language, in terms of type frequency. Morphological 'universals' and strong cross-linguistic tendencies can be explained in 'evolutionary' terms by considering how morphological systems develop and what kinds of systems are most likely to result from natural language change, without positing any inherent differences in the desirability of various structures and patterns.

8

Morphological Change and Morphological Theory

8.1 Introduction

Grammatical theory and historical linguistics have always informed each other. Language change is one kind of evidence for what is going on inside speakers' heads, and can thus help us refine our theories and influence our choices among competing theories. Conversely, how we think about language change is highly dependent on our theory of grammar.

It has often been pointed out that the term 'grammar' itself is used ambiguously by modern linguists. It refers to (among other things): (1) the mental system of categories and relations in speakers' heads that allows them to use their language productively; (2) the model of that system that a linguist comes up with. A 'grammar' in the latter sense is a kind of theory. When linguists talk about the 'theory of grammar' or 'grammatical theory', they usually mean something more general: a universal framework of principles that is supposed to hold for the grammars (in both senses) of all human languages.

A general theoretical framework is useful, first of all, simply for the notational conventions it provides for characterizing grammatical categories and relations. The more standardized and familiar these conventions are, the easier it is for linguists to communicate with each other. Accounts formulated in different frameworks sometimes amount to notational variants of each other: the same analysis is simply expressed in different terms. There may also be important conceptual differences between different theories: To the extent that a theory of grammar is understood to model what is 'really going on' inside speakers' heads, different theories might give very different pictures of that psychological reality, even where they make exactly the same predictions about observable phenomena. Of greatest interest are empirical differences among theories. Almost all theoretical linguists strive for theories that embody substantive hypotheses about grammars. The theory itself is supposed to constrain possible grammars. By ruling out certain kinds of grammars, a theory makes predictions about what observable phenomena, including what kinds of innovations and changes, should and should not occur.

Analogical innovations are an important kind of empirical evidence that should allow us to test the predictions that follow from different theories of morphology. In principle, we should be able to examine evidence from historical changes and individual innovations, and as soon as we find an example that is at odds with the predictions of a given theory, we could consider that theory disproven. In practice, it does not work that way, for a number of reasons. First of all, observed phenomena are often open to a variety of interpretations. Secondly, not all of the innovations that speakers come up with can be attributed to their productive grammars. Some are simply slips of the tongue, or reflect deliberate flouting of grammatical rules. In the end, a linguist's choice of one theory over another often has more to do with aesthetic preferences and personal relationships than with empirical evidence. Sometimes, however, a great accumulation of evidence pointing in one direction can sway at least a few opinions.

8.2 Grammatical theory and acquisition

At the heart of a theory of morphology is a model of the mental system that allows speakers to produce and comprehend wordforms that they have never before encountered. This mental system cannot just be a long list of memorized wordforms, or – to use a spreadsheet metaphor – a big table with the value of every cell filled in. If our mental morphological system is indeed like a spreadsheet, it must include something like formulas that allow us to calculate values for some cells based on values in other cells.

In addition to offering a model of the productive mental system, many theories also address the question of how speakers/learners could acquire/construct such a system given the input that they receive from other speakers. Structuralist/descriptivist theories tend to pay little attention to the acquisition issue, but it was as central to Neogrammarian theoretical work as it has been in a wide variety of frameworks in recent decades. Paul's (1886) account of analogy begins with a discussion of how learners construct their mental networks. Chomsky equates 'the problem of constructing a theory of language acquisition' with the 'explanatory adequacy' of a theory of grammar (1965: 27). Today, linguists of many different theoretical persuasions would concur with this assessment of the importance of acquisition for grammatical theory.

Our understanding of acquisition and its relation to productive language use is closely tied to the questions about the synchrony–diachrony dichotomy raised in Chapter 2. Janda and Joseph point out that 'children's acquisition of language is usually treated as a clearly synchronic phenomenon' (2003: 122), which seems paradoxical at first since acquisition is clearly a process that unfolds over time. If Joseph and Janda (1988: 194) are right that all change involves 'cross-generational and cross-lectal transmission', then it does not matter that acquisition takes time. If, on the other hand, the linguists are right who argue that 'asocial individual' forces such as repetition have a significant gradual impact on individuals' mental grammars and thereby play an important role in language change, then the clean split between acquisition and language use breaks down and the synchrony–diachrony dichotomy with it. A growing number of linguists are once again thinking about grammar, acquisition and language history in ways that are incompatible with a synchrony–diachrony model, 'maybe without even being aware of it' (Paul 1886: 20, Peter Auer's translation).

One way to characterize the differences among grammatical theories is in terms of how they see the relationship and the division of labor between acquisition and language use (Booij 2010: 93). If we look at the whole course of an analogical formation, we can describe it in theory-neutral terms as a process that takes an unstructured set of wordforms as input (the forms that a learner hears in utterances from other speakers) and ultimately produces a form as output that was not among the input forms. (Compare the theory-neutral interpretation of proportional equations described in §1.7.) Theories differ in their answers to two questions: (1) Can we draw a clear line between the parts of this process that belong to acquisition and those that belong to productive language use? (2) To the extent that we can draw such a line, which parts of the process belong to which? As we will see in more detail below, **static** conceptions of the grammar draw a clear line, while **dynamic** conceptions do not. The second question allows us to distinguish between **rule-based** and **analogy/exemplar-based** models (§8.5; §8.6) as well as between **syntagmatic/compositional** and **paradigmatic/configurational** theories (§8.8). In any rule-based model, the centerpiece of acquisition is learners' abstraction of rules and the explicit conditions on their application from the patterns they discern across perceived forms (see e.g. Albright and Hayes 2002). In an analogy/exemplar-based model, the learner's primary task – at least as far as morphology is concerned – is one of organization rather than abstraction; it is a matter of organizing whole wordforms into some sort of multi-dimensional mental structure. As Goldsmith (2006) points out, this kind of organization is in fact an obvious prerequisite to any abstraction of explicit rules, and thus a necessary first step in any comprehensive model of acquisition. Most existing models of morphological learning – generative, connectionist, or otherwise – have ignored this crucial first step and 'assumed that some "oracle" – some outside source of information – provides the ... learner with the information that two words are morphologically related' (Goldsmith 2006).

Syntagmatic/compositional theories have learners breaking forms down into the smallest possible components and language users putting them back together again. In a paradigmatic/configurational theory, by contrast, speakers know how to get from one wordform to another, rather than how to construct a wordform out of smaller pieces, and to the extent that analyzing words into component parts is a necessary step in the computation that produces analogical formations as output, this step belongs to productive language use rather than to acquisition (again, assuming a static conception of grammar that draws a clear line between acquisition and use).

8.3 The nature and significance of linguistic universals

As mentioned above (§8.1), most linguists understand grammatical theory to be about properties that all mental grammars of all languages (must) have in common. There are many different views, however, about the general nature and the specific substance of these properties. One important split is between those, including Chomsky and his followers, who believe that many of these universal properties are specific to language (features of an innate human 'language faculty') and others who argue that most or all of them are attributable to a combination of general properties of human cognition, the way language is used, and the way it naturally develops.

An even older divide concerns the extent to which universals should be the focus of linguists' attention. Obviously, human languages are all the same in some ways and different in others. Especially in the first half of the twentieth century, the primary focus was on exploring and characterizing linguistic diversity. The Chomskyan paradigm brought a dramatic shift, treating differences among languages as largely superficial and regarding the invariant core of grammar as the main object of serious theoretical interest.

Of course, the historical linguist cannot focus exclusively on universals, since they are invariant across time as well as across languages. The appropriateness of thinking primarily in universal terms is also more questionable in morphology than in any other area of grammar. Many regard morphology as the language-specific branch of grammar that deals with the overt expression ('spell-out') of grammatical relations. Saussure (1995 [1916]: 228–30) suggested that even the basic question of whether morphology is about words and paradigms or about concatenation of morphemes (see §8.8) might not have a universal answer. Early generative work of the 1950s and 1960s theorized morphology out of existence, dividing its terrain between syntax (the morpheme structure of words) and phonology (allomorphy/morphophonemics). Since the resurrection of morphology in the 1970s, prominent generativists (e.g. Chomsky 1995: 3) have endorsed Jespersen's (1924: 52) assertion that '[n]o one ever dreamed of a universal morphology.' This is also consistent with Aronoff's view that morphologists should 'try to understand each system on its own terms' (1994: 166).

8.4 Static vs. dynamic conceptions of grammar

For our understanding of the nature of analogy$_2$ and morphological change, there may be no more important distinction than the one between static and dynamic (or 'fluid') conceptions of grammar. Under a 'static' view, using one's adult grammar to comprehend and produce utterances does not affect or alter the mental grammar in any (interesting) way. Saussure articulates an essentially static view of 'synchronic' grammar, and since the mid-twentieth century, generativists and many others have largely taken this view for granted.

This contrasts sharply with the conception of mental grammar that Paul presents in the *Prinzipien*, where the system is in constant flux, with each form and utterance that an individual produces, analyzes, or merely thinks about leaving its mark. Through the twentieth century, the dynamic view was represented by the work of scholars such as Jespersen, Householder and Bybee. Bolinger (1968: 88) sums it up especially well: 'Never a word spoken but language becomes a bit different from what it was, however microscopically. What we say displaces what we might have said and strengthens those words at the expense of others.'

Explicit arguments against a dynamic conception of grammar are relatively rare. Many linguists clearly regard the correctness of the static view as an issue that was settled long ago and are either unaware of current advocacy for a dynamic view, or consider it unworthy of comment. An exception is Joseph and Janda (1988: 194; quoted in Janda and Joseph 2003: 121; see also Janda 2001):

> In denying ... [the sharp distinction between] synchrony and diachrony, the view that there is only a panchronic or achronic dynamism in language suggests that there exist grammatical principles or mechanisms which direct speakers to change their languages in certain ways other than through cross-generational and cross-lectal transmission. To the best of our knowledge, however, there is absolutely no evidence suggesting that this kind of asocial individual causation of linguistic change really exists.

There is certainly no shortage of purported 'evidence ... of asocial individual causation of linguistic change' in the recent literature, so what Joseph and Janda presumably mean is that they do not find this evidence convincing. Bybee, for example, provides an overview of work which in her opinion shows that 'certain facets of linguistic experience, such as the frequency of use of particular instances of constructions, have an impact on representations that we can see evidenced ... in the nature of language change' (2006: 711). There are many cases, for example, where a word or construction takes on a new meaning based on a context in which it happens to be used with great frequency. Temporal conjunctions and prepositions such as *since* often take on causal meanings because they are often used pragmatically to invite a causal inference, as shown in (29).

(29a) *Since he started working on that project, he hasn't gotten much sleep.* (original meaning with temporal semantics and causal implicature)
(29b) *Since the project has to be finished by next week, he won't be getting much sleep.* (new meaning with causal semantics)

Bybee and many others would argue that such shifts occur within the mental grammars of individuals due to frequent repetition. At age 20, my mental representation of *since* might show only temporal semantics, but if over the next twenty years I hear it, utter it and/or think it very often in connection with a causal implicature, my semantic representation might shift by age 40, and this shift in my semantic representation would go hand in hand with me using the word in ways that I would not have earlier. Crucially, this kind of change could truly involve 'asocial individual causation', since my own uses of the word – even in talking to myself or my cat, or in writing private notes or diary entries – count as repetitions for me just as much as do uses that I hear from others.

As we saw in Chapter 2, few linguists dispute that some aspects of change are attributable to the transmission of language to new learners – but in a dynamic, usage-based model where the mental grammar 'is strongly tied to the experience that a speaker has had with language' (Bybee 2006: 711), or in Paul's words is 'a product of everything that has ever entered consciousness through listening to others, through one's own speech and through thinking in linguistic forms' (Paul 1886: 23, Peter Auer's translation), transmission to new learners is at best irrelevant to some aspects of change.

To the extent that psychological effects such as 'habituation' (Haspelmath

1998: 319) play an important role in shaping an individual's mental grammar, one might even wonder whether transmission to new learners could sometimes act as a brake on change. In general, however, the utterances produced by the members of a speech community at a given point in time should reflect the states of their mental grammars at that moment, including any shifts in representations attributable to the effects of repetition. Grammars constructed by learners on the basis of those utterances should thus also roughly reflect these shifts. The shifts in mental representations are attributable to *individuals'* cumulative experience over the course of their lives. They can be transmitted to new learners because language evolution is Lamarckian rather than Darwinian (Janda and Joseph 2003: 65), but the role of transmission is entirely passive here. New learners to whom the shifted representations are transmitted would presumably pick up where their predecessors left off, and to the extent that repetition continues to have the same kinds of effects on their mental representations as it had on those of speakers before them, we could see a historical process of change in a particular direction spanning multiple generations.

One possible response to such arguments from those who advocate attributing all significant grammatical change to 'cross-generational and cross-lectal transmission' would be that individuals generally do not unlearn things that they have already learned. They can keep piling new knowledge on top of old knowledge, but the old knowledge does not go away. Apparent 'unlearning' plays a crucial role in most grammatical change, and this only makes sense if we realize that it is not really a matter of individuals unlearning what they once knew, but rather of new learners failing to acquire this knowledge in the first place – presumably in many cases because previous speakers who had the knowledge failed to provide evidence in their output that would allow new learners to acquire it. In the case of *since*, for example, one could argue that the semantic representation always remains more or less stable for a given individual. There may be shifts in speakers' usage; they may gradually come to use *since* more often to invite a causal inference than they did earlier in their lives, but whatever form the knowledge associated with such shifts in usage might take, it does not replace what these speakers initially learned about the purely temporal semantics of *since*. Only new learners – in their ignorance, so to speak – would be capable of creating a new representation for *since* by reanalyzing the causal implicature as being inherent in the word's semantics. Scholars on both sides of this debate tend to have their minds made up, but the dynamic, usage-based view seems to be gaining some ground (Blevins and Blevins 2009: 5).

In §2.4, we saw some indication of how consequential this static-vs.-dynamic distinction is for our understanding of the nature of analogical innovations and the associated changes in mental grammar. In a static model, (most) analogical innovations are attributed to imperfect learning. Learners produce innovations where, for example, they have not (yet) acquired the corresponding tradtional forms or some of the conditions on the application of a rule. The relevant changes in the mental grammar are entirely attributed to transmission to new learners, and the analogical innovations are simply the overt manifestations of these mental-grammar changes. At least in the case of inflectional regularization, the innovative forms do not even have mental representations in the grammar. Since they are generated by default rules whenever necessary, there is no need for a stored representation.

In a dynamic model, by contrast, every wordform that an individual has ever encountered, regular or irregular, has a representation in the mental grammar, and one's own production plays just as great a role as the input one receives from other speakers in shaping and reinforcing one's representations of forms and patterns. There are no true default rules. The form produced by a speaker on a given occasion is determined by the relative strength at the moment of speaking of the mental representations of the candidate forms and patterns. Rather than being a mere manifestation of an underlying change in the mental grammar, overt analogical innovations play a key role in giving rise to grammatical changes by first creating and then reinforcing the mental representations of new forms and patterns.

In his 'generalized and reinterpreted version of the traditional concept of analogy' (1968: 176) as grammar 'simplification' or 'optim(al)ization' (1978: 83), Kiparsky explicitly rejects the dynamic, usage-based conception of the mental grammar and the associated view of the relationship between overt analogical innovations and grammatical change described above – a view which he associates with 'a theory of language acquisition based on substitution-in-frames techniques and equivalent "taxonomic" devices' (1978: 78). Since wordforms that can be generated by rules do not have mental representations, the correspondence between an underlying grammatical change and its overt consequences is generally much less direct in Kiparsky's theory than in Paul's. The underlying change in the mental grammar might, for example, consist of a simplification in the lexicon (e.g. eliminating an indication that an item is an exception to a rule) or a simplification of a rule's 'structural analysis' (the elimination of some of the conditions on the rule's application). The observable consequences of such a change would be the production of forms that had not been produced before, but these new forms would not be represented as such anywhere in the mental grammar (Anderson 1992: 368).

The notion of analogical change as formal simplification/optimization of the grammar is sometimes presented as an alternative to Paul's proportional model. This is valid in one respect, but there is quite a bit of confusion over which aspect of Paul's theory is relevant here. 'Simplification vs. proportions' (Kiparsky 1978: 77; Hock 1986: 238–79; Lahiri 2000: 10) is a potentially misleading way to characterize the contrast because, once again, proportional equations per se are not the issue. The kind of word-and-paradigm theory of morphology embodied in Paul's proportional model is, in principle, entirely compatible with the essence of Kiparsky's conception of analogical change as grammar simplification: Learners could construct proportional equations – or, more abstractly, 'schematic paradigms' (James Blevins 2004: 20) – which they would then apply when needed in order to generate unlisted wordforms (Anderson 1992: 369). Forms generated in this way would not be added to the mental grammar, and would have no effect on it. The next time the same form was needed, it would necessarily be generated again via proportional equation in exactly the same way, because the only forms represented in the mental grammar would be the ones that were involved in the initial construction of the proportional equations during acquisition. (Abstract schematic paradigms would make represention of regularly inflected forms entirely unnecessary.) Analogical innovations would be attributable to simplifications such as the loss of a stored irregular form or of an entire proportional equation, which would in turn be attributable to 'imperfect learning', just as in Kiparsky's theory.

This is of course radically different from Paul's conception of grammar, but the point is that the difference is not inextricably linked to proportions. Kiparsky's theory differs from Paul's in two essential ways: (1) Kiparsky's conception of grammar is static while Paul's is dynamic (usage-based); (2) Kiparsky's model of morphology is based on abstract rules that operate on abstract underlying lexical stems, while Paul's 'proportional' word-and-paradigm model is based on relationships among inflected wordforms. We should not lose sight of the fact that these two differences are, in principle, independent of each other. The following sections examine several closely related issues.

8.5 Exemplar-based vs. rule-based models

The dominant approaches to linguistic theory for most of the last century have characterized speakers' grammatical knowledge in terms of explicit, abstract rules. These rules take many different forms, but in morphology they typically can be paraphrased as statements like: 'The regular past tense in English is formed by adding the suffix <-ed> to the verbal base.' Acquisition is seen as a matter of figuring out these rules based on the forms the learner is exposed to. In many theories, the learner is guided in this process by innate knowledge of universal properties of grammar.

An alternative 'exemplar-based' approach holds that learners store representations of the forms they hear in some kind of associative network. This network allows them to discern patterns across the forms, to generalize, and ultimately to produce forms that they have never heard without (necessarily) ever abstracting out any explicit representations of rules and, most crucially, without discarding any of the information contained in the representations of the concrete forms.

Exemplar-based models tend to be associated with dynamic conceptions of grammar and rule-based models with static conceptions, but in principle these are indepedent distinctions. Many connectionist implementations, for example, amount to exemplar-based, static models because they strictly separate the 'learning phase' from the 'testing phase' or 'production phase', with no further learning occurring during the latter (e.g. Hare and Elman 1995).

Since the influential sketch of an exemplar-based model laid out by Paul in the *Prinzipien* (see §8.8.2 below), many linguists have closely associated such models with the notion of analogy$_2$ itself. In the first half of the twentieth century, more abstract, rule-based (and static) approaches to grammar became increasingly popular. This kind of approach dates back to the work of the great grammarians of Ancient India, such as Pāṇini (probably sixth c. BCE). It became familiar to Europeans with the growing knowledge of Sanskrit starting in the late eighteenth century, and has long been popular among linguists more concerned with the conciseness and elegance of the grammars they write than with realistic models of the representations and processes inside speakers' heads.

The Chomskyan generative paradigm that became dominant in the second half of the twentieth century proposed that maximally concise, redundancy-free, abstract grammars are not just masterpieces of scholarly ingenuity, but are in fact good models of speakers' unconscious grammatical knowledge. Although this view is still widely held today, exemplar-based models have been steadily gaining ground over the past few decades (Blevins and Blevins 2009). This development has been greatly enhanced by computational implementations that address the objections of many generativists and others to the lack of explicitness in this approach.

At least for our purposes, the most important empirical differences between exemplar-based and rule-based theories involve wordform token frequency and gradient similarity. Token frequency (§7.5) is not represented at all in models based on abstract rules, and it can thus have no effect on the operation of the productive grammar. An abstract rule does not know or care how often it has been applied; it functions exactly the same way the first time and the millionth time. This is analogous to a conventional computer program, which is not affected in any way by being run again and again. In a usage-based model, by contrast, the mental representation of a form is reinforced by each occurrence. The more often an individual encounters or uses a form, the stronger its representation becomes.

In a rule-based model, similarity of forms is only relevant to the extent that it involves the necessary and sufficient condtions for membership in a category, such as the domain of a rule. If it satisfies the criteria, the rule applies; otherwise it does not apply; end of story. There are no degrees of membership, and properties of forms other than those referred to by the necessary and sufficient condtions are completely irrelevant. In an exemplar-based model, by contrast, every aspect of similarity among forms is potentially relevant to the likelihood that they will display similar morphological behavior. Falling within the domain of a rule is not just a question of 'in' or 'out', but rather a matter of degree. Wordform frequency and gradient similarity have figured especially prominently in the dual-mechanism debate (§8.6.1).

Of course, rule-based models can always account for observed token-frequency and gradient-similarity effects as something extra-grammatical, as a matter of 'performance' rather than 'competence'.

8.6 Analogy vs. rules

As explained in Chapter 1, historical linguists of all theoretical persuasions use the terms 'analogy' and 'analogical', and for this reason I have tried to keep my definitions of analogy$_2$ and analogical innovation/change as theory-neutral as possible. In the Neogrammarian tradition, 'rule' is often used in a non-technical sense to refer to any regularity or valid generalization, and informally 'analogy' and 'rule' are sometimes used more or less interchangeably (MacWhinney 1975: 66). Where the two are contrasted, rules are usually understood to be explicit and abstract, in the sense of being dissociated from any words that instantiate them, whereas analogy is based on relations among mental representations of words in something like an associative network (Anshen and Aronoff 1988; Skousen 1989, 1992, 2009; Becker 1990; Moder 1992; Booij 2010: 88–93). This is very closely related to the rule-based vs. exemplar-based distinction discussed in the previous section. In heavily rule-based models of grammar, it is common to allow analogy, in the present sense, to play a marginal role as a 'supplementary mechanism' (Kiparsky 1992: 56; Blevins and Blevins 2009: 9).

There is increasingly widespread acceptance among linguists that some kind of associative network plays an important role in morpho(phono)logy, perhaps alongside abstract rules. A number of scholars go much further in this direction and maintain that all morphology – and perhaps syntax as well – is based entirely on an associative network (e.g. Householder 1971; Rumelhart and McClelland 1986, 1987; Skousen 1989, 2009; Becker 1990; Burzio 2005; Bybee 2006). For some applications of recent developments in this area to the modeling of grammatical change, see Hare and Elman 1995; Wanner 2006; Fischer 2007.

8.6.1 Dual-mechanism models

One does not necessarily have to take sides in an all-or-nothing way on the rule-based vs. exemplar/analogy-based question. Several types of hybrid models have been proposed that see a role for both abstract rules and concrete exemplars in grammatical representation and processing. The best known of these is probably the dual-mechanism model of morphological processing developed by Pinker and many collaborators (Pinker and Prince 1988; Pinker 1999; Marcus et al. 1995; Clahsen 1999), which posits a fundamental distinction between irregular inflection, which involves wordforms stored in some kind of associative/analogical network, and regular (default) inflection, which is based on abstract, concatenative rules. Crucially, most regularly inflected forms are not stored in memory. Speakers produce them anew by rule whenever they are needed, whereas much of what was said above about exemplars, analogy and usage-based models of grammar would apply to irregular morphology under this approach.

The potential relevance of the dual-mechanism hypothesis for our understanding of analogical change, and conversely, the relevance of historical evidence to the dual-mechanism debate, is often mentioned in the literature (e.g. Pinker 1999) but rarely explored in any depth. Arguably, we should expect a fundamental distinction between regularizing and non-regularizing analogical change as a historical counterpart to the dual-mechanism distinction between regular and irregular morphology (Fertig 1999b). Regularization would work essentially as it does in Kiparsky's theory. It would amount to falling back on a default rule whenever an irregular form has not (yet) been transmitted successfully to new learners. The resulting regularized form would not be stored in memory. By contrast, non-regularizing analogical changes, whether they be irregularizations of previously regular forms (e.g. *dived > dove*; *weared > wore*) or shifts from one irregular pattern to another (e.g. *spake > spoke*; participial *hid > hidden*), would work essentially as they do in Paul's theory. They would involve the attractive force of a form or cluster of forms that compete with the traditional form, and – most crucially – would result in the creation of an innovative form with its own representation in the mental grammar. The memory traces of innovative forms could thus play a role in non-regularizing analogical change that would have no parallel in regularization. Specifically, repetition of an innovative irregular form would have a positive feedback ('snowball') effect. The more often this form is repeated, the stronger its representation becomes, increasing the likelihood that it will eventually triumph completely over the traditional form.

What predictions does this theory make about the relationship between analogical change and token frequency? In the case of regularization, the prediction is the familiar one: The lowest-frequency irregular items will have the weakest memory traces and will thus be most likely to be lost completely, allowing the product of the default rule to surface in their place. For non-regularizing analogical change, the situation is less straightforward. Imagine that the attractive force of a pattern is strong enough that it results in occasional analogical innovations for all items that fall under its sway (based on phonetic and perhaps semantic similarity), regardless of their token frequency. For low-frequency items, the memory traces of these occasional innovative forms might fade before they ever occur again, whereas the innovative forms of the highest-frequency items might occur often enough to gain a permanent foothold, such that the representation of the new form could then gradually strengthen with each subsequent occurrence. Variation between the old and new forms might continue for an indefinite period, but it is also possible that the innovative form would eventually replace the older form completely. It does indeed appear to be the case that the correlation between high token frequency and resistance to analogical change only holds for regularization, whereas non-regularizing analogical change frequently affects very high-frequency items, including grammatical function words such as pronouns and auxiliary verbs (Fertig 1998a). By emphasizing the differences between regular and irregular morphology, the dual-mechanism model points us toward a possible explanation for this difference between regularizing and non-regularizing historical developments, although a similar explanation could also be available within a usage-based framework which – while rejecting the 'rule/list fallacy' (Langacker 1987) – allows for associative generalizations that approach the behavior of abstract rules.

Nübling (2000) proposes a very different kind of explanation for the correlation of low token frequency with regularization and high token frequency with non-regularizing change. She emphasizes the communicative advantages of formal shortness and paradigmatic differentiation for the most commonly used lexical items. English *be*, the most irregular of all English verbs, illustrates both of these points. All forms of this word other than *being* are monosyllables made up of just two or three segments, and this is the only English verb that has a distinct form for the infinitive (*be*) and for the first person singular (*am*), as well as two different forms in the past tense (*was*, *were*). Such functional accounts can be regarded either as alternatives or as complements to a strictly non-teleological positive feedback account like that sketched out above (see also Croft 2003: 110–17).

8.7 Rules vs. constraints

When linguists distinguish between rules and constraints, they mean something different by 'rule' than when they distinguish between rules and exemplar-based analogy. Here, 'rule' refers to a procedural statement that tells you what changes you have to make to turn a representation of one type into a representation of another. A constraint, by contrast, is a declarative statement that tells you what properties a representation of a particular type should or should not have. In the case of German final devoicing, for example, a rule would say something like 'make all syllable-final obstruents voiceless', whereas a constraint would say 'syllables ending in voiced obstruents are not permitted'. Constraints are most often applied to surface representations of wordforms and longer strings, but in principle they can apply to any level of representation posited in a theory of grammar (Kiparsky 2000).

Optimality theory (see §5.1) is by far the best known constraint-based approach to grammar today, but it is by no means the only one. Many linguists have proposed that output constraints play an important role in morphology and morphophonology. Whereas the constraints of orthodox optimality theory are all universal, morphological output constraints often seem to be language-specific or even construction-specific.

Paul's solvable proportional equations amount to rules, in the current sense, rather than output constraints. They imply: (1) a formula that tells you how to transform the form on the top of a proportion into the corresponding form on the bottom; and (2) conditions on the input to this formula (the form on top). Bybee and Moder (1983: 263) argue that such proportional equations cannot account for certain attested analogical changes and that we therefore need to recognize a kind of morphological output constraint that they call a 'product-oriented schema' (see also Bybee and Slobin 1982a). Their examples include the class of irregular English verbs that is characterized by having the vowel /ʌ/ in the past tense and participle. They point out that the original members of this class all had the vowel /ɪ/ in the present tense (*sling, spin, cling*, etc.). Strictly proportional extension of this pattern would thus only have licensed application to other verbs with /ɪ/, but in fact, verbs with other vowels have also been attracted into this class historically: e.g. *strike, sneak, drag* (in my dialect). This suggests that the class is defined not by a procedural rule that says 'change /ɪ/ to /ʌ/' but rather by a declarative constraint that says 'the vowel of the past tense/participle is /ʌ/'. Bybee and Slobin further argue that even the regular English past tense is better characterized by a constraint that says essentially: 'the past tense and participle end in -*t* or -*d*' rather than by a rule that says: 'add -*ed*'. This would account for the stability of the relatively large class of verbs that already end in -*t* or -*d* in the present tense and do not add any past suffix: *hit, cut, hide, bleed, send* and so on.

The kind of analogical change that Bybee and her collaborators are talking about can arguably be accounted for in proportional terms if we relax Paul's very strict interpretation of the input conditions implied in a proportional equation. Paul believed that the part of a wordform that changes from the top to the bottom of a proportion has to match exactly across all the items in a solvable equation. So, for example, the Latin pattern in *amīcus* (nom. sg.) : *amīcī* (gen. sg.) can only be extended to other nouns that end in -*us* in the nom. sg. Similarly, the *sling* : *slung* pattern could, in Paul's view, only be extended to other verbs with the vowel /ɪ/ in the present. We could relax this requirement so that a wider range of inputs count as matches. The proportion *sling* : *slung* could still be interpreted as essentially a procedural rule, but the rule would say: 'Change the vowel of the present (whatever it might be) to /ʌ/.' Such rules become indistiguishable, however, from combinations of output constraints and 'correspondence' constraints that require the past-tense form to be as similar as possible to the present-tense form provided that it satisfies the output constraints (Kenstowicz 1996; Benua 1997; McCarthy 2005).

In any case, output constraints clearly do play an important non-proportional role in analogical change, in much the same way that general phonotactic and prosodic generalizations do (§6.5). We see these effects, for example, with morphological output constraints of a prosodic nature, which have been identified in many languages (e.g. Wiese 1996; Booij 1998).

8.8 Syntagmatic/compositional vs. paradigmatic/configurational approaches to morphology

The terms syntagmatic/compositional and paradigmatic/configurational have been suggested by Ackerman and Malouf (2009) to capture what they and many others regard as a very fundamental distinction among theories of morphology. Saussure is widely credited for laying out the syntagmatic–paradigmatic distinction, although he used the term 'associative' (1995 [1916]: 173) rather than paradigmatic. A syntagmatic relation holds between forms that occur together within an utterance, such as the subject and verb of a simple sentence like *Debbie sang*. A paradigmatic relation holds between forms that could be substituted for each other in a particular position (perhaps requiring other concomitant changes in other positions). Since any other name could be substituted for *Debbie* in the sentence above, we can say that all personal names stand in a paradigmatic relationship to each other. Similarly, *sings, sang, danced, dances* and so on all stand in a paradigmatic relationship to each other. In syntax, paradigmatic relationships define classes of words, many of which are large and open, in the sense that new items can be freely added to the class: nouns, verbs, adjectives, as well as subclasses of these such as abstract nouns and transitive verbs. Other classes of words can be much smaller and (relatively) closed (prepositions, conjunctions), and some are extremely small and entirely closed (articles, demonstratives).

It is fairly uncontroversial that the basic productive rules of syntax are largely syntagmatic, in that they specify legal sequences of words and larger constituents. Through much of the twentieth century, most mainstream theories posited mainly syntagmatic rules for morphology as well. Words can be divided into **morphs** or **morphemes** in much the same way that a sentence can be divided into words: *untied* can be broken down into *un + tie + (e)d*, with each part making a pretty straightforward contribution to the meaning of the whole word. Productive syntagmatic rules tell speakers how they can combine meaningful elements to produce more complex meaningful forms. Productive paradigmatic rules tell speakers how they can transform one meaningful form to produce a different meaningful form, whereby the input and the output may have the same degree of grammatical complexity. Syntactic transformations, such as that which defines the relationship between an active and the corresponding passive sentence (*Peter ate the apples* :: *The apples were eaten (by Peter)*), are paradigmatic rules, but it would become quite unwieldy to try to do syntax entirely with paradigmatic rules. In morphology, however, models based exclusively on paradigmatic rules are a viable and venerable alternative. The appeal of such models is perhaps not so obvious in a language with as little inflectional morphology as English, but starts to become more apparent even in a language with a slightly more complex system, such as German. Consider the paradigm of the indicative forms of the modern German verb *lachen* 'laugh' in (30).

(30) pres. sg   pl
      1st   *lache*   *lachen*
      2nd   *lachst*   *lacht*
      3rd   *lacht*   *lachen*
      past sg   pl
      1st   *lachte*   *lachten*
      2nd   *lachtest* *lachtet*
      3rd   *lachte*   *lachten*

A syntagmatic/compositional approach would identify a lexical stem *lach-* and a number of inflectional affixes, *-t(-)*, *-e*, *-st*, *-en* and so on, and then formulate rules for combining these elements to produce the various forms. The rule for the second sg. pret., for example, would say that it is made up of the lexical verb stem *lach-* + the preterite morpheme *-t-* + the second sg. morpheme *-(e)st*. Since this is a productive rule, speakers can apply it to arrive at the second sg. pret. forms of other verbs of which they know the stems. The grammar would make no reference to relationships between this inflected wordform and any another.

One type of paradigmatic approach would instead state rules that allow one to derive the shape of any of these wordforms from that of any other. One such rule might say, for example, 'to go from the third sg. to the first pl., remove the final *-t* and replace it with *-en*'. One argument in favor of paradigmatic rules is that they provide a natural way of capturing systematic identity relations within paradigms. We see in (30) that the first pl. and third pl. are the same. This identity turns out to hold without exception in German. In a syntagmatic approach, it would be treated as essentially a coincidence. A paradigmatic rule, however, can capture it directly by saying something like 'to go from the first pl. to the third pl. (or vice versa) do not make any formal changes at all' (Zwicky 1985).

Exemplar/analogy-based models are always paradigmatic/configurational; rule-based models can be either paradigmatic or syntagmatic. A current rule-based framework that is especially clear about its syntagmatic/compositional orientation is Distributed Morphology (Halle and Marantz 1993), and Andersen (1980) approaches morphological change from an emphatically syntagmatic/compositional perspective. Albright (2005, etc.), by contrast, provides a good example of a paradigmatic, rule-based model. Much recent work in optimality theory posits important roles for both syntagmatic and paradigmatic relationships in morphology (see §5.1).

Some scholars are apparently unaware (or unconvinced) that it is possible to formulate abstract paradigmatic rules that map whole wordforms onto other whole wordforms. (See the related discussion of 'simplification vs. proportions' in §8.4 above.) Generativists and others who argue that explicit rules are superior to Paul's proportions (as a theory of morphology as well as in accounting for analogical change) generally assume that adequate explicitness requires abstract underlying stems (King 1969; Kiparsky 1992; Anderson 1992; Lahiri 2000: 6). Similarly, proponents of dual-mechanism models of morphological processing generally portray 'concatenative' rules as the only alternative to associative analogical networks (§8.6.1; Pinker and Prince 1988; Pinker 1999; Clahsen 1999). In fact, however, some current approaches to inflectional morphology posit explicit, abstract rules that map fully inflected forms onto other fully inflected forms (James Blevins 2004; Albright 2005). Abstract derivational rules of 'cross-formation' (e.g. Becker 1994; Haspelmath and Sims 2010: 49–51), also known as 'paradigmatic word formation' (Booij 2002: 6–9, 2007: 13) have long been invoked to account for cases like English *profusion-profusive*, where there is no verb *profuse (or *profude) in English from which these words could be deirved, as *possession* and *possessive* are derived from *possess*. Some theories posit that speakers' grammars do contain unrealized base forms like *profuse* for purposes of derivation, but many prefer to posit a rule that directly relates *profusion* and *profusive*. The formal portion of such a rule could be as simple as 'replace word-final *-ion* with *-ive*'. (A phonologically adequate formulation would of course be slightly more complex.)

Paradigmatic rules that differ from analogy only in that they have become completely dissociated from the words that instantiate them raise the possibility of abstractness being a matter of degree. As the mental representation of a morphological pattern grows stronger, its links to particular lexical items could become weaker, and in the limiting case these links could (virtually) disappear, leaving a completely abstract pattern that can be applied productively to any item that fits it. Most linguists who believe that morphological relations map surface forms onto other surface forms see things in these gradient terms (e.g. Bybee 1995, 2007; James Blevins 2006; Booij 2010), but the important point is that evidence and arguments that seem to support a rule-based as opposed to exemplar/analogy-based model of morphology do not necessarily bear one way or the other on the question of whether the rules should directly capture: (1) paradigmatic relationships among wordforms; (2) syntagmatic relationships among morphemes; or (3) relationships between complex forms and abstract underlying stems (Hockett 1954).

At least in Germanic languages, paradigmatic word formation plays an especially important role in compounding. For example, parallel compounds ending in *-man/-woman/-person* or *-boy/-girl* are often clearly not independent of each other. The creation of the words *chairwoman* (1699) and *chairperson* (1971) was not simply a straightforward matter of combining the elements *chair* and *woman/person*. The analogy of the established word *chairman* (1654) was clearly crucial. Booij (2007: 13) offers a similar example from Dutch: *boeman* 'ogre'–*boevrouw* 'ogre woman'. This phenomenon is analogical in the sense that the meaning of the newer compounds depends on that of particular existing compounds (Anderson 1992: 297–9).

As with so many other theoretical distinctions, there is a great conceptual difference between syntagmatic/compositional and paradigmatic/configurational approaches to morphology, but the empirical differences tend to be quite subtle. Some linguists argue that even the conceptual differences between the two approaches are more apparent than real. If we take an inflected surface form as the input to a morphological rule that yields another inflected form as output, the first thing the rule typically has to do is lop a chunk off one end of the input form, yielding what amounts to a stem as an intermediate step in the derivation. Why not just start with the stem in the first place? James Blevins (2004) offers a good synchronic reason why not: The part that you lop off of the input form is often precisely what identifies the item as belonging to a particular inflectional class. If you populate your mental lexicon with abstract stems that have already had those identifying parts lopped off, then your lexical entries need to include abstract class features that tell you how to inflect items. Why not just represent the fully inflected form directly in the lexical entry so that its inflectional properties can be determined by matching it with a paradigm, eliminating the need for any abstract class features? More generally, Blevins' model has the following characteristics, the first of which sets it apart from certain other 'word-and-paradigm' approaches but aligns it very closely with Paul's proportional theory: (1) The phonological and morphological information in lexical entries consists exclusively of representations of full wordforms. This means that there are neither abstract underlying representations of stems nor diacritic class features in the lexicon; (2) Inflectional affixes have no independent representation; they only exist as parts of larger sturctures – on the syntagmatic axis as parts of words, and on the paradigmatic axis as parts of paradigms.

Certain analogical changes may also provide empirical support for a paradigmatic/configurational model (Haspelmath and Sims 2010: 174–6). As mentioned above, paradigms often include one or more identical forms, and these identity relationships can be encoded directly in paradigmatic rules (Zwicky 1985; Stump 1993). As we have seen, quite a few analogical changes are most naturally characterized as extensions of identity relations. The historical spread of identity between the English past tense and past participle is an obvious example. Non-standard varieties have pushed this development even further than in the standard language, with past-tense forms such as *seen* and *done* (*he done it*) and, conversely, participial use of *took*, *drove*, *went* and so on (*I should've went with you*). This development does not involve the extension of any particular inflectional marker, but rather of the paradigmatic identity relationship: past tense = past participle (Whitney 1867: 85).

It is sometimes claimed that a paradigmatic approach offers a more natural way of accounting for analogical innovation and change in general (Haspelmath and Sims 2010: 166–7), but as explained above in §8.2, syntagmatic models of morphology merely shift the paradigmatic work onto the shoulders of the language learner, making morphology more like syntax.

8.8.1 Asymmetric vs. symmetric paradigmatic models

Ackermann and Malouf also call attention to an important distinction among paradigmatic/configurational theories of morphology. Such theories can be either asymmetric, in the sense that some forms are identified as basic and others are derived from them by directional rules, or they can be symmetric, with the relationships among forms having no inherent directionality. In principle, one could then use any (set of) known form(s) as a basis for predicting the shape of any unknown forms. Ackermann and Malouf advocate a symmetric theory. Proponents of asymmetric models include Wurzel (1984, 1989), James Blevins (2004) and Albright (2005, 2008, 2009). This distinction is especially relevant to backformation (§3.6.3) and the intraparadigmatic directionality of analogical change (§7.4).

8.8.2 Paul's proportional model

The widespread use of proportional equations (only) to portray analogical innovations/changes has resulted in a great deal of misunderstanding concerning their theoretical status. I will try to clear some of that up here.

For Paul, proportional equations are not only, or even primarily, a device for visualizing analogical formations. In other words, proportional equations are not just there to be solved. The basic function of a (morphological) proportional equation is to represent the systematic intersecting structure of the grammatical and lexical categories of a speaker's mental system. A complete proportional equation is typically a vast multi-dimensional array of forms. In a language like English, with a very simple inflectional system, we can largely make do with a two-dimensional table. Imagine a very wide spreadsheet with a column for each of the thousands of verbs in English and five rows: (1) base form (*walk*); (2) third sg. pres. indic. (*walks*); (3) *-ing* form (*walking*); (4) past tense (*walked*); (5) past participle (*walked*). This spreadsheet would be the complete proportional equation for English verbs. Descriptive and pedagogical grammars of inflecting languages almost always present morphological paradigms in just such arrays, although they usually only use a single lexical item to exemplify each inflectional pattern. What Paul is claiming with his notion of proportional groups/equations is that this kind of representation is not just a convenient invention of linguists and grammarians. It is a good model of the way morphological knowledge is organized in speakers' mental grammars.

Paul points out that these vast tables typically contain gaps – cells that are not filled in with memorized wordforms because an individual has never heard that form, or has not heard it often enough to memorize it, or did not recognize it for what it was, or has forgotten it. An 'X' in a proportional equation represents such a gap. When we look at the other forms in the table, it is often obvious what form belongs in an empty cell. With English verbs, for example, gaps in the *-ing* row can be filled in with essentially 100 per cent confidence if the base form is known. The past tense and participle are a little iffier, but suffixing *-(e)d* to the base is a good guess in most cases. In some cases we might decide there are several plausible candidates to fill a gap. A complete proportional equation is thus Paul's model of a morphological (sub)system, and solving such an equation is his model of how such a system operates productively to generate forms.

The familiar four-part equations like those in (4) in Chapter 1 are, in most cases, simply convenient abbreviations. As Paul points out, three known terms is the minimum required for a solvable equation. There are analogical innovations that appear to be based on just three known forms (§7.3.6), but this is certainly the exception rather than the rule.

Proportional equations are most often used in historical work as a post hoc way of showing or suggesting an analogical model for an attested innovation. The four-part abbreviation is usually adequate for this purpose, and many linguists are undoubtedly unaware that there might be more to proportional equations than this, but Paul regarded the solving of proportional equations as a good model of analogical innovation only because he regarded proportional equations as a good model of mental grammar.

One important point specific to Paul's morphological equations bears repeating here (see §3.4): As a staunch believer in word-and-paradigm morphology, Paul emphatically rejected the possibility that a term in a proportion could be anything smaller than a complete wordform. Abstract roots, stems and affixes have no separate representation in Paul's model of the mental grammar, and thus cannot be terms of proportions.

In the decades of the twentieth century when almost all linguists assumed that our mental grammars must contain explicit morphological and syntactic rules, proportional equations were widely regarded as deficient because they do not explicitly state the rules that relate the forms on the top to those on the bottom. A related, legitimate criticism is that Paul's theory does not provide any explicit model of the computation in speakers' heads that takes a proportional group as input and yields candidate forms to fill gaps as output. The idea that speakers' mental grammars include explicit, abstract rules is a hypothesis about one aspect of this computation, but this in itself is hardly an advance over Paul, since until recently (Albright and Hayes 2002) no one had developed any testable model of how learners might arrive at the explicit rules. Connectionist networks (Rumelhart and McClelland 1986, 1987) and Analogical Modeling (Skousen 1989, 1992, 2009) offer alternative models of the computation that do not rely on explicit rules.

Another widespread criticism is that the proportional model is 'unconstrained' or 'too strong', in the sense that equations for improbable or even preposterous innovations can be formulated just as easily as those for the most likely developments. A closely related point is that the model does not account for any correlation between the likelihood of an analogical innovation and the degree of phonological similarity between the model and the target (Hermann 1931; Albright 2009). We must keep in mind, however, that the proportional model is just one small part of Paul's account of analogical change (see Chapter 7).

8.9 Chapter summary

Our theoretical assumptions have a profound effect on how we think about analogical innovation and change. Most significantly, if we adopt a static, rule-based model of the mental grammar, then essentially all grammatical change is attributed to the transmission of language to new learners, who reanalyze some of the forms and patterns they encounter and simply fail to acquire others ('imperfect learning'). Overt analogical innovations reveal the default forms that surface when traditional, irregular forms or non-default rules are no longer there to block them, but these overt innovations themselves do not really play any role in change. They merely provide convenient evidence of the grammatical changes that have occurred.

In a dynamic, exemplar/analogy-based model, imperfect learning is just one of many factors that can contribute to the emergence of overt analogical innovations, which are not merely symptoms of underlying changes in the mental grammar but rather play a vital role in grammatical change by creating mental representations of forms that previously had none and reinforcing those representations through repetition. This is the essence of analogical change in a dynamic model. Dual-mechanism models raise the possibility that both sides could be right in this debate: static models for regularization; dynamic models for non-regularizing analogical change.

Other theoretical choices further shape our understanding of the nature of mophologically-motivated change in a variety of less fundamental ways.

References

Ackerman, F. and R. Malouf (2009), 'Parts and wholes: Patterns of relatedness in complex morphological systems and why they matter', in James P. Blevins and Juliette Blevins (eds), *Analogy in Grammar: Form and Acquisition*, Oxford: Oxford University Press, pp. 54–82.

Aitchison, Jean (2001), *Language Change Progress or Decay?*, 3rd edn, New York: Cambridge University Press.

Albright, Adam (2005), 'The Morphological Basis of Paradigm Leveling', in Laura J. Downing, T. A. Hall and Renate Raffelsiefen (eds), *Paradigms in Phonological Theory*, Oxford: Oxford University Press, pp. 17–43.

Albright, Adam (2008), 'Explaining Universal Tendencies and Language Particulars in Analogical Change', in Jeff. Good (ed.), *Language Universals and Language Change*, New York: Oxford University Press, pp. 144–81.

Albright, Adam (2009), 'Modeling analogy as probabilistic grammar', in James P. Blevins and Juliette Blevins (eds), *Analogy in Grammar: Form and Acquisition*, Oxford: Oxford University Press, pp. 185–204.

Albright, Adam and Bruce Hayes (2002), 'Modeling English Past Tense Intuitions with Minimal Generalization', in *Morphological and Phonological Learning: Proceedings of the 6th Workshop of the ACL Special Interest Group in Computational Phonology (SIGPHON)*, Philadelphia: Association for Computational Linguistics, pp. 58–69.

Algeo, John and Thomas Pyles (2004), *The Origins and Development of the English Language*, 5th edn, Boston: Thomson Wadsworth.

Andersen, Henning (1973), 'Abductive and Deductive Change', *Language* 49, 765–93.

Andersen, Henning (1974), 'Towards a Typology of Change: Bifurcating Changes and Binary Relations', in J. M. Anderson and C. Jones (eds), *Historical Linguistics II*, New York: American Elsevier, pp. 17–60.

Andersen, Henning (1980), 'Morphological Change: Towards a Typology', in Jacek Fisiak (ed.), *Historical Morphology*, New York: Mouton, pp. 1–50.

Andersen, Henning (2001a), 'Markedness and the Theory of Linguistic Change', in Henning Andersen (ed.), *Actualization Linguistic Change in Progress*, Philadelphia: Benjamins, pp. 21–57.

Andersen, Henning (2001b), 'Actualization and the (Uni)directionality of Change', in Henning Andersen (ed.), *Actualization Linguistic Change in Progress*, Philadelphia: Benjamins, pp. 225–48.

Andersen, Henning (2006), 'Synchrony, diachrony and evolution', in Ole Nedergaard Thomsen (ed.), *Competing Models of Linguistic Change*, Amsterdam: Benjamins, pp. 59–90.

Anderson, Stephen R. (1992), *A-Morphous Morphology*, New York: Cambridge University Press.

Anshen, Frank and Mark Aronoff (1988), 'Producing Morphologically Complex Words', *Linguistics* 26, 641–55.

Anttila, Raimo (1972), *An Introduction to Historical and Comparative Linguistics*, New York: Macmillan.

Anttila, Raimo (1977), *Analogy*, New York: Mouton.

Anttila, Raimo (1989), *Historical and Comparative Linguistics*, 2nd edn, Philadelphia: Benjamins.

Anttila, Raimo (2003), 'Analogy: The Warp and Woof of Cognition', in Brian D. Joseph and Richard D. Janda (eds), *Handbook of Historical Linguistics*, Oxford: Blackwell, pp. 425–40.

Aronoff, Mark (1976), *Word Formation in Generative Grammar*, Cambridge, MA: MIT Press.

Aronoff, Mark (1994), *Morphology by Itself*, Cambridge, MA: MIT Press.

Aronoff, Mark (1998), 'Isomorphism and Monotonicity: Or the Disease Model of Morphology', in Steven G. Lapointe, Diane K. Brentari and Patrick M. Farrell (eds), *Morphology and its Relation to Phonology and Syntax*, Stanford: CSLI Publications, pp. 411–18.

Bauer, Laurie (2001), *Morphological Productivity*, Cambridge: Cambridge University Press.

Bauer, Laurie (2003), *Introducing Linguistic Morphology*, 2nd edn, Washington, DC: Georgetown University Press.

Bauer, Laurie (2004), *A Glossary of Morphology*, Washington, DC: Georgetown University Press.

Becker, Thomas (1990), *Analogie und morphologische Theorie*, Munich: Fink.

Becker, Thomas (1994), 'Back-formation, Cross-formation, and "Bracketing Paradoxes" in Paradigmatic Morphology', in Geert Booij and Jaap van Marle (eds), *Yearbook of Morphology 1993*, Boston: Kluwer, pp. 1–25.

Benua, Laura (1997), *Transderivational Identity: Phonological Relations Between Words*, Doctoral diss., University of Massachusetts, Amherst (Rutgers Optimality Archive ROA-259-0498, <http://roa.rutgers.edu/files/259-0498/roa-259-benua-2.pdf>, last accessed 31 January 2013)

Benware, W. A. (1996), 'Processual Change and Phonetic Analogy: Early New High German <s> <sch>', *American Journal of Germanic Linguistics and Literatures*, 8.265–87.

Besch, Werner (1967), *Sprachlandschaften und Sprachausgleich im 15. Jahrhundert*, München: Francke.

Blevins, James P. (2004), 'Inflection Classes and Economy', in Gereon Müller, Lutz Gunkel and Gisela Zifonun (eds), *Explorations in Nominal Inflection*, New York: de Gruyter, pp. 41–85.

Blevins, James P. (2006), 'Word-based morphology', *Journal of Linguistics* 42, 531–73.
Blevins, James P. and Juliette Blevins (2009), 'Introduction: Analogy in grammar', in James P. Blevins and Juliette Blevins (eds), *Analogy in Grammar: Form and Acquisition*, Oxford: Oxford University Press, pp. 1–12.
Blevins, Juliette (2004), *Evolutionary Phonology*, Cambridge: Cambridge University Press.
Blevins, Juliette (2008), 'Consonant Epenthesis: Natural and Unnatural Histories', in Jeff Good (ed.), *Language Universals and Language Change*, New York: Oxford University Press, pp. 79–107.
Bloomfield, Leonard (1933), *Language*, New York: Holt.
Bod, Rens (2006), 'Exemplar-based syntax: How to get productivity from examples', *Linguistic Review* 23, 291–320.
Bolinger, Dwight (1968), *Aspects of Language*, New York: Harcourt.
Booij, Geert (1998), 'Phonological output constraints in morphology', in Wolfgang Kehrein and Richard Wiese (eds), *Phonology and Morphology of the Germanic Languages*, Tübingen: Niemeyer, pp. 143–63.
Booij, Geert (2002), *The Morphology of Dutch*, New York: Oxford University Press.
Booij, Geert (2007), *The Grammar of Words: An Introduction to Morphology*, 2nd edn, New York: Oxford University Press.
Booij, Geert (2010), *Construction Morphology*, New York: Oxford University Press.
Brugmann, Karl (1876), 'Nasalis Sonans in der indogermanischen Grundsprache', in Georg Curtius and Karl Brugmann (eds), *Studien zur griechischen und lateinischen Grammatik*, vol. 9, Leipzig: Hirzel, pp. 285–338.
Brugmann, Karl (1877), 'Zur Geschichte der Nominalsuffixe *-as-*, *-jas-* und *-vas-*', *Zeitschrift für vergleichende Sprachforschung auf dem Gebiete der Indogermanischen Sprachen* 24 (n.s. 4), 1–99.
Brugmann, Karl (1878), 'Das verbale suffix *â* im indogermanischen, die griechischen passivaoriste und die sogen. aeolische flexion der verba contracta', in Hermann Osthoff and Karl Brugmann, *Morphologische Untersuchungen auf dem Gebiete der Indogermanischen Sprachen*, vol. 1, Leipzig: Hirzel, pp. 1–91.
Brugmann, Karl (1885), *Zum heutigen Stand der Sprachwissenschaft*, Straßburg: Trübner.
Burzio, Luigi (2005), 'Sources of Paradigm Uniformity', in Laura J. Downing, T. A. Hall and Renate Raffelsiefen (eds), *Paradigms in Phonological Theory*, Oxford: Oxford University Press, pp. 65–106.
Bybee, Joan (1980), 'Morphophonemic Change from Inside and Outside the Paradigm', *Lingua* 50, 45–89.
Bybee, Joan (1985), *Morphology. A Study of the Relation between Meaning and Form*, Philadelphia: Benjamins.
Bybee, Joan (1988), 'Morphology as Lexical Organization', in Michael Hammond and Michael Noonan (eds), *Theoretical Morphology*, New York: Academic Press, pp. 119–41.
Bybee, Joan (1991), 'Natural Morphology: the Organization of Paradigms and

Language Acquisition', in Thom Huebner and Charles A. Ferguson (eds), *Crosscurrents in Second Language Acquisition and Linguistic Theories*, Philadelphia: Benjamins, pp. 67–91.

Bybee, Joan (1995), 'Regular Morphology and the Lexicon', *Language and Cognitive Processes* 10, 425–55.

Bybee, Joan (1996), 'Productivity, Regularity and Fusion: How Language Use Affects the Lexicon', in Rajendra Singh (ed.), *Trubetzkoy's Orphan, Proceedings of the Montréal Roundtable "Morphonology: Contemporary Responses"*, Philadelphia: Benjamins, pp. 247–69.

Bybee, Joan (2001), *Phonology and Language Use*, Cambridge: Cambridge University Press.

Bybee, Joan (2006), 'From usage to grammar: the mind's response to repetition', *Language* 82, 711–33.

Bybee, Joan (2007), *Frequency of Use and the Organization of Language*. Oxford: Oxford University Press.

Bybee, Joan (2009), 'Grammaticization Implications for a Theory of Language', in Elena Lieven and Jiansheng Guo (eds), *Crosslinguistic Approaches to the Psychology of Language*, New York: Taylor and Francis, pp. 345–55.

Bybee, Joan L. and Carol Lynn Moder (1983), 'Morphological Classes as Natural Categories', *Language* 59, 251–70.

Bybee, Joan L. and Jean E. Newman (1995), 'Are Stem Changes as Natural as Affixes?', *Linguistics* 33, 633–54.

Bybee, Joan L. and Dan I. Slobin (1982a), 'Rules and Schemas in the Development and Use of the English Past Tense', *Language* 58, 265–89.

Bybee, Joan L. and Dan I. Slobin (1982b), 'Why Small Children Cannot Change Language on Their Own: Suggestions from the English Past Tense', in Anders Ahlqvist (ed.), *Papers from the 5th International Conference on Historical Linguistics*, Amsterdam: Benjamins, pp. 29–37.

Bybee, Joan, Revere Perkins and William Pagliuca (1994), *The Evolution of Grammar*, Chicago: University of Chicago Press.

Cable, Thomas (2002), *A Companion to Baugh & Cable's History of the English Language*, 3rd edn, Upper Saddle River, NJ: Prentice Hall.

Campbell, Lyle (2004), *Historical Linguistics: An Introduction*, 2nd edn, Cambridge, MA: MIT Press.

Carstairs-McCarthy, Andrew (1992), *Current Morphology*, New York: Routledge.

Carstairs-McCarthy, Andrew (2010), *The Evolution of Morphology*, Oxford: Oxford University Press.

Chapman, Graham, John Cleese, Terry Gilliam, Eric Idle, Terry Jones and Michael Palin (1989), *The Complete Monty Python's Flying Circus: All the Words*, vol. 1, New York: Pantheon.

Chomsky, Noam [1959] (1964), 'Review of *Verbal Behavior* by B.F. Skinner (New York, 1957)', in Jerry A. Fodor and Jerrold J. Katz (eds), *The Structure of Language*, Englewood Cliffs, NJ: Prentice-Hall, pp. 547–78. [Reprinted from *Language* 35, 26–58.]

Chomsky, Noam (1965), *Aspects of the Theory of Syntax*, Cambridge, MA: MIT Press.

Chomsky, Noam (1986), *Knowledge of Language: Its Nature, Origin, and Use*, New York: Greenwood.
Chomsky, Noam (1995), *The Minimalist Program*, Cambridge, MA: MIT Press.
Chomsky, Noam and Morris Halle (1968), *The Sound Pattern of English*, New York: Harper and Row.
Clahsen, Harald (1999), 'Lexical Entries and Rules of Language: A Multidisciplinary Study of German Inflection', *Behavioral and Brain Sciences* 22:6, 991–1060.
Clahsen, Harald and Monika Rothweiler (1993), 'Inflectional Rules in Children's Grammars: Evidence from German Participles', in Geert Booij and Jaap van Marle (eds), *Yearbook of Morphology 1992*, Boston: Kluwer, pp. 1–34.
Clark, Eve V. (1987), 'The Principle of Contrast: A Constraint on Language Acquisition', in Brian MacWhinney (ed.), *Mechanisms of Language Acquisition*, Hillsdale, NJ: Erlbaum, pp. 1–33.
Coseriu, Eugenio [1969] (1970), 'System, Norm und "Rede"', in Eugenio Coseriu, *Sprache Strukturen und Funktionen, XII: Aufsätze zur Allgemeinen und Romanischen Sprachwissenschaft*, ed. by Uwe Petersen, Tübingen: Tübinger Beiträge zur Linguistik, pp. 193–212. [German translation of 'Sistema, norma e "parola"', in *Studi Linguistici in onore di Vittore Pisani*, vol. 1, pp. 235–53. Brescia: Paideia.]
Croft, William (2000), *Explaining Language Change,* New York: Longman.
Croft, William (2003), *Typology and Universals*, 2nd edn, New York: Cambridge University Press.
Curtius, Georg (1885), *Zur Kritik der neuesten Sprachforschung*, Leipzig: Hirzel.
Davies, Anna Morpurgo (1978), 'Analogy, Segmentation, and the Early Neogrammarians', *Transactions of the Philological Society* 1978, 36–60.
Delbrück, B. (1893), *Einleitung in das Sprachstudium*, 3rd edn, Leipzig: Breitkopf & Härtel.
Deutscher, Guy (2001), 'On the mechanisms of morphological change', *Folia Linguistica Historica* 22, 41–8.
Deutscher, Guy (2002), 'On the misuse of the notion of "abduction" in linguistics', *Journal of Linguistics* 38, 469–85.
Deutscher, Guy (2005), *The Unfolding of Language*, New York: Holt.
Dresher, B. Elan (2000), 'Analogical levelling of vowel length in West Germanic', in Aditi Lahiri (ed.), *Analogy, Levelling, Markedness*, New York: Mouton de Gruyter, pp. 47–70.
Dressler, Wolfgang U. (1987), 'Word Formation (WF) as Part of Natural Morphology', in Wolfgang U. Dressler (ed.), *Leitmotifs in Natural Morphology*, Philadelphia: Benjamins, pp. 99–126.
Dressler, Wolfgang U., Willi Mayerthaler, Oswald Panagl and Wolfgang U. Wurzel (1987), 'Introduction', in Wolfgang U. Dressler (ed.), *Leitmotifs in Natural Morphology*, Philadelphia: Benjamins, pp. 3–24.
Dryer, Matthew (2009), 'The Branching Direction Theory of Word Order Correlations Revisited', in Sergio Scalise, Elisabetta Magni and Antonietta Bisetto (eds), *Universals of Language Today*, Heidelberg: Springer, pp. 185–207.

DWB = Grimm, Jacob and Wilhelm Grimm (1854–1971), *Deutsches Wörterbuch*, 33 vols., Leipzig: Hirzel.
Eckert, Penelope (2012), 'Three Waves of Variation Study: The Emergence of Meaning in the Study of Sociolinguistic Variation', *Annual Review of Anthropology* 41, 87–100.
Esper, Erwin A. (1973), *Analogy and Association in Linguistics and Psychology*, Athens: University of Georgia Press.
Fertig, David (1998a), 'Suppletion, Natural Morphology, and Diagrammaticity', *Linguistics* 36, 1065–91.
Fertig, David (1998b), 'The *ge-* Participle Prefix in Early New High German and the Modern Dialects', *American Journal of Germanic Linguistics and Literatures* 10, 237–78.
Fertig, David (1999a), 'Analogical "Leveling" from Outside the Paradigm: Stem-vowel Changes in the German Modals', *Diachronica* 16, 233–60.
Fertig, David (1999b), 'Diachronic Evidence for a Dual-mechanism Approach to Inflection (Commentary on Clahsen 1999)', *Behavioral and Brain Sciences* 22:6, 1023–4.
Fertig, David (2000), *Morphological Change Up Close*, Tübingen: Niemeyer.
Fertig, David (2005), 'Review of *The Morphology of Dutch* by Geert Booij', *Journal of Germanic Linguistics* 17, 141–8.
Fischer, Olga (2007), *Morphosyntactic Change: Functional and Formal Perspectives*, New York: Oxford University Press.
Fortson, Benjamin W., IV (2003), 'An Approach to Semantic Change', in Brian D. Joseph and Richard D. Janda (eds), *Handbook of Historical Linguistics*, Oxford: Blackwell, pp. 648–66.
Garrett, Andrew (2001), 'Reduplication and Infixation in Yurok: Morphology, Semantics, and Diachrony', *International Journal of American Linguistics* 67:3, 264–312.
Garrett, Andrew (2008), 'Paradigmatic uniformity and markedness', in Jeff Good (ed.), *Linguistic Universals and Language Change*, Oxford: Oxford University Press, pp. 125–43.
Garrett, Andrew (2012), 'The historical syntax problem: reanalysis and directionality', in Dianne Jonas, John Whitman and Andrew Garrett (eds), *Grammatical Change Origins, Nature, Outcomes*, New York: Oxford University Press, pp. 52–72.
Garrett, Andrew and Juliette Blevins (2008), 'Analogical Morphophonology', in Kristin Hanson and Sharon Inkelas (eds), *The Nature of the Word: Studies in Honor of Paul Kiparsky*, Cambridge, MA: MIT Press, pp. 527–45.
Gerken, LouAnn (2006), 'Decisions, decisions: infant language learning when multiple generalizations are possible', *Cognition* 98, B67–B74.
Gerken, LouAnn, Rachel Wilson, Rebecca Gómez and Erika Nurmsoo (2009), 'The relation between linguistic analogies and lexical categories', in James P. Blevins and Juliette Blevins (eds), *Analogy in Grammar: Form and Acquisition*, Oxford: Oxford University Press, pp. 101–17.
Goldberg, Adele (2006), *Constructions at Work: the Nature of Generalization in Language.* Oxford: Oxford University Press.

Goldsmith, John (2006), 'An algorithm for the supervised learning of morphology', *Natural Language Engineering* 12, 353–71.
Greenberg, Joseph H. (1966), *Language Universals*, The Hague: Mouton.
Gries, Stefan T. (2004), 'Shouldn't it be breakfunch? A quantitative analysis of blend structure in English', *Linguistics* 42, 639–67.
Grosse, Rudolf (1988), 'Zur Wechselflexion im Singular Präsens der starken Verben – Lautwandel oder Analogie?' in Peter Wiesinger (ed.), *Studien zum Frühneuhochdeutschen Festschrift für Emil Skála*, Göppingen: Kümmerle, pp. 161–6.
Haiman, John (1985), *Natural Syntax*, New York: Cambridge University Press.
Hale, Kenneth (1973), 'Deep-surface canonical disparities in relation to analogy and change: an Australian example', in Thomas S. Sebeok (ed.), *Diachronic, Areal, and Typological Linguistics*, The Hague: Mouton, pp. 401–58.
Hale, Mark and Charles Reiss (2008), *The Phonological Enterprise*, Oxford: Oxford University Press.
Halle, Morris and Alec Marantz (1993), 'Distributed Morphology and the Pieces of Inflection', in Kenneth Hale and Samuel Jay Keyser (eds), *The View from Building 20*, Cambridge, MA: MIT Press, pp. 111–71.
Hare, Mary and Jeffrey L. Elman (1995), 'Learning and Morphological Change', *Cognition* 56, 61–98.
Harris, Alice C. and Lyle Campbell (1995), *Historical Syntax in Cross-Linguistic Perspective*, New York: Cambridge University Press.
Haspelmath, Martin (1995), 'The Growth of Affixes in Morphological Reanalysis', in Geert Booij and Jaap van Marle (eds), *Yearbook of Morphology 1994*, Boston: Kluwer, pp. 1–29.
Haspelmath, Martin (1998), 'Does Grammaticalization Need Reanalysis?', *Studies in Language* 22, 315–51.
Haspelmath, Martin (1999), 'Why is grammaticalization irreversible?', *Linguistics* 37, 1043–68.
Haspelmath, Martin (2006), 'Against markedness (and what to replace it with)', *Journal of Linguistics* 42:1, 25–70.
Haspelmath, Martin and Andrea D. Sims (2010), *Understanding Morphology*, 2nd edn, London: Hodder.
Havet, M. L. (1875), 'Préface du traducteur', in Franz Bücheler, *Précis de la Déclinaison Latine*, trans. by M. L. Havet, Paris: Vieweg, pp. i–xxii.
Heine, Bernd (1993), *Auxiliaries*, New York: Oxford University Press.
Hempen, Ute (1988), *Die starken Verben im Deutschen und Niederländischen*, Tübingen: Niemeyer.
Henry, Victor (1883), *Étude sur l'analogie en général et sur les formations analogiques de la langue Grecque*, Paris: Maisonneuve.
Hermann, Eduard (1931), *Lautgesetz und Analogie* (*Abhandlungen der Gesellschaft der Wissenschaften zu Göttingen, Philologisch-Historische Klass, neue Folge* 23, 3), Berlin: Weidmannsche Buchhandlung.
Hill, Eugen (2007), 'Proportionale Analogie, paradigmatischer Ausgleich und Formerweiterung: ein Beitrag zur Typologie des morphologischen Wandels', *Diachronica* 24, 81–118.

Hock, Hans Henrich (1986), *Principles of Historical Linguistics*, New York: Mouton.
Hock, Hans Henrich (2003), 'Analogical Change', in Brian D. Joseph and Richard D. Janda (eds), *Handbook of Historical Linguistics*, Oxford: Blackwell, pp. 441–60.
Hock, Hans H. and Brian D. Joseph (2009), *Language History, Language Change, and Language Relationship*, 2nd edn, Berlin: Mouton de Gruyter.
Hockett, Charles F. (1954), 'Two models of grammatical description', *Word* 10, 210–34.
Hockett, Charles F. (1958), *A Course in Modern Linguistics*, New York: Macmillan.
Holt, D. Eric (2003), 'Remarks on Optimality Theory and Language Change', in D. Eric Holt (ed.), *Optimality Theory and Language Change*, Dordrecht: Kluwer, pp. 1–30.
Hopper, Paul (1987), 'Emergent Grammar', *Berkeley Linguistics Society* 13, 139–57.
Hopper, Paul J. and Elizabeth Closs Traugott (1993), *Grammaticalization*, New York: Cambridge University Press.
Hopper, Paul J. and Elizabeth Closs Traugott (2003), *Grammaticalization*, 2nd edn, New York: Cambridge University Press.
Householder, Fred W. (1971), *Linguistic Speculations*, New York: Cambridge University Press.
Hyman, Larry M. (2003), 'Sound Change, Misanalysis, and Analogy in the Bantu Causative', *Journal of African Languages and Linguistics* 24, 55–90.
Itkonen, Esa (2005), *Analogy as Structure and Process Approaches in Linguistics, Cognitive Psychology and Philosophy of Science*, Philadelphia: Benjamins.
Jacobs, Neil G. (2005), *Yiddish: A Linguistic Introduction*, New York: Cambridge University Press.
Jaeger, Jeri J., Alan H. Lockwood, David L. Kemmerer, Robert D. Van Valin, Brian W. Murphy and Janif G. Khalak (1996), 'A Positron Emission Tomographic Study of Regular and Irregular Verb Morphology in English', *Language* 72, 451–97.
Janda, Richard (2001), 'Beyond "pathways" and "unidirectionality": on the discontinuity of language transmission and the counterability of grammaticalization', *Language Sciences* 23, 265–340.
Janda, Richard D. and Brian D. Joseph (2003), 'On Language, Change, and Language Change – Or, Of History, Linguistics, and Historical Linguistics', in Brian D. Joseph and Richard D. Janda (eds), *Handbook of Historical Linguistics*, Oxford: Blackwell, pp. 3–180.
Jeffers, Robert J. and Ilse Lehiste (1979), *Principles and Methods for Historical Linguistics*, Cambridge, MA: MIT Press.
Jespersen, Otto (1922), *Language: Its Nature, Development and Origin*, London: Allen & Unwin.
Jespersen, Otto (1924), *The Philosophy of Grammar*, New York: Holt.
Jespersen, Otto (1928), *A Modern English Grammar on Historical Principles, part 1: Sounds and Spellings*, 4th edn, Heidelberg: Winter.
Joseph, Brian D. (1998), 'Diachronic Morphology', in Andrew Spencer and

Arnold M. Zwicky (eds), *The Handbook of Morphology*, Malden, MA: Blackwell, pp. 351–73.

Joseph, Brian D. and Richard D. Janda (1988), 'The How and Why of Diachronic Morphologization and Demorphologization', in Michael Hammond and Michael Noonan (eds), *Theoretical Morphology*, New York: Academic Press, pp. 193–210.

Kager, René (1999), *Optimality Theory*, New York: Cambridge University Press.

Keller, Rudi (1994), *On Language Change: the Invisible Hand in Language*, London: Taylor and Francis.

Keller, Rudi (2005), 'Sprachwandel als invisible-hand-Phänomen', in Thomas Stehl (ed.), *Unsichtbare Hand und Sprecherwahl*, Tübingen: Narr, pp. 27-42.

Kenstowicz, Michael (1996), 'Base Identity and Uniform Exponence: Alternatives to Cyclicity', in Jacques Durand and Bernard Laks (eds), *Current Trends in Phonology: Models and Methods*, vol. 1, Manchester: University of Salford, 363–93.

King, Robert D. (1969), *Historical Linguistics and Generative Grammar*, Englewood Cliffs, NJ: Prentice-Hall.

Kiparsky, Paul (1965), *Phonological Change*, PhD dissertation, MIT.

Kiparsky, Paul (1968), 'Linguistic Universals and Linguistic Change', in Emmon Bach and Robert T. Harms (eds), *Universals in Linguistic Theory*, New York: Holt, Rinehart and Winston, pp. 170–202.

Kiparsky, Paul (1971), 'Historical Linguistics', in William O. Dingwall (ed.), *A Survey of Linguistic Science*, College Park: University of Maryland Linguistics Program.

Kiparsky, Paul (1972), 'Explanation in Phonology', in Stanley Peters (ed.), *Goals of Linguistic Theory*, Englewood Cliffs, NJ: Prentice-Hall, pp. 189–227.

Kiparsky, Paul (1973), 'Phonological Representations', in O. Fujimura (ed.), *Three Dimensions of Linguistic Theory*, Tokyo: TEC Co, pp. 1–136.

Kiparsky, Paul (1974), 'Remarks on Analogical Change', in J. M. Anderson and C. Jones (eds), *Historical Linguistics II*, New York: American Elsevier, pp. 257–75.

Kiparsky, Paul (1978), 'Analogical Change as a Problem for Linguistic Theory', in Braj B. Kachru (ed.), *Linguistics in the Seventies: Directions and Prospects*, Urbana: Dept. of Linguistics, University of Illinois, pp. 77–96.

Kiparsky, Paul (1992), 'Analogy', in William Bright (ed.), *International Encyclopedia of Linguistics*, vol. 1, New York: Oxford University Press, pp. 56–61.

Kiparsky, Paul (1995), 'The Phonological Basis of Sound Change', in John A. Goldsmith (ed.), *The Handbook of Phonological Theory*, Oxford: Blackwell, pp. 640–70.

Kiparsky, Paul (2000), 'Analogy as optimization: "exceptions" to Sievers' Law in Gothic', in Aditi Lahiri (ed.), *Analogy, Levelling, Markedness*, New York: Mouton de Gruyter, pp. 15–46.

Kiparsky, Paul (2012), 'Grammaticalization as optimization', in Dianne Jonas, John Whitman and Andrew Garrett (eds), *Grammatical Change Origins, Nature, Outcomes*, New York: Oxford University Press, pp. 15–51.

Kluge, Friedrich (1975), *Etymologisches Wörterbuch der deutschen Sprache*, 21st edn, New York: de Gruyter.
Krahe, Hans (1969), Germanische Sprachwissenschaft, vol. 3: Wortbildungslehre, 7th edn, ed by Wolfgang Meid, Berlin: de Gruyter.
Kroesch, Samuel (1926), 'Analogy as a Factor in Semantic Change', *Language* 2, 35–45.
Kuha, Mai (2004), 'Investigating the Spread of "so" as an Intensifier: Social and Structural Factors', *Texas Linguistic Forum* 48, 217–27.
Kuryłowicz, Jerzy (1964), *The Inflectional Categories of Indo-European*, Heidelberg: Winter.
Kuryłowicz, Jerzy [1945–9] (1966), 'La Nature des procès dits "analogiques"', in Eric P. Hamp, Fred W. Householder and Robert Austerlitz (eds), *Readings in Linguistics II*, Chicago: Chicago University Press, pp. 158–74. [Reprinted from *Acta Linguistica* 5, 121–38.]
Kuryłowicz, Jerzy (1977), *Problèmes de Linguistique Indo-Européenne*, Wrocław: Zakład Narodowy Imienia Ossolińskich Wydawnictwo Polskeij Akademii Nauk.
Labov, William (1966), *The Social Stratification of English in New York City*, Washington, DC: The Center for Applied Linguistics.
Labov, William (1994), *Principles of Linguistic Change*, vol. 1: *Internal Factors*, Cambridge, MA: Blackwell.
Lahiri, Aditi (2000), 'Introduction', in Aditi Lahiri (ed.), *Analogy, Levelling, Markedness*, New York: Mouton de Gruyter, pp. 1–14.
Langacker, Ronald W. (1977), 'Syntactic Reanalysis', in Charles N. Li (ed.), *Mechanisms of Syntactic Change*, Austin: University of Texas Press, pp. 57–139.
Langacker, Ronald (1987), *Foundations of Cognitive Grammar*, vol. 1: *Theoretical Prerequisites*, Stanford: Stanford University Press.
Lass, Roger (1990), 'How to Do Things with Junk: Exaptation in Language Evolution', *Journal of Linguistics* 26, 79–102.
Lass, Roger (1997), *Historical Linguistics and Language Change*, New York: Cambridge University Press.
Lehmann, Christian (1985), 'Grammaticalization: Synchronic Variation and Diachronic Change', *Lingua e stile* 20, 303–18.
Lehmann, Winfried (1962), *Historical Linguistics: An Introduction*. New York: Holt, Rinehart and Winston.
Lehmann, Winfried (1973), 'A structural principle of language and its implications', *Language* 49, 47–66.
Leskien, August (1876), *Die Declination im Slavisch-Litauischen und Germanischen*, Leipzig: Hirzel.
Lightfoot, David W. (1979), *Principles of Diachronic Syntax*, New York: Cambridge University Press.
Lucas, Robert (1976), 'Econometric Policy Evaluation: A Critique', in K. Brunner and A. Meltzer (eds), *The Phillips Curve and Labor Markets,* New York: American Elsevier, pp. 19–46.
McCarthy, John J. (2005), 'Optimal Paradigms', in Laura J. Downing, T. A. Hall and Renate Raffelsiefen (eds), *Paradigms in Phonological Theory*, Oxford: Oxford University Press, pp. 170–210.

McCarthy, John J. and Alan Prince (1995), 'Prosodic Morphology', in John Goldsmith (ed.), *A Handbook of Phonological Theory*, Oxford: Basil Blackwell, pp. 318–66.
McMahon, April M. S. (1994), *Understanding Language Change*, New York: Cambridge University Press.
MacWhinney, Brian (1975), 'Rules, rote, and analogy in morphological formations by Hungarian children', *Journal of Child Language* 2, 65–77.
Mańczak, Witold (1958), 'Tendences générales des changements analogiques', *Lingua* 7, 298–325 and 387–420.
Marcus, Gary F., Ursula Brinkmann, Harald Clahsen, Richard Wiese and Steven Pinker (1995), 'German Inflection: The Exception that Proves the Rule', *Cognitive Psychology* 29, 189–256.
Mayerthaler, Willi (1980), 'Aspekte der Analogietheorie', in Helmut Lüdtke (ed.), *Kommunikationstheoretische Grundlagen des Sprachwandels*, Berlin: de Gruyter, pp. 80–130.
Mayerthaler, Willi (1981), *Morphologische Natürlichkeit*, Wiesbaden: Athenaion.
Mayerthaler, Willi (1987), 'System-independent Morphological Naturalness', in Wolfgang U. Dressler (ed.), *Leitmotifs in Natural Morphology*, Philadelphia: Benjamins, pp. 25–58.
Meillet, A. [1908] (1965), 'Linguistique Historique et Linguistique Générale', *Linguistique Historique et Linguistique Générale*, Paris: Honoré Champion, pp. 44–60. [Reprinted from *Scientia (Rivista di scienza)* 4.]
Merton, Robert K. (1968), 'The Matthew Effect in Science', *Science* 159, 56–63.
Middleton, G. (1892), *An Essay on Analogy in Syntax*, London: Longmans, Green and Co.
Milroy, James (1992), *Linguistic Variation and Change*, Cambridge, MA: Blackwell.
Milroy, James (1999), 'Toward a Speaker-based Account of Language Change', in Ernst Håkon Jahr (ed.), *Language Change: Advances in Historical Sociolinguistics*, New York: Mouton de Gruyter, pp. 21–36.
Millward, C. M. (1996), *A Biography of the English Language*, 2nd edn, New York: Harcourt Brace.
Misteli, Franz (1879–80), 'Lautgesetz und Analogie', *Zeitschrift für Völkerpsychologie* 11, 365–475 and 12, 1–27.
Moder, Carol Lynn (1992), 'Rules and analogy', in Garry W. Davis and Gregory K. Iverson (eds), *Explanation in Linguistics*, Philadelphia: Benjamins, pp. 179–91.
Moulton, William G. (1961), 'Lautwandel durch innere Kausalität: die ostschweizerische Vokalspaltung', *Zeitschrift für Mundartforschung* 28, 227–51.
Moulton, William G. (1967), 'The Mapping of Phonemic Systems' in Ludwig Erich Schmitt (ed.), *Verhandlungen des 2. Internationalen Dialektologenkongresses*, vol. 2, Wiesbaden: Steiner, pp. 574–91.
Nichols, Johanna (2003), 'Diversity and Stability in Language', in Brian D. Joseph and Richard D. Janda (eds), *Handbook of Historical Linguistics*, Oxford: Blackwell, pp. 283–310.
Norde, Muriel (2009), *Degrammaticalization*, New York: Oxford University Press.

Nübling, Damaris (2000), *Prinzipien der Irregularisierung*, Tübingen: Niemeyer.
Nunberg, Geoffrey (2002), 'Going Nucular', "Fresh Air" commentary, October 2, 2002 <http://people.ischool.berkeley.edu/~nunberg/nucular.html> (last accessed 31 January 2013).
Oertel, Hanns (1901), *Lectures on the Study of Language*, New York: Scribner's.
Ohala, John (1993), 'The phonetics of sound change', in Charles Jones (ed.), *Historical Linguistics: Problems and Perspectives*, London: Longman, pp. 237–78.
Ohala, John, Leanne Hinton and Johanna Nichols (eds) (1994), *Sound Symbolism*, New York: Cambridge University Press.
Osthoff, Hermann (1878a), *Das Verbum in der Nominalkomposition*, Jena: Costenoble.
Osthoff, Hermann (1878b), 'Formassociation bei Zahlwörtern', in Hermann Osthoff and Karl Brugmann, *Morphologische Untersuchungen auf dem Gebiete der Indogermanischen Sprachen*, vol. 1, Leipzig: Hirzel, pp. 92–132.
Osthoff, Hermann (1879a), 'Das physiologische und psychologische Moment in der sprachlichen Formenbildung', in Rud. Birchow and Fr. v. Holtzendorff (eds), *Sammlung gemeinverständlicher wissenschaftlicher Vorträge*, vol. 14, no. 337, Berlin: Habel, pp. 505–52.
Osthoff, Hermann (1879b), 'Kleine beiträge zur declinationslehre der indogermanischen sprachen II', in Hermann Osthoff and Karl Brugmann, *Morphologische Untersuchungen auf dem Gebiete der Indogermanischen Sprachen*, vol. 2, Leipzig: Hirzel, pp. 1–147.
Osthoff, Hermann (1899), *Vom Suppletivwesen der indogermanischen Sprachen. Akademische Rede zur Feier des Geburtsfestes des höchstseligen Grossherzogs Karl Friedrich*, Heidelberg: Hörning.
Osthoff, Hermann and Karl Brugmann (1878), 'Vorwort', in Hermann Osthoff and Karl Brugmann, *Morphologische Untersuchungen auf dem Gebiete der Indogermanischen Sprachen*, vol. 1, Leipzig: Hirzel, pp. iii–xx.
Palmer, A. Smythe (1882), *Folk-Etymology, a Dictionary of Verbal Corruptions or Words Perverted in Form or Meaning, by False Derivation or Mistaken Analogy*, London: Bell.
Paul, Hermann (1877), 'Die Vocale der Flexions- und Ableitungs-Silben in den aeltesten germanischen Dialecten', *Beiträge zur Geschichte der deutschen Sprache und Literatur* 4, 315–475.
Paul, Hermann (1879), 'Zur geschichte des germanischen vocalismus', *Beiträge zur Geschichte der deutschen Sprache und Literatur* 6, 1–256.
Paul, Hermann (1880), *Principien der Sprachgeschichte*, 1st edn, Halle: Niemeyer.
Paul, Hermann (1886), *Principien der Sprachgeschichte*, 2nd edn, Halle: Niemeyer.
Paul, Hermann (1897), 'Ueber die Aufgaben der Wortbildungslehre', *Sitzungsberichte der philosophisch-philologischen und der historischen Classe der k.b. Akademie der Wissenschaften zu München* 1896.692-713.
Paul, Hermann (1920), *Prinzipien der Sprachgeschichte*, 5th edn, Halle: Niemeyer.

Paul, Hermann (1989), *Mittelhochdeutsche Grammatik*, 23rd edn, ed. Peter Wiehl and Siegfried Grosse, Tübingen: Niemeyer.
Pfeifer, Wolfgang (ed.) (1993), *Etymologisches Wörterbuch des Deutschen*, 2nd edn, Munich: Deutscher Taschenbuch Verlag.
Phillips, Betty S. (2006), *Word Frequency and Lexical Diffusion*, New York: Palgrave Macmillan.
Piñeros, Carlos Eduardo (1998), *Prosodic Morphology in Spanish: Constraint Interaction in Word Formation*, PhD dissertation, Ohio State University.
Piñeros, Carlos Eduardo (2004), 'The creation of portmanteaus in the extragrammatical morphology of Spanish', *Probus* 16, 203–40.
Pinker, Steven (1999), *Words and Rules*, New York: HarperCollins.
Pinker, Steven and Alan Prince (1988), 'On Language and Connectionism: Analysis of a Parallel Distributed Processing Model of Language Acquisition', *Cognition* 28, 73–194.
Pinker, Steven and Alan Prince (1994), 'Regular and Irregular Morphology and the Psychological Status of Rules of Grammar', in Susan D. Lima, Roberta L. Corrigan and Gregory K. Iverson (eds), *The Reality of Linguistic Rules*, Philadelphia: Benjamins, pp. 321–51.
Pope, M. K. (1952), *From Latin to Modern French with Especial Consideration of Anglo-Norman*, rev. edn, Manchester: Manchester University Press.
Prokosch, E. (1939), *A Comparative Germanic Grammar*, Philadelphia: Linguistic Society of America.
Raffelsiefen, Renate (2000), 'Constraints on schwa apocope in Middle High German', in Aditi Lahiri (ed.), *Analogy, Levelling, Markedness*, New York: Mouton de Gruyter, pp. 125–70.
Rajaona, Siméon (2004), *Les phénomènes morphologiques Eléments de morphologie inflexionelle du malgache*, Antananarivo: Ambozontany.
Rajemisa-Raolison, Regis (1971), *Grammaire Malgache*, 7th edn, Fianarantsoa: Ambozontany.
Reiss, Charles (2006), 'Morphological Change, Paradigm Leveling and Analogy', in Keith Brown (ed.), *Encyclopedia of Language & Linguistics*, 2nd edn, Amsterdam: Elsevier, pp. 277–8.
Rigney, Daniel (2010), *The Matthew Effect: How Advantage Begets Further Advantage*, New York: Columbia University Press.
Robins, R. H. (1978), 'The Neogrammarians and their nineteenth-century predecessors', *Transactions of the Philological Society* 1978, 1–16.
Rogge, Christian (1925), 'Die Analogie im Sprachleben, was sie ist und wie sie wirkt', *Archiv für die gesamte Psychologie* 52, 441–68.
Ronneberger-Sibold, Elke (1987), 'Verschiedene Wege zur Entstehung von suppletiven Flexionsparadigmen, Deutsch *gern - lieber - am liebsten*', in Norbert Boretzky, Werner Enninger and Thomas Stolz (eds), *Beiträge zum 3. Essener Kolloquium über Sprachwandel und seine bestimmenden Faktoren*, Bochum: Brockmeyer, pp. 243–64.
Ronneberger-Sibold, Elke (1988), 'Entstehung von Suppletion und Natürliche Morphologie', *Zeitschrift für Phonetik, Sprachwissenschaft und Kommunikationsforschung* 41, 453–62.
Ross, Malcolm and Mark Durie (1996), 'Introduction', in Mark Durie and

Malcolm Ross (eds), *The Comparative Method Reviewed: Regularity and Irregularity in Language Change*, New York: Oxford University Press, pp. 3–38.

Rumelhart, David E. and James L. McClelland (1986), 'On Learning the Past Tenses of English Verbs', in David E. Rumelhart and James L. McClelland (eds), *Parallel Distributed Processing: Explorations in the Microstructure of Cognition*, vol. 1, Cambridge, MA: Bradford, pp. 216–71.

Rumelhart, David E. and James L. McClelland (1987), 'Learning the Past Tenses of English Verbs: Implicit Rules or Parallel Distributed Processing?', in Brian MacWhinney (ed.), *Mechanisms of Language Acquisition*, Hillsdale, NJ: Erlbaum, pp. 195–248.

Samuels, M. L. (1972), *Linguistic Evolution*, Cambridge: Cambridge University Press.

Saussure, Ferdinand de [1916] (1995), *Cours de linguistique générale*, ed. Charles Bally and Albert Sechehaye, Paris: Payot.

Scherer, Wilhelm (1868), *Zur Geschichte der deutschen Sprache*, Berlin: Duncker.

Schirmunski, V. M. (1962), *Deutsche Mundartkunde*, Berlin: Akademie-Verlag.

Schuchardt, Hugo [1885] (1972), *Über die Lautgesetze: Gegen die Junggrammatiker*, Berlin: Oppenheim. [Reprint and translation in Vennemann and Wilbur 1972, 1–72.]

Schürr, Friedrich (1925), *Sprachwissenschaft und Zeitgeist*, 2nd edn, Marburg: Elwert.

Shapiro, Michael (1991), *The Sense of Change*, Bloomington: Indiana University Press.

Skousen, Royal (1989), *Analogical Modeling of Language*. Boston: Kluwer.

Skousen, Royal (1992), *Analogy and Structure*, Boston: Kluwer.

Skousen, Royal (2009), 'Expanding Analogical Modeling into a general theory of language prediction', in James P. Blevins and Juliette Blevins (eds), *Analogy in Grammar: Form and Acquisition*, Oxford: Oxford University Press, pp. 164–84.

Steriade, Donca (2000), 'Paradigm uniformity and the phonetics–phonology boundary', in Michael Broe and Janet Pierrehumbert (eds), *Papers in Laboratory Phonology* 5, Cambridge: Cambridge University Press, pp. 313–34.

Stump, Gregory T. (1993), 'Rules of Referral', *Language* 49, 449–79.

Sturtevant, Edgar H. (1917), *Linguistic Change*, Chicago: University of Chicago Press.

Sturtevant, Edgar H. (1947), *An Introduction to Linguistic Science*, New Haven: Yale University Press.

Tiersma, Peter Meijes (1982), 'Local and General Markedness', *Language* 58, 832–49.

Timberlake, Alan (1977), 'Reanalysis and actualization in syntactic change', in Charles N. Li (ed.), *Mechanisms of Syntactic Change*, Austin: University of Texas Press, pp. 141–80.

Tomasello, Michael (2003), *Constructing a Language: A Usage-based Theory of Language Acquisition*, Cambridge, MA: Harvard University Press.

Trask, R. L. (1996), *Historical Linguistics*, London: Arnold.
Traugott, Elizabeth C. and Graeme Trousdale (2010), 'Gradience, gradualness and grammaticalization: How do they intersect?', in Elizabeth Closs Traugott and Graeme Trousdale (eds), *Gradience, Gradualness and Grammaticalization*, Philadelphia: Benjamins, pp. 19–44.
Vennemann, Theo (1972a), 'Rule Inversion', *Lingua* 29, 209–42.
Vennemann, Theo (1972b), 'Phonetic Analogy and Conceptual Analogy', in Theo Vennemann and Terence H. Wilbur (eds), *Schuchardt, the Neogrammarians, and the Transformational Theory of Phonological Change*, Frankfurt: Athenäum, pp. 181–204.
Vennemann, Theo (1974), 'Topics, subjects and word order: from SXV to SVX via TVX', in J. M. Anderson and C. Jones (eds), *Historical Linguistics*, vol. 1, Amsterdam: North Holland, pp. 339–76.
Vennemann, Theo (1993), 'Language change as language improvement', in Charles Jones (eds), *Historical Linguistics: Problems and Perspectives*, London: Longman, pp. 237–78.
Vennemann, Theo and Terence H. Wilbur (1972), *Schuchardt, the Neogrammarians, and the Transformational Theory of Phonological Change*, Frankfurt: Athenäum.
Vincent, Nigel (1974), 'Analogy Reconsidered', in J. M. Anderson and C. Jones (eds), *Historical Linguistics II*, New York: American Elsevier, pp. 427–45.
Vossler, Karl (1905), *Sprache als Schöpfung und Entwicklung*, Heidelberg: Winter.
Wackernagel, Jacob (1926), *Vorlesungen über Syntax*, vol. 1, Basel: Birkhäuser.
Wanner, Dieter (2006), *The Power of Analogy: An Essay on Historical Linguistics*, New York: Mouton de Gruyter.
Wedel, Andrew (2009), 'Resolving pattern conflict: Variation and selection in phonology and morphology', in James P. Blevins and Juliette Blevins (eds), *Analogy in Grammar: Form and Acquisition*, Oxford: Oxford University Press, pp. 83–100.
Weinreich, Uriel [1968] (1977), *Modern English–Yiddish Yiddish–English Dictionary*, New York: Schocken Books [reprint of the YIVO edition].
Weinreich, Uriel, William Labov and Marvin Herzog (1968), 'Empirical foundations for a theory of language change', in Winfried Lehmann and Yakov Malkiel (eds), *Directions for Historical Linguistics*, Austin: University of Texas Press, pp. 95–198.
Wheeler, Benjamin Ide (1887), *Analogy and the Scope of its Application in Language*, Ithaca, NY: John Wilson and Son University Press.
Whitney, William Dwight (1867), *Language and the Study of Language: Twelve Lectures on the Principles of Linguistic Science*, London: Trübner.
Wiese, Richard (1996), *The Phonology of German*, New York: Oxford University Press.
Wurzel, Wolfgang Ullrich (1984), *Flexionsmorphologie und Natürlichkeit*, Berlin: Akademie-Verlag.
Wurzel, Wolfgang Ullrich (1987), 'System-dependent Morphological Naturalness in Inflection', in Wolfgang U. Dressler (ed.), *Leitmotifs in Natural Morphology*, Philadelphia: Benjamins, pp. 59–96.

Wurzel, Wolfgang Ullrich (1989), *Inflectional Morphology and Naturalness*, Boston: Kluwer [Translation of Wurzel 1984].

Wurzel, Wolfgang Ullrich (1990a), 'Gedanken zu Suppletion und Natürlichkeit', *Zeitschrift für Phonetik, Sprachwissenschaft und Kommunikationsforschung* 43, 86–91.

Wurzel, Wolfgang Ullrich (1990b), 'The Mechanism of Inflection: Lexicon Representations, Rules, and Irregularities', in Wolfgang U. Dressler, Hans C. Luschützky, Oskar E. Pfeiffer and John R. Rennison (eds), *Contemporary Morphology*, New York: Mouton de Gruyter, pp. 203–16.

Yang, Charles D. (2002), *Knowledge and Learning in Natural Language*, New York: Oxford University Press.

Zwicky, Arnold M. (1985), 'How to describe inflection', *Berkeley Linguistics Society* 11, 372–86.

Index

abductive and deductive innovations, 19
ablaut, 27–8, 33, 65, 73–4, 77, 81, 90, 107–8
acquisition, 3, 7, 8, 23–6, 76, 94, 112, 115–17, 123–4, 127–9; *see also* child language; imperfect learning
across-the-board change *see* change: across-the-board
actualization, 19, 28
adaptive rule, 22
adjective, strong and weak declensions in Germanic, 38–40; *see also* backformation; participle; reanalysis; reinterpretation
Albright, Adam, 91, 115, 117–18, 135–6, 139
Algic *see* Yurok
allomorphy, 34, 42, 106–7, 125; *see also* alternations; morphophonology
alternations, 27, 47–51, 53, 56, 65, 71–7, 79, 81–2, 90–2, 96, 99, 105–18; *see also* ablaut; allomorphy; devoicing; lengthening; leveling; morphophonology; rhotacism; shortening; umlaut; Verner's Law
ambiguity, 20, 22, 25, 32–3, 53, 67, 91
analogical change *see* analogical innovation; analogy
analogical extension *see* extension
analogical formation, 4, 10, 12–14, 21, 81, 87, 96, 124, 138
analogical innovation, 4–7, 9–22, 24–9, 32, 34, 37, 40, 44–6, 48–9, 82, 85, 87, 90, 97, 100, 102, 116, 122, 127–30, 132, 137–40
Analogical Modeling, 139
analogy
  conceptual, 97
  constraints on *see* constraints: on analogy
  definitions of, 4, 9–13
  false, 5, 98, 102, 120
  four-part, 47–8, 83, 138–9
  non-proportional, 6, 12, 21, 43–7, 57–70, 72–6, 83, 92–3, 114, 134
  phantom, 77–83
  phonetic, 95
  preventive, 98–101
  proportional, 9–12, 14, 15–16, 18, 21, 42–56, 58, 65–6, 71–6, 83, 89–91, 100, 102, 104–5, 116, 133
  semantic *see* semantics
  syntactic *see* syntax
  vs. rules, 130–1
analysis *see* reanalysis

Andersen, Henning, 19, 22, 27, 37, 42, 64, 73, 107, 112–13, 135
Anttila, Raimo, 12–14, 43, 64, 118–20
applicative, 33, 51, 73
Aronoff, Mark, 70, 115, 125
assimilation, 50, 96
  analogical change as, 93, 103
  leveling as, 64
  non-proportional analogy as, 59, 64
associative interference, 12–13, 21, 43, 47, 57, 74, 92; *see also* analogy: non-proportional
asymmetric vs. symmetric paradigmatic models, 137–8

backformation, 1, 18, 29–30, 48, 51–5, 83, 116, 138
Bantu, 33, 50, 72; *see also* Bemba; Nyakyusa; Nyamwezi
basicness, 116–17
Basque, 59
Belarusian, 73
Bemba, 73, 75
Bible, 115–16
biuniqueness, 106
blend, 18, 27, 32, 62–70
Blevins, James, 3, 71, 128, 136–8
Blevins, Juliette, 59, 71, 114
blocking, 25, 36, 50, 139
Bloomfield, Leonard, 7, 8, 13, 24–5, 43, 88–9, 101
borrowing, 52, 58–9; *see also* contact
Brugmann, Karl, 6, 96, 99
Bybee, Joan, 24–5, 30, 110, 112, 114–18, 125–7, 133

Campbell, Lyle, 14, 17, 29, 58, 64; *see also* Harris, Alice
Carstairs-McCarthy, Andrew, 80–3, 89, 98, 114
causative, 33, 51, 73
change
  across-the-board, 56, 95
  analogical *see* analogical innovation; analogy
  lexical *see* semantics
  morphophonological *see* morphophonology
  phonetic *see* sound change
  phonological *see* sound change
  semantic *see* semantics
  syntactic *see* syntax
  vs. innovation *see* innovation: vs. change
  see also non-change
child language, 17, 23–4, 29, 32, 57–9, 115, 123; *see also* acquisition

Chomsky, Noam, 6, 23–4, 123–5, 130
Clahsen, Harald, 30, 131–2
Clark, Eve *see* Principle of Contrast
competence and performance, 23, 130
compounding, 10, 25, 54–5, 60–1, 66, 68–70, 87, 136
concatenation, 44, 125, 131, 136
conceptual analogy *see* analogy: conceptual
confusion
 of similar-sounding words, 61–2
 terminological and conceptual, 5, 21–2, 42–4, 128
connectionism, 3, 124, 129, 139
constraints
 on analogy, 102–21
 vs. rules, 132–4; *see also* Optimality Theory
contact, 14, 33–4
contamination, 6, 14, 21, 43–6, 51, 57, 62–6, 69, 78, 83, 92
contractions, 67
conversion, 30, 36, 116; *see also* derivation; verb: denominal
Coseriu, Eugenio, 26
covert vs. overt innovation, 13, 16, 19–21, 25, 32, 36–7, 40, 77, 88; *see also* reanalysis
creativity, 26–7, 62, 58–9, 66, 120, 123
Croft, William, 8, 12, 86–7, 106–7
cross-formation, 136
cumulative exponence *see* portmanteau
Czech, 113

dative, 31, 85–6, 91
Davies, Anna Morpurgo, 16, 18n, 44
deductive *see* abductive and deductive innovations
default, 22, 25–6, 30, 34, 55, 82, 93, 128, 131–2, 139
Delbrück, B., 103
deliberate innovation *see* creativity
demorphologization, 77
denominal verb *see* verb: denominal
derivation, 27–31, 35–6, 38, 49–52, 54–5, 66, 87, 136
Deutscher, Guy, 12, 119–20
devoicing, final, 76, 90, 92, 105, 114, 133
diachronic correspondence (vs. change), 7
diachrony *see* synchrony-diachrony dichotomy
diagram, 12, 109; *see also* iconicity
dissimilation, 45
Distributed Morphology, 135
Dressler, Wolfgang U., 103, 115
dual-mechanism model, 55, 118, 130–2, 136, 140
Dutch, 30–1, 34–6, 38, 40, 77, 136
dynamic vs. static models of grammar, 3, 22–3, 25–7, 124–9, 140

Eckert, Penelope, 26
economics, micro- and macro-, 6
economy, 107
Elman, Jeffrey L., 3, 119, 129, 131
emergent grammar, 3
empiricism, 24, 88; *see also* rationalism
English
 Middle, 7, 24, 31, 53, 60–1, 72–4, 80–2
 Old, 7, 10, 27, 31–2, 34–5, 37–8, 45, 49–50, 52–4, 60–3, 73, 76, 78–83, 87, 107, 109
equations, proportional *see* analogy: proportional; proportional equation
evolutionary grammatical theory, 3, 114–16, 121
exaptation, 20, 37–40, 77, 116
exemplar-based models, 3, 118, 124, 129–32, 135–6, 140
expressiveness *see* creativity
extension, 17–18, 19, 33, 35, 38, 46–51, 53, 55–6, 71–2, 77–9, 83, 89–93, 107–8, 113, 115–16, 133, 137

false analogy *see* analogy: false
family resemblance, 106, 112
final devoicing *see* devoicing: final
folk etymology, 1, 6, 10–11, 14, 21, 27, 33, 43–6, 51, 54, 57–63, 75, 83, 92–3
four-part analogy *see* analogy: four-part
French, 28, 31, 34, 54, 59, 63–4, 67–8, 70, 93, 113
frequency
 token, 107, 117–18, 121, 130, 132
 type, 55, 108, 110, 113, 118, 121; *see also* inflectional-class stability

Garrett, Andrew, 33, 49, 51, 71, 72, 76
generative linguistics, 9, 23–4, 47, 92, 125, 130
German, 14, 25, 27–8, 30–2, 34–6, 38, 40, 46, 49–50, 53, 55–6, 58–63, 65–8, 71–4, 77–80, 85–6, 90–2, 105–8, 111–14, 116–17, 133, 135
 Central, 79
 dialects of, 14, 31, 50, 53, 65, 79–80, 91–2, 110
 Middle High, 8–9, 14, 31, 50, 60–2, 72, 76, 79–80, 108
 Northern, 92
 Old High, 25, 30–1, 46, 62, 77–8, 107, 113
 Upper, 65
Germanic, 28, 30–2, 34–5, 38–40, 50, 55, 60, 63–4, 73, 77, 81, 90, 107, 113–14, 136
 West, 30, 38, 71, 77, 80, 107
 see also Dutch; English; German; Gothic; Old Norse
Goldsmith, John, 124
Gothic, 35, 39–40
grammaticalization, 15, 28, 84n
Greek, Ancient, 34, 38, 51, 63–4, 99, 113
groups, 96, 119
 formal and material, 28, 94
 proportional *see* proportional equation

Hare, Mary, 3, 119, 129, 131
harmony, 95, 97–8, 110–12, 120; *see also* system congruity
 in word order, 86–7
Harris, Alice, 20, 31–2, 48, 87, 98
Haspelmath, Martin, 19–20, 26–7, 34, 36, 106, 126, 137
Havet, M. L., 18n
Hebrew, 59
Hermann, Eduard, 7, 11, 95, 99, 139
Hock, Hans Henrich, 13, 27, 47–8, 51, 56n, 60–3, 71, 87, 91, 96, 104, 108–9
Hockett, Charles, 55, 136
humor, 15, 18, 26–7, 55, 57, 59, 120
Hyman, Larry M., 33, 51, 72
hypercorrection, 14, 18n, 48, 59–60, 70n
hypocorrection, 59–60

Icelandic *see* Old Norse
icon *see* iconicity
iconicity, constructional, 100, 109–10, 114; *see also* diagram
identity relation, 89–90, 111, 116, 135, 137; *see also* referral, rule of
imperfect learning, 25–6, 118, 127, 129, 139–40
implicature, 126–7
inflection, 3, 8, 27–30, 38–40, 46–7, 49–50, 53–6, 73–4, 80–2, 87, 89, 96, 110–15, 117, 135–8
inflectional-class stability, 110, 112, 114, 133; *see also* type frequency
innate knowledge, 5, 23, 125, 129; *see also* empiricism; generative linguistics; rationalism; Universal Grammar; universals

Index

innovation
  abductive and deductive *see* abductive and deductive innovations
  analogical *see* analogical innovation; analogy
  deliberate *see* creativity
  in segmentation *see* resegmentation
  in valuation *see* revaluation
  intentional *see* creativity
  vs. change, 7–9
intentional innovation *see* creativity
intraparadigmatic and interparadigmatic dimensions, 49, 104–18, 138
inversion *see* rule inversion
invisible hand, 119
irregularization, 27, 30–1, 55–6, 80–3, 131
isomorphism, 106–7; *see also* iconicity; Natural Morphology; naturalness

Janda, Richard, 24, 27–8, 76–7, 80, 123, 126
Jespersen, Otto, 17, 19, 26, 99, 125
jocular language *see* humor
Joseph, Brian, 12, 18, 24, 27–8, 76–7, 80, 87, 108–9, 123, 126

Keller, Rudi, 119
King, Robert D., 6, 17, 23–4, 56, 76, 92, 105
Kiparsky, Paul, 6, 13, 20, 23–5, 27–8, 43–8, 56, 66, 72–6, 93, 99, 105, 112, 128–9, 131, 133
Kuryłowicz, Jerzy, 28, 99, 104, 108, 116–17

Labov, William, 8, 18n
Langacker, Ronald W., 20, 25, 132
Lass, Roger, 4, 6, 37–40, 77, 119
Latin, 38–9, 49, 62–4, 69, 75, 93, 96–9, 106, 114, 133
  Classical, 80
  Late, 64, 113
  Vulgar, 62, 64
learning *see* acquisition
lengthening, 62
  open-syllable, 61, 74
leveling, 42, 47–9, 53, 64, 71–8, 83, 89–91, 96, 99, 105, 107, 115–18
  direction of, 91, 104, 107, 116–18
  formal vs. material, 48, 72
  non-regularizing, 72, 83
  partial, 21, 38, 71–3
lexical diffusion, 93–4
Lightfoot, David W., 98
loss, 15, 22, 76, 129

McCarthy, John, 70, 75n
Malagasy, 34, 53
Mańczak, Witold, 114
markedness, 106, 117
Matthew effect, 115–16
Mayerthaler, Willi, 106–10, 117
mechanism, 11, 19–41, 59, 63, 74, 76, 92, 112, 131
metanalysis, 19
metaphor, 90
metathesis, 45
Milroy, James, 6, 9
mishearing, 10–11, 21, 58–9, 75, 92
modal verb *see* verb: modal
morpheme, 38, 44, 63, 66–8, 90–2, 125, 134–6
morphologization, 15, 20, 27–8, 37, 77, 116
morphology
  derivational *see* derivation
  Distributed *see* Distributed Morphology
  inflectional *see* inflection
  Natural *see* Natural Morphology
  non-concatenative, 70

  see also compounding; morpheme; word-and-paradigm theory
morphonology *see* morphophonology
morphophonemics *see* morphophonology
morphophonology, 5, 9, 17, 42, 47–9, 86, 90–2, 94–6, 115, 133; *see also* allomorphy; alternations
morphotactic transparency *see* transparency: morphotactic

Natural Morphology, 106, 115, 118
naturalness
  system-dependent, 74, 110–14, 121
  system-independent, 106–10, 114, 121
  see also markedness; Natural Morphology
Neogrammarian, 2–7, 10, 14, 17–19, 22, 42, 44–5, 48, 56, 71–2, 83, 90, 92, 94–6, 98–103, 113, 120, 123, 130
network model, 3, 23, 94, 123, 129–31, 136, 139
neural *see* connectionism
Nichols, Johanna, 9
non-change, 9, 76–7
non-concatenative morphology *see* morphology: non-concatenative
non-proportional *see* analogy: non-proportional
Nübling, Damaris, 55–6, 107, 132
Nyakyusa, 33
Nyamwezi, 50–1

Oertel, Hanns, 11, 14, 21, 43, 47
Ohala, John, 18n, 59, 65
Old Church Slavonic, 113
Old Norse, 60
one-form-one-function, 74, 106–9, 114, 121; *see also* isomorphism
onomasiological and semasiological perspectives, 62, 88–9, 101
opacity, 33, 70, 98, 105; *see also* transparency
open-syllable lengthening *see* lengthening: open-syllable
Optimality Theory, 75–6, 133, 135; *see also* constraints
optimization, 43, 104–16, 128
Osthoff, Hermann, 3, 6–7, 27, 42–3, 46, 99, 103
overt *see* covert vs. overt innovation

panchrony, 22–3; *see also* synchrony-diachrony dichotomy; universals
paradigm leveling *see* leveling
paradigmatic/configurational theory *see* word-and-paradigm theory
participle, 1–2, 8, 27–8, 30–2, 35–6, 50, 53–5, 65–6, 73, 78, 81–2, 88, 104, 111, 113, 131, 133, 137–8
Paul, Hermann, 2–18, 23–4, 37, 43–50, 56, 58, 64–5, 70, 72, 85, 87, 91–2, 94–5, 97–9, 103, 110, 123–6, 128–9, 131, 133, 135, 137–9
perception, 21, 41, 46, 57, 63, 74–5, 92–3, 115
performance *see* competence and performance
phantom analogy *see* analogy: phantom
phonetic analogy *see* analogy: phonetic
Piñeros, Carlos Eduardo, 70
Pinker, Steven, 112–13, 131–2, 136
phonaesthesia, 65
phonologization, 75
phonological change *see* sound change
phonology *see* hypercorrection; hypocorrection; lexical diffusion; morphophonology; phonologization; sound change
portmanteau, 66–7; *see also* blend; contractions
preference theory, 74–6, 83, 106–10, 114–16, 121; *see also* Natural Morphology; universals

prefix, 33, 35–6, 53, 60–1, 65, 74, 79, 111
preventive analogy *see* analogy: preventive
Prince, Alan, 70, 112–13, 131, 136
Principle of Contrast, 76
Prinzipien der Sprachgeschichte see Paul, Hermann
processing, 8, 70, 106, 115, 131
production, 5, 21, 26, 41, 46, 57, 63, 74, 92–3, 128
 vs. reproduction, 9–11, 13, 46, 95
productivity, 49, 69, 113
pronoun, 15, 31–2, 132
prophylaxis, 98–100
proportion *see* proportional equation
proportional *see* analogy: proportional; proportional equation
proportional equation, 10, 15–16, 18n, 21, 28–37, 44, 46, 65, 70, 74, 87–91, 94, 105, 124, 128–9, 133, 138–9
Prosodic Morphology, 70
prosody, 17, 36, 67–70, 98, 134; *see also* Prosodic Morphology
proto-Bantu *see* Bantu
proto-Germanic *see* Germanic
proto-Indo-European, 38
prototype, 112–13
psycholinguistics, 3, 8, 17

rationalism, 24; *see also* empiricism; innate knowledge
reality TV, 115
reanalysis, 13, 16, 19–41, 50, 53–4, 57–9, 61, 65, 67, 75, 77, 88, 97, 116
 paradigmatic vs. syntagmatic, 20, 27
 phonological *see* hypercorrection; hypocorrection
 types of, 27–40
 see also morphologization; reinterpretation; resegmentation
recomposition, 60–1
recutting *see* resegmentation
referral, rule of, 135; *see also* identity relation
regularization, 2, 8, 31, 55–6, 71–4, 80–3, 93, 96, 104, 109, 118, 127, 131–2, 140
reinterpretation, 19, 27
rephoneticization, 75
reproduction *see* production: vs. reproduction
resegmentation, 27, 32–4, 41, 70
revaluation, 27–8, 37, 41
rhotacism, 38, 75, 99, 114
Romance, 28, 80, 113, 115; *see also* French; Latin; Spanish
Rückumlaut, 72
rule inversion, 91–2
Russian, 73, 113

Samuels, M. L., 65, 107
Saussure, Ferdinand de, 12, 19, 22–6, 44, 76, 103, 125, 134
Schuchardt, Hugo, 7, 18n, 92, 95, 97, 101
semantics, 15, 88–90, 101
semasiological *see* onomasiological and semasiological perspectives
semiotics, 109
shortening, 63, 75, 81, 93
simplification *see* optimization
Skousen, Royal, 130–1, 139
Slavic *see* Belarusian; Czech; Old Church Slavonic; Russian
Smith, Adam *see* invisible hand
sociolinguistics, 3, 17, 70n
sound change, 3, 7–8, 10–11, 13, 17, 23, 33, 38, 40, 42, 45–6, 59, 71–2, 80–1, 85, 87, 92–101, 107–8, 114
 interaction with analogy, 25, 34, 61, 95–101, 105

Spanish, 31, 58–9
speaker-oriented approach, 6–7
speech community, 3, 7–8, 12, 24, 26, 127
static *see* dynamic vs. static models of grammar
Sturtevant, Edgar H., 43, 47, 58–9, 72, 95, 97–8
style, 26; *see also* variation
suppletion, 28–9, 78, 111
sweeping change *see* change: across-the-board
symmetric *see* asymmetric vs. symmetric paradigmatic models
synchrony-diachrony dichotomy, 3, 22–3, 25, 123–6
syntagmatic/compositional theory, 124, 134–7;
 see also concatenation; Hockett, Charles; morpheme; word-and-paradigm theory
syntax, 1, 5, 15, 28, 31–2, 44, 46–7, 50, 56, 70, 85–7, 94–5, 98, 101, 109, 125, 131, 137
system congruity, 100, 110–11, 114, 119–20; *see also* harmony
system-defining structural properties, 111–12

teleology, 13, 26, 118–20, 132
therapy *see* prophylaxis
Timberlake, Alan, 19–20
token frequency *see* frequency: token
Tolkien, J. R. R., 60
Transmission, 30–1, 61, 70; *see* acquisition
transparency
 morphotactic, 106
 Transparency Principle, 98, 105
 see also opacity
Trask, R. L., 20, 59, 66
Traugott, Elizabeth, 13, 15, 19, 21–2, 36–7
type frequency *see* frequency: type

umlaut, 28, 50, 53, 55, 65, 72–3, 77, 91, 96, 106–9, 114, 116
Universal Grammar, 22, 24
universals, 3, 23, 74–6, 83, 114–15, 117, 121, 122, 124–5, 129, 133
usage-based model, 3, 126–32; *see also* exemplar-based models

variation, 3, 9, 17, 30, 36, 39–40, 61, 74, 82–3, 86, 132; *see also* style
Vennemann, Theo, 74, 91, 98, 117–18, 120
verb
 denominal, 30–1, 35, 78, 82, 96
 irregular weak in English, 81–3
 modal, 46–7, 86
 strong and weak in Germanic, 27, 30–1, 72, 78, 80–3, 111–12; *see also* dual-mechanism model; irregularization; regularization
 see also participle; Rückumlaut
Verner's Law, 73–4, 114
vowel lengthening *see* lengthening
vowel shortening *see* shortening

Wheeler, Benjamin Ide, 13, 21, 37, 42, 93, 102, 117–19
Whitney, Dwight, 18n, 89, 137
word-and-paradigm theory, 3, 10, 44–6, 128–9, 134–9
word formation
 paradigmatic *see* cross-formation
 see also compounding; derivation
Wurzel, Wolfgang Ullrich, 97, 107, 110–14, 138

Yang, Charles, 26, 112, 118
Yurok, 33, 49

zero derivation *see* conversion
Zwicky, Arnold, 135, 137

EU representative:
Easy Access System Europe
Mustamäe tee 50, 10621 Tallinn, Estonia
Gpsr.requests@easproject.com

www.ingramcontent.com/pod-product-compliance
Lightning Source LLC
Chambersburg PA
CBHW061840300426
44115CB00013B/2458